DATE DUE

MAY 0 4 '92	FEB 0 9 1995
JUL 2 1 '92 MAY 0 2 '95	MAR 2 8 '95
JUN 1 3 1993	
MAR 2 0 '94	
MAY 1 0 '94	
JUN 1 1 1994	
JUN 1 3 1994	
DEC 1 1994	

BRODART, INC   Cat. No. 23-221

Victimization in Schools

Gary D. Gottfredson
and
Denise C. Gottfredson

Center for Social Organization of Schools
The Johns Hopkins University
Baltimore, Maryland

Plenum Press • New York and London

Library of Congress Cataloging in Publication Data

Gottfredson, Gary D.
  Victimization in schools.

  (Law, society, and policy; v. 2)
  Bibliography: p.
  Includes index.
  1. School violence—United States. 2. School vandalism—United States. 3. School disci-
pline—United States. 4. School environment—United States. I. Gottfredson, Denise C. II.
Title. III. Series.
LB3013.3.G67   1985   371.5'8   85-17010
ISBN 0-306-42023-6

©1985 Plenum Press, New York
A Division of Plenum Publishing Corporation
233 Spring Street, New York, N.Y. 10013

Printed in the United States of America

Preface

The perception that our nation's public schools are disorderly and unsafe is widespread, and the image of the public school is deteriorating. Since 1974, the Gallup organization has gathered opinions about the public schools. The percentage giving the schools an "A" rating declined from 18% to 6% between 1974 and 1983 (Gallup, 1974, 1984). In a recent survey of America's teenagers, only 9% gave the schools an "A" rating (Bahner, 1980, p. 106). Lack of discipline tops the list of the problems adults see facing schools, and class disturbances and theft are reported by teenagers to be "very big" or "fairly big" problems in their schools (Bahner, 1980, p. 107).

These public perceptions are fostered by and reflected in national media attention ("City Schools in Crisis," 1977; "Help! Teacher Can't Teach!" 1980; "High Schools under Fire," 1977). Public concern is also reflected in Congressional hearings where testimony creates the image of grave disorder within our schools (U.S. Senate, Committee on the Judiciary, 1975, 1976b; U.S. House of Representatives, Subcommittee on Elementary, Secondary, and Vocational Education, 1980). The public has given the schools low marks, and the Senate Judiciary Committee (1975) gave the schools an "A" in violence and vandalism.

In short, parents, students, and public officials are alarmed at what they see as a rising tide of violence and disorder in the schools and are concerned about how much learning can occur in a disruptive environment, and about the safety of teachers and students.

These concerns have undoubtedly contributed to middle-class flight from our urban schools. The wholesale departure of the children of middle-class families from city public schools (often called "white flight") will, if not stemmed, result in the big city schools being an impoverished "dumping ground" for the poor—children of minority families without resources to flee and without resources to improve their schools. This specter implies that maintaining order in the public schools, and maintaining the appearance of order, is a school-management problem of great importance.

The work reported in this book was undertaken during a period of heightened awareness of the problems of the public schools, and in a time when the spirit of many school administrators and public officials has been defeatist. Schools, it is often said by those who run them, inherit their problems from the community and from the families that fail to control their children and do not instill in them a sense of value of education. The Coleman report (Coleman, Campbell, Hobson, McPartland, Mood, Weinfeld, & York, 1966) has engendered a 20-year legacy of research concluding that schools make little difference, that input (student characteristics) determines output (achievement). Thus, the fatalism of school administrators has to some degree been clothed in sociological respectability.

Yet if the public schools are to be improved, if we are to achieve educational equity rather than leaving the have-nots of our cities to founder in deteriorating schools, then we must understand what makes some schools orderly and others havoc-ridden. More specifically, we must determine what sources of school orderliness are amenable to administrative control and to intervention. The search for those sources is the subject of this book.

Any single investigation of a social problem can aspire only to increase knowledge somewhat, to add a modicum of understanding, or to bring a different perspective to the problem. Scientific breakthroughs seldom occur in social science (Janowitz, 1979). By this standard, we judge our work successful. This book adds to knowledge about the nature and distribution of school disruption, increases understanding about the social ecology of secondary schools, and claims that schools (and those who run them) can make a difference.

The research reported here was conducted over a period of several years at the Johns Hopkins University, Center for Social Organization of Schools, and was supported in part by grants from the National Institute of Education, U.S. Department of Education (formerly Health, Education, and Welfare). We are grateful for the assistance of Lois Hybl, Richard D. Joffe, Robert Kirchner, and Mary K. Roberts who helped with word processing and research. Robert Crain, Michael R. Gottfredson, and John Hollifield read and commented on parts of the manuscript; and Robert Kirchner was especially helpful to us in preparing Chapter 13. Henry J. Becker, Michael S. Cook, Robert Crain, Richard Scott, Michael Wiatrowski, Shi-Chang Wu, and James M. Richards, Jr., helped us with advice or comments in discussions about our research. In addition, we are grateful for the feedback from colleagues in other universities who used earlier drafts of parts of this book in their graduate seminars in research methods and mental health. This feedback prompted us to make the work more widely available.

The data used in this research, based on the responses of thousands of students and teachers and the principals in over 600 schools, were made available by the Inter-University Consortium for Political and Social Research. These data were originally collected by the Research Triangle Institute on behalf of the National Institute of Education for its Congressionally mandated Safe School Study (David Boesel, project director).

Most important, we are grateful to the students, teachers, and principals who contributed information about their schools, their experiences in those schools, and their perceptions of the social relations that affect their day-to-day lives. Without their help, this work could not have been done. We earnestly hope that their contributions will be rewarded by having the data heeded by researchers, policymakers, educators, and the public so that schools become more pleasant, orderly places.

Much of the work to prepare this manuscript was accomplished in an isolated house on the Chesapeake Bay built in 1895 by Albert LaVallette. The warm, humid days of the Maryland summer made the writing pads soggy but usable, and the ghost said to inhabit the house never interfered with the writing.

None of those who helped us—those who collected the data, those who made it available to us, our colleagues who gave advice, the ghost at LaVallette's, nor the National Institute of Education that supported part of this work—is responsible for the analyses or interpretations presented here. Opinions expressed, and any errors, are ours alone.

Contents

CHAPTER 1

The Problem of School Disorder

The public's concern with what is widely perceived as burgeoning crime and violence in the nation's public schools is reflected in and fostered by spectacular media attention to the topic, the results of public opinion surveys, and continuing Congressional hearings. Testimonial accounts of school crime, such as the national magazine reports (e.g., "City Schools in Crisis." 1977; "High Schools under Fire," 1977), the Congressional hearings, and a book titled *Violence in Schools* (McPartland & McDill, 1977) are useful, but they are sensationalized accounts.

HOW MUCH VIOLENCE IS THERE?

Many schools are deeply troubled by fear and lack of safety. The typical public school is not, however, the hotbed of violence and disorder that popular accounts suggest. In this introductory chapter, we describe some basic facts about school disorder—insofar as they may accurately be known. The facts, although by no means reassuring, are not as terrible as the reader of *Time* or *Newsweek* who has no occasion to visit the schools may think.

Two main sources of systematic information about disorder in schools are available. The first is the *Safe School Study Report to Congress* (National Institute of Education, 1978). As one reflection of Congressional concern about crime in schools, the Ninety-Third Congress required the Secretary of Health, Education and Welfare to

1

conduct a study of school crime (Public Law 93—380). The study was to provide information about the nature and extent of violence and vandalism in schools, and to suggest strategies to reduce these problems. The principal response to this requirement was the Safe School Study conducted by the National Institute of Education (NIE). Many of the data collected in that study are used in the research reported later in this book. In the Safe School Study, thousands of teachers and students reported about their experiences of victimization. The second source of information is the victimization surveys made by the Census Bureau and the Law Enforcement Assistance Administration. In these surveys, thousands of households were approached to find out who had recently been victimized, where, when, and by whom.

The following paragraphs draw on these two sources of information to provide a summary of the evidence about the nature and extent of violence in schools.

Teacher Victimization

Teachers experience a variety of indignities in schools-ranging from rare but serious offenses, such as rape or serious assault, to frequent and pervasive experiences of verbal abuse. The percentages of teachers experiencing several kinds of personal victimization in schools in major metropolitan, small city, suburban, and rural areas in a typical month are displayed in Figure 1 (based on unpublished tabulations from the National Institute of Education's Safe School Study). For most types of teacher victimization, lowest rates are found in rural schools, followed by suburban, and then small city schools; highest rates are found in schools in major cities. Although experiences of serious victimization are relatively rare in a proportionate sense, so many teachers work in the nation's public schools that in a typical month an estimated 6,000 junior or senior high school teachers experience at least one robbery; 128,000 have something worth more than $1.00 stolen; and 5,200 are physically attacked. Other types of indignities are experienced more frequently: 48% of junior or senior high school teachers report that students swore or made obscene gestures at them in a typical month, 12% report that a student threatened to hurt them, and an equal percent report hesitating to confront misbehaving students for fear of their own safety.

An alternative way to put the nature and extent of teacher victimization into perspective is to examine the relative frequency of victimization in school. According to Census Bureau—Law Enforce-

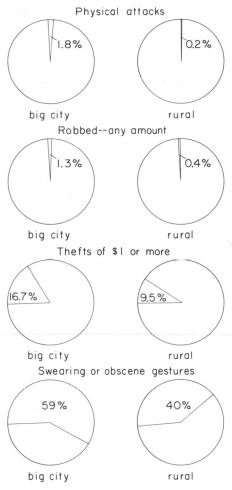

FIGURE 1. Percentage of teachers reporting various events (typical month, source: NIE, 1978).

ment Assistance Administration (LEAA) surveys conducted in 28 cities (McDermott & Hindelang, 1977), about 8% of the approximately 3.3 million victimizations reported in a 1-year period occurred in school, and about 8% of these were victimizations of teachers or school administrators. The vast majority of these crimes involve theft (larceny without contact, 79%). Other crimes are experienced less often: simple assault (11%), aggravated assault (7%), robbery (2%), larceny with contact (1%), and rape (nearly 0%).

In short, although many teachers have something stolen from a desk, locker or coat, and many are the butt of nasty remarks or gestures, few are raped or suffer serious physical harm. Put another way, the main problems of disruption are the day-to-day indignities suffered by school staff, not wholesale mayhem and plunder.

Student Victimization

Students experience a similar range of indignities. Rapes and serious assaults occur so rarely that obtaining reasonably precise estimates of their frequency or distribution is nearly impossible. Figure 2 (based on the Safe School Study survey) shows information about student victimizations that corresponds to the Figure 1 information for teachers. Student victimizations are less concentrated in big-city schools than are teacher victimizations—about the same proportion of students

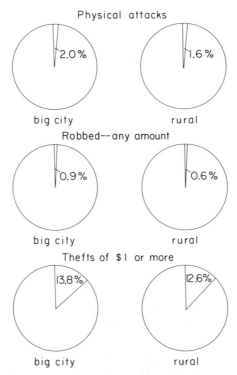

FIGURE 2. Percentage of students reporting various events (typical month, source: NIE, 1978, student interviews).

experience attacks in suburban schools as in big-city schools, for example. Evidence in the Safe School Study report (NIE 1978, Chap. 3), implies that boys are victimized much more than are girls, and that boys are usually victimized by boys, girls by girls, blacks by blacks, and whites by whites.

To summarize, the typical student or teacher experience of personal victimization in schools is of a minor incident. Serious victimizations are rare. But the frequency of minor victimizations and indignities, and public and student opinion about school disorder, imply that these kinds of victimizations are major social problems.

THE IMPERATIVE TO DO BETTER

Although the foregoing paragraphs imply that media reports of extreme disorder and the impassioned testimony of some big-city teachers' unions and school security personnel may exaggerate the extent of public school disorder, disorder is a serious problem. Schools must do a better job of maintaining order and they must improve their public image. Why?

Tocqueville (1898) long ago noted a source of tension in American society. On the one hand we cherish an egalitarian ethic: all are created equal. On the other hand, we seek a meritocracy: the cream should rise to the top. Blau and Duncan (1967), in their landmark empirical work that founded the modern sociology of attainment, convincingly argue that the route to success in our society is through educational attainment. Most good jobs—those that bring affluence or confer prestige—require not only literacy and computational competency, but also educational credentials (Daily, 1971). Postsecondary education is increasingly necessary to get ahead, and the research of the 15 years since the Blau and Duncan report has strengthened the evidence, tying later-life success to success and persistence in school (Featherman & Hauser, 1978 Jencks, 1977).

The race and class inequality noted by Tocqueville in his 19th century travels are still painfully obvious today. Because getting ahead means learning in and persisting in school, the challenge for America is to (a) provide equality of access to education of high quality, or (b) break down needless barriers to employment based on educational credentials. Despite reason to believe that the latter course has merit (Berg, 1971;

Daily, 1971), it has never been a popular idea. The view that education not only is, but also *ought to be* the way to get ahead is widespread.

Recognizing that equality of educational opportunity is essential, the Supreme Court ended legally segregated public schools in *Brown v. Board of Education*. Since the 1960s progress has been made in the integration of education, but school segregation persists. This segregation has its roots in residential segregation and in the differential ability to pay for private schooling. Our urban public schools are often predominantly minority schools; they suffer the highest rates of disruption, and have poor public images.

This disruption and this poor image are management problems of the greatest urgency. Unfortunately, these problems are not always seen as management problems. The afflictions suffered by urban public schools are variously attributed to race, social class, economic, and geographic causes. But competent public administrators in our urban centers must act as creative and responsible managers of resources and political power to (a) stem the flow of the children of the affluent to private schools, (b) retain middle-class families in the cities where they contribute to the tax base, and (c) develop and maintain a positive public image so that businesses and industries are encouraged to locate in the cities where they will provide jobs and tax revenues.

To bring about these outcomes, school managers must do many things, but two are salient. The image of the public schools depends largely on perceptions: first, that they are doing a good job of education, and second, that they are safe and orderly. A vast literature on achieving academic goals exists (Brophy, 1982; Peterson & Walberg, 1979; Slavin, 1982). The research reported in this book is aimed primarily at the second of these issues facing educational administrators and policy makers. It examines the characteristics of schools, their governance, and their administration, and it seeks to learn whether and how school management contributes to the levels of disruption schools experience.

PREVIOUS RESEARCH AND ADVICE

There is no shortage of theory and advice linking youths' experiences in school—and even the institution of traditional schooling itself—to youth misconduct or delinquent behavior.[1] Greenberg (1977), in a compelling analysis, argues that "any society that excluded juveniles from the world of adult work for long periods of mandatory attendance at schools organized like ours would have a substantial amount of delinquency" (pp. 213—214).

But few studies have involved the comparative analysis of schools with different social composition and different administrative and governance practices to learn what arrangements under the control of policy makers and school administrators might reduce disorder. Three exceptions are the forerunners of the present research: Johnston's (1973) study of schools, McPartland and McDill's (1977) review of advice and original research, and the NIE's (1978) Safe School Study. Other exceptions were published after the bulk of the research reported here was complete: Rutter, Maughan, Mortimore, and Ouston's (1979) study of twelve urban secondary schools and Coleman, Hoffer, and Kilgore's (1982) study of achievement in public and private high schools (based in part on earlier work by DiPrete, 1981).

Early Forerunners

The first of these attempts to study school characteristics and delinquency rates was an enterprising study by Johnston (1973). That research was fraught with difficulties arising from the attempt to detect reliable school effects of many kinds (i.e., not limited to delinquency, but including achievements and many other dependent measures) in a small ($n = 87$) sample of schools. Delinquency rates did not turn out to be highly predictable in that study, but no effort was made to focus specifically on that criterion or to engineer the measures of school differences in a way that would enhance the predictability of variance of delinquency across schools. As a result, clear interpretations of that project's results with respect to delinquency rates in school are hard to make. As the author put it,

> Given the post hoc nature of our search, we must accept the fact that we might well miss some predictors which validly relate to one or two specific

---

[1]See Howard (1978) and Johnson, Bird and Little (1979) for practical advice; and see G. D. Gottfredson (1981) for a review of research and theory. A compendium of theory of uneven quality and limited accessibility is provided by National Council on Crime and Delinquency (1978).

criteria, in order to avoid reaching a great number of false positive
conclusions. (p. 105)

Johnston's effort is valuable, however, because it points out the
need to (a) focus clearly on a criterion of interest (disorder), and (b) to
study a sample of schools of sufficient size that dependable conclusions
are possible.

In a second forerunner of our work, McPartland and McDill (1977)
analyzed data from three surveys, each involving from 14 to 20 schools,
to search for school-contextual effects on delinquent behavior. They
found that small schools, schools where grades were high, and schools
where student participation in decisions about how the school is
governed tend to have students reporting less misconduct. Although the
number of schools was small, and although one may quibble with the
technical details of their research (especially where they draw conclusions about a small number of schools as ecological units based on
statistics about individuals), their conclusions seem sensible and accord
with speculations and advice offered by others (Garbarino, 1978;
Howard, 1978). This research is valuable because it provides some clues
about where to look for school effects, and it reminds us of the need for
better data: more appropriate outcome measures, larger sample sizes,
and a broader range of school practices and other characteristics to
examine.

The NIE Safe School Study Report

The direct precursor of this book is the National Institute of
Education's (1978) Safe School Study. That study contributed greatly to
our understanding of the extent and patterning of disorder in the public
schools. In addition to the original 357 page report published by NIE,
several other accounts summarizing the Safe School Study are now
available (Boesel, 1978; Crain & Wu, 1978; Hollifield, 1978; "How
safe," 1978; Rubel, 1979; Subcommittee on Economic Opportunity,
1978; Wyne, 1979). For this reason, only a few highlights of the report
that are closely related to the present research will be reviewed here.

The Safe School Study was conducted for Congress in the context
of intense interest by a variety of stakeholders. One stakeholder was the
American Federation of Teachers (AFT), which was concerned that its
big-city teachers were engaged in hazardous work. A second stakeholder
was the National Association of School Security Directors (NASSD), a

vocal group with a clear point of view about ways to reduce school violence and vandalism: more security staff.

The study had three parts: (a) a mail survey of elementary and secondary principals in several thousand public schools to collect information about the nature and incidence of disruptive activities, (b) an intensive study of 642 public junior and senior high schools in which thousands of students and teachers answered questionnaires, and (c) case studies of 10 schools.

Among the conclusions drawn in the NIE report are that misbehavior can be controlled by decreasing the size and impersonality of schools, by making school discipline more systematic, by decreasing arbitrariness and student frustration, by attention to a school's reward structure, by increasing the relevance of schooling, and by decreasing students' sense of powerlessness and alienation. In short, a clear theme permeates the NIE interpretations—school administration and policies make a difference. The NIE report's message to administrators and teachers is that they have a role in reducing school disruption.

The NIE report has serious limitations. Most of the analyses reported in the NIE report are crosstabulations of personal or school characteristics with victimization status. For example, an item intended to measure students' sense of internal control is crosstabulated with students' victimization status. The report contains hundreds of such crosstabulations. These tabulations provide a valuable portrait of who is victimized, but they provide only a weak basis for policy recommendations in which one could have confidence. The possible explanations for any particular association discovered through this kind of analysis are nearly endless, and such individual-level analyses do not focus on variations across schools.

Most relevant to the questions regarding differences in disorder among schools is a 57 page appendix to the NIE report, authored by Shi-Chang Wu. In that section of the report a more systematic attempt was made to examine some theoretical notions about the causes of school disruption. School violence—defined in those analyses as the percentage of students who reported that they had been physically attacked at least once at school in the past month, and the percentage of students who reported that they had been robbed at least once in the past month—was hypothesized to be a function of

1. Crime levels in the surrounding community
2. The age of the studentry

3. The sex composition of a school's students
4. The sense of internal control among a school's students
5. The quality of school governance or rule enforcement
6. The degree of fairness in the treatment of students
7. The extent of student–teacher interaction
8. The perceived relevance of the subject matter to which students are exposed in school

The first four characteristics in this list were construed as control or background variables, and an attempt was made to determine whether the second four variables added to the explanation of school violence. The Safe School Study report concluded that the four background variables accounted for from 15% to 26% of the variance in school violence, and that the other four variables accounted for an additional 2% to 18% of the variance after the background factors were controlled. These percentages have a range because data were analyzed separately for six sets of schools: junior and senior high schools in metropolitan central cities, suburban metropolitan areas, and nonmetropolitan areas (called urban, suburban, and rural for short). The report goes on to explore the potential of several additional variables to explain school violence when the eight basic predictors mentioned earlier are statistically controlled.[2]

The Safe School Study's data base provides social scientists and policy makers with the best source of information about school characteristics and school disruption currently available. Considerable thought and theoretical work went into the design of the research (Williams, Moles, & Boesel, 1975). Furthermore, despite the demands of Congress for quick answers to difficult questions and the difficult circumstances under which the research was conducted, the NIE staff worked hard to preserve the scientific quality and integrity of the research process (Boesel, 1978). The report's major conclusions therefore require careful consideration. Before summarizing those conclusions, however, it is important to note several limitations of the research that weaken confidence in those conclusions. Such limitations are to be expected in a report produced under severe constraints of time, as was the Safe School Study. Even superhuman effort and skill could not have produced a comprehensive and thoroughgoing report. Those who want

[2]Hundreds of potential predictors were explored in preliminary analyses. We thank Shi-Chang Wu for discussing this work with us and showing us copies of detailed correlation matrices used in his work.

sound information on which to base policy recommendations cannot expect quick and easy answers.

The following appear to be the major limitations of the Safe School Study report:

1. The analyses are devoid of tests of statistical significance. One cannot have confidence even in the sign of a regression coefficient when this information is omitted. This problem is especially severe when sample sizes are small as they were in these analyses of subgroups of schools (n's range from 76 to 121), and many of the results shown may be expected to be nonsignificant.[3]

2. Comprehensive evidence is lacking about the statistical relations among potential predictors of school violence that are plausibly related to both violence and the predictors that were examined in the report. As a result, the interpretation of weights assigned by the regression procedure to variables that were examined is rendered suspect. For example, although we know that crime rates differ greatly across social areas (Block, 1979; Shaw & McKay, 1972), measures of community characteristics—with the exception of student and teacher reports of parental victimization and neighborhood crime—were not explicitly included in the analyses. Furthermore, the examination of additional explanatory variables was done in a piecemeal fashion that does not allow one to disentangle potential redundancy among them. A result of this problem of lack of completeness in the statistical models developed in the Safe School Study report is that one does not know whether one should regard a statistically derived weight for any particular variable as meaningful or as spurious (Blalock, 1964).

3. The analyses are devoid of information about the quality of the measurement of any of the variables examined. Lack of predictive power in a variable may be the result only of poor measurement and may tell us little about the actual relations among the constructs for which the measurements were intended to stand (Stanley, 1971).

4. The implicit assumptions about the causal ordering of explanatory variables are often suspect. For example, some analyses implicitly assume that the perceived relevance of a school's curriculum may cause

[3]The NIE researchers appear to have attended to patterns of consistency in directions of regression coefficients across the six subsamples of schools. This is a reasonable approach if adhered to consistently, but because the method of arriving at inferences was not formally specified it is unclear just how a determination that a finding is dependable was made. Furthermore, the report argues (p. A-5) that schools ought to be compared only with others in the same subset.

the racial composition of the school. Such an assumption, if explicitly stated, would have little plausibility, and the consequence of the procedures used is potentially to overestimate the contribution of intermediary school characteristics, such as governance practices and perceived relevance of the curriculum, to the explanation of school disruption.[4]

The foregoing notwithstanding, the univariate and multivariate analyses in the Safe School Study have provided a wealth of descriptive data and clues that inform the present research. Several interesting patterns in the results of the NIE study appear to accord with expectations about the causes of school violence or disruption. The following list, adapted from Chapter 5 (p. 129) of the NIE report, summarizes the suggestive evidence about schools with relatively little violence:

1. Schools whose attendance areas have low crime rates and few or no fighting gangs
2. Schools with a small percentage of male students
3. Schools that are composed of higher grade levels
4. Small Schools
5. Schools where students rate classrooms as well disciplined, where rules are strictly enforced, and where the principal is considered strict
6. Schools where students consider school discipline as being fairly administered
7. Schools where class sizes are small and where teachers teach a few rather than many different students each week
8. Schools where students say that classes teach them what they want to learn

---

[4]One additional technical problem sometimes arises. The comparisons sometimes made among different types of schools on the basis of differences in regression slopes are suspect not only because of the lack of statistical tests, but also because these comparisons involved the inspection of unstandardized regression coefficients that may be expected to fluctuate when any population is partitioned. When the sample of schools was divided into subgroups on the basis of characteristics which are related to the criterion (for example, urban vs. rural location), even unstandardized regression slopes are expected to vary simply due to the implicit selection on the criterion measure (Lord & Novick, 1968, pp. 141—143). Such fluctuations in regression coefficients among subpopulations do not necessarily imply that different processes are occuring in the various subpopulations (Hannan & Burstein, 1974, pp. 382—384; Kim & Mueller, 1976; Richards, 1979).

9. Schools where students consider grades important and plan to go on to college
10. Schools where students believe they can influence what happens in their lives by their efforts, rather than feeling that things happen to them which they cannot control

To this list we may append some additional suggestions derived from earlier review and research by McPartland and McDill (1976):

1. Schools where report card grades tend to be high
2. Schools where student participation in decisions about how the school is governed is relatively high

This list provides a useful starting point for the present research. It implies that a thoroughgoing examination of school size, school governance, grading practices, and a variety of studentry attitudes may provide increased insight into the ways school administration may contribute to the prevention of disorder. As the foregoing enumeration of difficulties in interpreting the original Safe School Study report's results illustrates, however, new research must carefully examine a wide range of potential explanatory variables simultaneously, and guard against spurious causal inferences. This means, in short, that community and demographic characteristics should certainly be statistically controlled when assessing whether the evidence from the Safe School Study supports the interpretation that school governance, school climate, and other school characteristics contribute to the explanation of disruption. The list generated by earlier researchers may be likened to an early explorer's map. We believe that there is treasure out there, but we also know that there are shoals and reefs—even though we do not yet know where they may be.

CHAPTER 2

Scope of the Research

It is the social body which forms the objects of our researches, and not the peculiarites distinguishing the individuals composing it.

—Quetelet (1842/1969, p. 7)

Our aims are to understand and predict school disorder so that we may suggest to policymakers and administrators a promising set of practical strategies to cope with delinquency and disruption in schools, and to find more efficient ways to prevent dilinquency in general. This book describes progress toward our goal by summarizing some ecological analyses of natural variations in the rates of disruptive behavior across schools. We seek to learn about the social behavior of human aggregates and the ways in which these behaviors are influenced by the characteristics of the broader community, the social composition of schools, and by specific practices and climates of the institutions involved. In contrast to most research on youth development or delinquency, the present research takes the school (not the individual person) as the unit of analysis.

AN ORGANIZATIONAL PERSPECTIVE

In conceiving the present research, we have thought of schools as meaningful entities—social organizations that have measurable features that distinguish them from other schools just as individual people have features that distinguish among them. Just as we can describe some

14

people as "persevering" or "conventional" or "conforming", we can describe schools as "academically oriented" or "orderly" or "safe." And just as behavioral scientists often assume that the behavior of individuals can often be explained by reference to differences in individual potential (e.g., potential for learning or for self-restraint) and to learning histories and resources that predispose them to behave certain ways in certain situations, we assume that the behaviors of schools as social organizations can often be explained by reference to differences in student and teacher input (the composition of the schools' inhabitants), the historical influences of political or administrative entities on their practices, and the particular situations with which they are confronted.

Readers not used to adopting an organizational perspective will have to mentally shift gears as they make their way through our research. We are examining school environments exclusively. None of our research bears directly on differences in the behavior of individuals within these environments. This will likely be a foreign perspective to many readers who are used to explaining behavior by reference to individual differences.

Most of the time when we ask questions in our day-to-day lives about the sources of behavior, we are asking questions about puzzling differences among the behavior of different individuals. For example, we may be interested in explaining the differences in the academic achievement or amount of delinquent behavior of different people in the same or similar environments. The typical explanations involve an account of the different peoples' socioeconomic background, family environment, intelligence, learning history, or stakes in conformity. Sometimes—but not always—we ask questions about the influence of different environments or situations on individual behavior or achievement. For example, Coleman, Hoffer, and Kilgore (1982) recently examined the academic achievement of students enrolled in different kinds of schools, and they attempted to explain differences in achievement by reference to these students' background characteristics and the characteristics of the schools they attended.

In contrast to this kind of question, we are asking questions about the sources of differences in schools as organizations. Differences in the behavior of individual people within these organizations, however interesting they may be, are not the primary topic of the present inquiry. These differences are relevant to the present research only insofar as they may contribute to understanding the behavior of the human aggregates—schools—we are examining. Put another way, the present research focuses on the roots of differences among schools in the amounts of personal victimization they display, not on why some individuals within these schools are more often victimized than others.

What Organizational Characteristics Are Important?

We have assumed that several kinds of organizational characteristics are likely to be important in explaining school disorder. These include (a) the characteristics of the environments in which the schools themselves operate—the communities within which they are located, (b) the composition of the schools' populations—the makeup of the body of teachers and students who inhabit them, (c) the sizes of the schools and the resources available to the them, (d) the way the school is run—its rules and practices, and (e) the schools' psychosocial climates—the ways teachers and students in the school perceive it.

Community Influences. It seems plausible that powerful community influences operate to mark schools with distinctive cachets. The common stereotypes of the large urban school on the one hand—and the small rural school on the other—probably have some validity, and the distinctive forms of schooling in these divergent communities may evolve to meet divergent community demands. Even such morphologically similar objects as the yellow school bus seem to have different symbolic meanings in rural areas than in large metropolitan areas. If some communities devote more resources to education or play a more active role in shaping their schools than do others, these community influences may also be important in determining school orderliness. Especially provocative is the possibility that the levels of social control prevalent in communities are imported into the schools operating within them.

School Composition. The populations of students served by different schools differ vastly. The students in some schools all come from poor minority families, and the students in other schools are almost all from advantaged white families. It is reasonable to expect that students with different family background or ethnicity may bring different predispositions to behave in an orderly way into the school. Similarly, schools differ in the kinds of teaching staff they are able to recruit and retain. These differences in the composition of the schools' population may contribute in important ways to school psychosocial climate and the orderliness of the organization.

School Size and Resources. The size of a school is an organizational feature that may be related to its orderliness. Larger organizations tend to be more highly structured than smaller ones, with greater specialization among different functional elements. Larger organizations may have weaker means of social control than smaller ones because of greater anonymity or because any individual can be more easily replaced by another available individual for filling roles required by the environment.

School Governance. Decisions made and implemented by the persons within a school about rules, rewards, and punishments may determine the ways students and teachers perceive the school environment and behave within it. In some schools, the school rules are well understood by students and teachers alike; in other schools it is easy to generate arguments among teachers and administrators about what the school's rules are—and students do not take the school's guidelines for behavior very seriously. Similarly, schools differ in the extent to which they emphasize academic achievement and in the extent to which teachers and administrators work together to make the school run effectively. These differences in styles of school governance are likely to affect school orderliness.

Perceptions of the School and Student Psychosocial Characteristics. Student and teacher perceptions of the school environment may influence behavior in the environment. For instance, if the school's inhabitants generally perceive rules to be firmly enforced and fairly administered, their behavior may tend more often to be guided by those rules. Or, if the typical student in the school is exposed to other students who undermine conventional authority or the pursuit of conventional goals, students may fail to behave in conventional ways.

In the research reported in subsequent chapters we examine all of the foregoing categories of organizational characteristics. The last two kinds of organizational characteristics describe intraorganizational conditions or processes, whereas the first three kinds of characteristics are potential ecological sources of influence on the schools. Seldom has research on schools combined both kinds of characteristics in the same study. Our explorations of the data about the 642 schools in the sample were guided broadly by this perspective that organizations can be measured in all these ways and by speculations or research-based clues about the features of schools that may determine school orderliness.

Speculations about Origins of School Disorder

Speculations about the ways in which schools may contribute to delinquency and disorder or to school orderliness range from the use of corporal punishment (Welsh, 1978), through notions about power relations (David & Lincoln, 1978) and rule generation process (Ianni, 1978), to calls for increasing student involvement and the accountability of students for their actions (Van Patten, 1976). Gold (1978) speculated and provided some evidence that school experiences affect self-esteem and thus affect delinquency. Others argue that the institution of schooling is fundamentally alienating, at least for some students, because it fails to offer them realistic promise of desired adult roles and isolates them from meaningful work (Chase-Dunn, Meyer, & Inverarity, 1977; Greenberg, 1977; Liazos, 1978; Stinchcombe, 1964) or because the nature of this "middle-class" institution provides obstacles for lower class youth that result in their involvement in delinquent behavior (Cohen, 1955). Taken together with the suggestions derived from the Safe School Study and from McPartland and McDill's work, these speculations construct a roulette wheel of potential approaches to the reduction of disruption in schools (cf. G. D. Gottfredson, 1981, 1983).

Howard (1978) has argued that many schools are "rigged" to ensure the failure of many students. That is, rewarding experiences in the school are available only to students who perform well academically. Often students who do not meet expectations in academic areas are also denied access to rewards in other areas, such as athletics or other extracurricular activities, because only students successful in academic pursuits are allowed to participate.

The scenario Howard (1978) portrays can easily be translated into Hirschi's (1969) theoretical terms. (Hirschi viewed *commitment* to conventional goals, *attachment* to prosocial others, *belief* in conventional rules, and *involvement* in conventional activities as stakes in conformity that restrain youths from misconduct.) Students who have difficulty with school—students with low academic or interpersonal skills—have difficulty with schoolwork, do not behave as model youth, and fail in school. They do not become attached to school because their social interaction in school is unrewarding and they do not become committed to educational goals they view as unrealistic. They are not involved in conventional activities because they are denied access to them, and they do not believe in conventional rules because they cannot make the system work for them.

The foregoing speculations, generally stated in terms of individual behavior, can often be translated into organizational terms. Schools located in high crime or poverty areas where education levels are low and a high proportion of the families are headed by females may serve many students who experience difficulty with traditional schooling. Many of these students may have developed only weak restraints against misconduct and therefore compose a school population that fails to restrain its members from misconduct in social interaction. The communities of such schools may have few resources to mobilize and have difficulty in recruiting the best administrators and teachers.

If, furthermore, such schools have climates that fail to increase students' stakes in conformity, they may tend to be disorderly. If they fail to create environments that offer all students opportunities to experience success, if their rules are unclear or inconsistently administered, then these school environments may be difficult for students to cope with. In such schools, belief in conventional rules may erode. Unless teachers and administrators create more constructive climates, the schools may be disorderly and the best personnel may become dissatisfied with the school and try to leave.

The Approach to the Research

Because these speculations are so diverse, the approach taken in the present research was to ransack the information on natural variations among schools that is contained in the Safe School Study data for measures that bear on as many of these speculations as possible. The amount of data collected in the Safe School Study was great, not only in terms of the number of schools, students, teachers, and principals surveyed, but also in terms of the number of different questions asked. For this reason we have adopted the strategy of searching for statistical regularities in the covariation among the many pieces of information about schools in an attempt to find a smaller number of dimensions that characterize schools. These dimensions are interpreted where possible in terms of the constructs used elsewhere in the literature on school disruption. In short, our measures of school characteristics were primarily derived empirically in a massive data reduction effort, but the selection and interpretation of measures derived in this way was influenced by our awareness of the speculations extant in the literature about school disruption.

This book therefore summarizes (a) the data reduction efforts, (b) the dimensions along which schools varied that are potentially related to disruption, (c) evidence about the relation of these naturally occurring differences among schools to school vicitimization rates, and (d) the development and tests of a set of hypotheses about the causes of school disorder.

We raise many questions that must be pursued in continuing research before one can have a confident understanding of the conditions that create orderly schools. We therefore caution the reader against an uncritical interpretation of any particular result, and we ourselves will be circumspect in suggesting policies and practices that might be implemented as one way of underscoring our belief that the issues involved have not yet received a thorough enough scrutiny to justify bold and confident conclusions.

It is our conviction in any case that the analysis of natural variation of the sort that characterizes the present research is exploratory in nature. Such research provides one way of sorting the promising from unpromising leads, and for uncovering practices that, if implemented in planned interventions, *may* lead to the consequences suggested. Only more rigorous research that involves stronger designs will ultimately tell us if strategies for reducing disruption will work in practical application (cf. Cook & Campbell, 1976; G. D. Gottfredson, 1979, 1984c). At the same time, however, we would be negligent if we did not learn as much as we can by organizing evidence arising from existing practices and forms of school social organization in order to choose, from the many possibilities available, those strategies most worthy of evaluation in future research.

CHAPTER 3

Overview of the Data, Plan, and Methods

This chapter describes the large sample of schools studied, the ways the data were collected, and our plan for the research. And it tells about our methods, and why we chose them.

Data

The data collected in 1976 by Research Triangle Institute as part of the NIE (1978) Safe School Study are the basis of all analyses. Specifically, we used the questionnaire data provided by principals, teachers, and students in phase II of that study, and data about the communities in which the schools were located, prepared from 1970 census counts by Dualabs.[1] The questionnaires solicited extensive information about students' and teachers' experiences of victimization, and about personal characteristics and characteristics of their schools. In this phase of the Safe School Study the target populations were 7th-through 12th-grade teachers and students in United States public schools.

Sampling. A multistage cluster sampling plan was used. Schools were secondary sampling units within primary sampling units (PSU's). The PSU's were Standard Metropolitan Statistical Area (SMSA) central cities with populations of 500,000 or more, the remaining SMSA central

[1]See Volume 2 of the Safe School Study report (NIE, 1978) for a complete account of survey methods, and Volume 3 for data file documentation. David Bayless headed the Research Triangle Institute Team. David Boesel was the NIE study director.

cities, the noncity portions of SMSA's, or non-SMSA counties or county groups. Clusters of schools within each PSU were selected for inclusion in incremental waves in order to achieve a target of 600 schools participating in the study. The details of the complicated sampling procedures are spelled out in Volume 2 of the *Safe School Study Report* (NIE, 1978, Appendix C). For the present purposes it is most important to note that some schools declined to participate in the study. Approximately 75% did agree to participate: of the 833 schools from which participation was sought, some data were obtained from 642. Principal questionnaires were available for 623 schools, teacher questionnaires for 623 schools, student questionnaires for 621, and census data were available for all 642 schools that participated in some form.

To obtain nationally representative estimates if all schools in the sample design had participated, responses would have to be weighted by the inverse of their (unequal) probabilities of selection. Due to the extensive nonresponse, however, such weighting would not result in a representative sample—biases of an unknown nature and extent would be present. The analyses reported in subsequent chapters use un-weighted data, and in all cases the school is the unit of analysis.

Data Collection Instruments. The principal questionnaire was mailed to junior and senior public high school principals for all phase II schools. Information was collected on 261 items from 623 principals. Of those who were sent the questionnaire, 76% responded.

The teacher questionnaire was self-administered. It requested information on 187 items. A total of 23,895 teachers responded, or 76% of all teachers in the selected schools. Although procedures for collecting the questionnaires differed, a ballot box procedure was often used to guard the confidentiality of the reports, some of which contained fairly sensitive information (e.g., reports about the principal).

The student questionnaire was self-administered in the schools to a randomly selected sample of about 50 students per school. The questionnaire asked for reports on 167 items, and usable questionnaires were retrieved from 31,373 students, or 81% of those asked to complete it.

Readers are encouraged to consult the original questionnaires, which are reproduced in an appendix, for insight into the scope and quality of the information gathered. In general, the questionnaires were exceptionally well executed and are quite comprehensive. Their major limitations are the absence of self-reported delinquency information and the absence of objective measures of student ability. The researchers

collecting the data were not permitted to collect self-reported delinquency information, and any attempt to collect objective ability data was
forgone because of fears that the response rate would be lowered by
attempts to collect these data. The questionnaires broadly assess school
composition, governance, security, social and academic climates, and the
victimization status of teachers and students.

Information about the Communities. The community data are
based on fourth-count data for census tracts, census places, or minor
civil divisions from the 1970 census. The appropriate geographical unit
for any particular school was chosen through a clerical process based on
the inspection of maps.[2] The exact process by which these units were
selected is not documented, and the *Safe School Study Report* (Volume
2) provides poor documentation of the data files. The *Census User's
Guide* (U.S. Bureau of the Census, 1970, Part 2) is an invaluable
resource for the use of these data. The community data based on the
1970 census were supplemented by certain additional information on
climate (weather) and unemployment rates. These additional data were
supplied by NIE staff and are undocumented. These community data are
extremely valuable, but nonetheless suffer from limitations. Chief
among these is the absence of information about the racial composition
of the communities. Fortunately, however, the availability of information about the racial composition of the schools themselves attenuates
this limitation.

Plan

In preparation for our ecological study of school disruption, we
were faced with a massive data reduction task—a task that challenged
the capacity of our research resources despite the availability of a large
modern computer. To aid in this data reduction task we distinguished at
the outset the following six broad categories of potentially explanatory
variables:

1. Exogenous community characteristics
2. Endogenous community characteristics (community crime)
3. School social compositional characteristics which are externally
   determined (i.e., largely beyond the control of the school)
4. School size, staffing, and resources

[2]David Bayless, personal communication, 1979.

5. Organizational climate
6. School security measures

Table 1 lays out the kinds of variables initially included in each of these broad categories and their major subcategories. This table is informed in part by the planning that originally guided the Safe School Study (Williams, Moles, & Boesel, 1975), in part by speculations in the literature and by earlier research, and in part by our own synthesis of this literature and our best judgments about the most plausible causal processes. It is a crude roadmap that was used to guide the research. As will be apparent later, it became necessary to revise this map to accord with what was learned as the research progressed.

TABLE 1

Potential Explanatory Variables in the Plan for the Research

1. Exogenous community characteristics:
   Community characteristics, such as social class, income, racial composition, and urbanicity.

2. Endogenous community characteristics:
   Community crime

3. School social compositional characteristics which are externally determined:
   Grades included in the school, sex, and racial composition, ability, family resources, social class origins of the studentry, desegregation activities.

4. School size, staffing, and resources:
   Total enrollment, student–teacher ratio, average classroom size, number of different students taught, teaching resources, teacher demographic and educational characteristics.

5. Organizational climate:
   (a) Principal and teacher attitudes, styles, and strategies for coping with delinquency.

   (b) School governance practices—
       Rules, sanctioning practices, clarity and enforcement of rules, control over decision making, parental involvement in the school, student involvement, equity.

   (c) Social climate—
       Academic competition, academic orientation, basic skills orientation, vocational orientation, subculture of delinquent opportunity, attachment, commitment, involvement, belief, internal control, racial attitudes.

6. Site hardening or security measures and opportunity to engage in delinquent activity:
   Security devices, surveillance, length of school day.

The general strategy was first to examine comprehensively the dimensionality or structure of each of these broad categories (or subcategories), and second to use the results of this examination to build reliable measures of the major dimensions in each group. As a third step, the association of these measures with school disorder was examined. Fourth, we attempted to judiciously apply statistical controls by specifying hypothetical models to explain school disruption. The aim of this fourth step was to learn whether one could have any confidence that the school variables should not be regarded as merely spurious predictors of school disruption. In general, the wisest course appeared to be to assume that those groups of variables listed first in Table 1 contribute to the explanation of those groups of variables following later in the table in the application of statistical controls.

This is a highly conservative approach. Therefore, in a final step, we examined a radically different conception of the underlying process to less conservatively estimate the influences of the major dimensions of school organization on school disorder. In this final step, the relations of major dimensions of school organization to school disorder were examined.

School Disorder

So far, little has been said of our conception of the criterion of school disorder. Careful attention must be paid to the way in which the criterion is measured in any study, because as a practical matter all else depends on this measurement. A poorly measured or unreliable criterion will not be very predictable, and the many possible alternative measures of school disruption could have different meanings.

The definition of the criterion as "crime" was eschewed because this word implies a legal definition (M. R. Gottfredson, 1976). No data allowing the use of such a definition were available to us in the present research. Furthermore, as Emrich (1978) has noted in a critique of the NIE Safe School Study, many of the measures of misconduct collected in the study are of a relatively minor sort in contrast to the image created by the term "crime," even though there can be little doubt that the type of misconduct covered is important in its consequences for those involved. For these reasons, the words *disorder, disruption*, and *victimization* have been used in the present report.

Disorder and *disruption* are used because they appear to capture the essence of the kinds of misconduct involved, some of which by themselves are relatively minor and some of which certainly do constitute crime. The word *victimization* is used not necessarily to imply that those who report having experienced any particular incident were necessarily victims. The situation is undoubtedly more complex than that, and those who report incidents may often have contributed to their occurrence. Victimization is used to convey the source of most information about school disruption. The victimization-survey approach was taken in data collection. Students and teachers were asked to report on their own experiences of various sorts. They were asked, for example, "Besides things under a dollar, did anyone take money or things directly from you by force, weapons, or threats at school in September?" Principals were also asked to report on problems that the school had experienced.

Later in the report we describe work to develop criterion measures of school disorder and describe results when alternative criterion measures are examined. At this point we note that our measures of disruption include primarily personal victimization reported by teachers and students, although principal reports were also used. We have not examined vandalism or property loss to the school.

Methods—General Overview

All analyses reported here are school-level ecological analyses. Community characteristics, principal reports, teacher reports, and student reports are all examined at this level. As a consequence, all results apply to the school. They do not necessarily apply to individuals (Robinson, 1950), and readers are cautioned against interpreting in terms of individual characteristics or individual-level phenomena. Student and teacher reports were first aggregated to the school level before any further analysis was performed. School means (or proportions, which are a special case of a mean) for teacher and student reports are examined.[3]

Using Table 1 as the guide, we examined sets of variables in turn. Items presumed to measure content associated with each of these blocks of variables were chosen from the community data file and the principal, teacher, and student questionnaires. Whenever it was apparent that redundancy among the variables was present, principal factor analysis was used to guide the development of composite measures which

[3]In one case—grades received—the standard deviation was also examined.

appeared to tap the dimensions underlying the observed covariation among items. Principal factor analysis assumes that observed redundancy (or correlations) among variables is due to their association with a smaller number of underlying, hypothetical dimensions or "factors." Well understood methods exist for discovering these factors, but considerable art and judgment is involved in making decisions about the appropriate number of factors, their orientation in the factor space that is defined once the dimensions are determined, and in their interpretation. See Harmon (1967) for a technical discussion of principal factor analysis, or for a briefer introductory account see Kim (1975) or Nunnally (1967).

Composites of items were formed in one of three ways:

1. Factor scores were computed for dimensions of community structure based on the community variable file, involving primarily 1970 census data. This is the *only* use made of factor scores *per se* in this research.

2. Scores were computed by adding together the standardized values of items (standardized with respect to their means and standard deviations across schools), with the appropriate sign for items that were closely related according to the factor analysis results.

3. For Likert-type items with similar standard deviations (or for yes-no items with similar standard deviations), items or item-school means for closely related variables—again according to the factor analysis results—were simply added together with the appropriate sign.

Occasionally, when feasible and when the data warranted,[4] single items were used without combination. In one instance—the internal control scale—a composite of the Likert-type items presumed by the authors of the NIE (1978) study to measure this construct was formed by adding together these items with the appropriate sign. This was done without regard to a factor analysis of their structure because it is widely assumed that the construct of internal control is well understood (cf. Coleman *et al.*, 1966; Rotter, 1966; Wittes, 1970).[5]

Correlation coefficients and multiple correlation were used to examine the relation of criterion measures to individual predictors or sets of predictors. For any particular prediction the zero-order correlation (r), and for any particular set of predictors the multiple correlation

---

[4]That is, the item in question had little variance in the factor space.

[5]In fact, however, reliabilities of such scales are often low (e.g., Little, 1979). We used this scale because others assume it to be important (Williams, Moles, & Boesel, 1975).

(R) provide useful information about the extent of association between the criterion and the predictor or predictor set. Draper and Smith (1966) and Kerlinger and Pedhazer (1973) provide technical accounts of multiple correlation, and brief introductory accounts are provided by Kim and Kahout (1975a) and Nunnally (1967).

The zero-order and squared multiple correlations convey information about the *total association* of each predictor or set of predictors with a criterion. Part of this total association is spurious. This means that the observed statistical relations may not be the result of these particular predictors causing the criterion, but rather due, at least in part, to the association of these predictors with some other variables that may be responsible for variation in the criterion or that may be responsible for variation in the predictor(s) under consideration and the criterion. These straightforward measures of association do not imply causality, and such interpretations should be guarded against. Alwin and Hauser (1975), Blalock (1964), and Kim and Kohout (1975b) provide useful accounts of the meanings of spurious association, causality, and correlation analysis.

In a more analytical attempt to conservatively test the consequences of some causal hypotheses we have used multiple correlation to disentangle spurious statistical associations and to search for associations that do not vanish when appropriate controls are applied. To perform this work we developed a path model, a kind of explicit statement of what we regard as the most appropriate statistical controls. The specific models are described in detail in Chapters 10 and 11.

Path analysis was used because it (a) provides a convenient way to structure the application of statistical controls in assessing the contributions of various ecological variables to the social phenomenon of interest, (b) allows the representation of considerable complexity in the relations among variables, and (c) provides a way to make some weak probes of causal hypotheses using correlational evidence, provided that some strong assumptions are plausible. The assumptions required for assessing our causal hypotheses are that all the causes of school disorder that are correlated with any predictors respresented in the model are included in the model, that measurement is without error, and that the directions of causality are as indicated in the model (i.e., that there is no reverse or mutual causality). These assumptions are sometimes violated. Although the assumption of error-free measurement is formally required in models without multiple measures of hypothetical variables

(Jöreskog & Sörbom, 1978), in practice we adopt the working assumption that measurement error is random and so structured that the pattern of direct and indirect contributions is not seriously distorted. Whether or not even this weaker assumption is warranted is often questionable. The assumption of unidirectional causality is also questionable, but is a necessary working assumption.

Because the methods used may not be familiar to all readers and because some of the terms we use differ from those usually applied, some introduction may be helpful. For other explanations see Blalock (1967), Harvey (1969), or Cook and Campbell (1976). In general the analytic strategy outlined by Alwin and Hauser (1975) is applied, although some of their terms are changed to emphasize the quasi-experimental nature of the research. Distinctions are made among total associations, total contributions, direct contributions, and indirect contributions. The total association between any predictor and the criterion is the zero-order (ordinary) correlation between them. In contrast, the total contribution is that association which, given the assumptions, is not due to a common cause of both the predictor and the criterion nor to separate causes of the two variables that are correlated with each other, nor to potential explanatory prior variables that have not been analyzed. The direct contribution of a predictor to the statistical explanation of the criterion is that part of its total contribution that is not transmitted, given the assumptions, via one or more intermediary variables. If the model is correctly specified and measurement is errorless, an indirect contribution would indicate how much of the total contribution to explanation of the criterion is gained because the predictor contributes to the explanation of intermediaries that in turn contribute to explanation of the criterion. The results and their reasonable interpretation require careful specification of the sequence via which variables are construed to influence each other.

In practical application, the criterion is sequentially regressed on predictors or sets of predictors whose causal positions in the model differ. The total contribution of a predictor is obtained by calculating the standardized partial regression coefficient in a regression of the criterion on only those predictors or sets of predictors that are assumed to enter the causal model at that point. Direct contributions, often called path coefficients, are obtained by calculating the standardized partial regression coefficients (beta weights) in a regression of the criterion on a set of predictors that includes all of the potentially explanatory variables simultaneously. The total indirect contribution may be obtained by subtraction.[6]

All significance tests used are two-tailed tests. In the case of a zero-order correlation or partial regression coefficient the indication that a value is significant at the .05 or .01 level implies that one may be confident in its sign (+ or −), not necessarily that it is important in an absolute sense. Readers should attend to the size rather than merely to the statistical significance of a value. The significance level shown for squared multiple correlations means that one may have some confidence that it is different from zero—only rarely of real interest. The size of these values should also be attended to. Finally, in Chapter 10, tests of the significance of increases in the value of R-squared are made to determine if the addition of a particular set of variables makes a reliable contribution to the predictor of the criterion beyond that obtained when other variables assumed to be causally prior are used.

In general, analyses were performed separately for junior and senior high schools. Occasionally, however, exploratory factor analyses were performed for both groups combined—when, for example, the community variables were examined for the pooled group of schools. This procedure is more economical than separate analyses, and pooled-group exploratory analyses were performed to save money.

Level of Analysis

All analyses are conducted at the school level. Individual-level data are always, as a first step, aggregated to the school level before any further analyses are performed. We focus on school-to-school variation in rates of disruption and attempt to specify characteristics of schools that are related to these rates. This focus accords with the human ecology tradition (Hawley, 1950) in treating schools—not individuals—as the objects of interest. Our concern here is with schools as human aggregates rather than as settings where individual-level processes are played out. Naturally, many of our results raise interesting questions for researchers with a reductionistic bent who may wish to pursue research and theory at a lower level, but implications of the research reported here for individual processes are ambiguous (G. D. Gottfredson, 1981;

[6]Standardized coefficients are reported throughout because no attempts are made to compare results for different populations, and because standardized coefficients are more directly interpretable when the metrics of criterion and predictor variables are arbitrary.

Gove & Hughes, 1980; Robinson, 1950) and we do not directly address them.

School-effects researchers are frequently concerned with the extent to which variation observed at the school level can be explained by aggregated individual-level processes. They might try to decompose the effects of school-level predictors on rates of victimization into "compositional" effects and "contextual effects." Compositional effects are due to group-level consequences of individual-level processes and are observed simply because students are not placed in schools according to a random process. For instance, if, at the individual level, consorting with prosocial others and receiving good grades reduce one's chance of being victimized, then we would expect schools with high proportions of prosocial others and students who receive high grades to have lower rates of victimization. This type of school effect would be regarded by some as an aggregated individual-level process rather than as a true school-level process.

It is desirable to decompose regression coefficients into their compositional and contextual components if the objective is to obtain estimates of the impact of the social structure on individuals that are not confounded by the aggregate attributes of individuals—attributes which are largely beyond the control of the school (Firebaugh, 1979). Because we are examining only between-school variation, such an adjustment is unnecessary.

One might also be inclined to decompose the school-level regression coefficients if one were interested only in those characteristics of the school whose between-school variation could not be explained by aggregated individual-level processes. We do not define school effects in this way. Many aggregate individual characteristics can indeed be influenced by changes in school policies and should not be adjusted out of the analyses. For example, schools whose students believe in conventional social rules and feel in control of their destinies experience less disorder (see Chapter 10). Although this observation may illustrate a compositional rather than a contextual effect, the distinction is irrelevant if schools can somehow alter their students' levels of belief in conventional rules and feelings of control. An observed relation between these aggregated individual characteristics and school disruption would provide evidence that attempts to reduce disruption levels should focus on altering these characteristics. The purpose of our research is to uncover such possible links between disruption and school characteristics, regardless of whether the link is due to true school-level processes or aggregate individual-level processes. Elsewhere, G. D. Gottfredson (1985) discusses the measurement of *compositional* school climate and *psychosocial* school climate. In our definition, the former is based on the aggregated characteristics of individuals and the latter on reports about the environment. Both kinds of climate measures can describe manipulable characteristics of a school.

Special Problems Associated with Aggregated Data

Multicollinearity. The use of aggregated data poses two special problems. The first of these is known as the problem of multicollinearity. Highly aggregated measures often have high correlations with each other. Gordon (1968) has provided a clear description of the problems which may occur when attempting to use the techniques of multiple correlation with such data.[7] Redundancy among measures often results in a splitting of predictable variance between two closely related measures leading to false conclusions regarding the importance of measures of any particular type. Worse yet, one sometimes finds supressor effects in which the *sign* of a valid predictor of a criterion is reversed in the partial regression coefficient associated with that variable when other similar variables are also used as predictors. In extreme cases it is impossible to calculate regression equations or perform factor analyses at all because it is impossible to invert a correlation matrix. (Matrix inversion is a computational procedure required by the techniques.) These difficulties sometimes arose in the research reported here, and we adopted various approaches to the problem and rejected others that are sometimes used.

One type of instance in which problems of multicollinearity arose was in our explorations of sets of variables using factor analysis. Paradoxically, while using factor analysis as a tool to guide the formation of composite measures, the redundancy we were attempting to reduce caused problems for the statistical techniques we were using. When it was clear that this was happening we followed one of two courses. If the program being used would invert the matrix, and if the

---

[7]No attempt will be made here to explain all the technical problems involved. We shall merely point out the problems and describe our approach. Interested readers should see Gordon (1968), Hoerl and Kennard (1970), or a textbook such as Hanushek and Jackson (1977).

results of the factor analysis appeared reasonable in terms of the way variables loaded onto factors, then we regarded the factor solutions as acceptable. In such cases the solutions sometimes show unusual results, such as exceedingly high communalities for some variables. These estimates are almost surely incorrect—quirks that result when the matrix being inverted has a tiny determinant. In other cases we could not invert the correlation matrix at all with the original set of variables. When this occurred the correlation matrix was inspected for very large values, and provided that a combination of variables seemed sensible, composite measures were produced. For example, a composite variable was formed from estimates of the percentage of a school's students that is white based on teacher and student reports. Or, when instances of ipsativity appeared responsible for the problem, a variable was sometimes dropped. For example, the percentage of students who are black is highly predictable from information about percentage white and percentage Spanish-speaking, and percentage black was therefore dropped from the matrix.

A second type of instance in which problems of multicollinearity arose was in performing some of the regression analyses. When two or more regressors share a substantial portion of their variance all the problems of tipping, variance splitting, and suppressor effects described by Gordon (1968) may, and in fact did, occur at some stage in our analyses. We have paid little attention to this problem in early chapters. The reason for not worrying too much in earlier chapters is that the focus is on how much of the variance in the school disruption measures is predictable from various categories of predictors. In these chapters we are interested in the size of the squared multiple correlations, and in the size of the zero-order correlations of predictors with criteria. The regression coefficients in these early chapters would have little meaning— not only because of the multicollinearity problem, but also because of the problem of lack of completeness. Many relevant variables are omitted from the prediction equations in the early chapters.

In Chapters 10 and 11 attempts are made to assess the consequences of specific causal models. Here, we have taken steps to avoid problems of interpretation of coefficients due to multicollinearity, because the interpretation of these coefficients is a major focus of the research. Several approaches have been used or suggested by others for coping with multicollinearity. Alwin (1976) has adopted the strategy of building equations in a step-wise fashion and not allowing a variable to enter unless it correlates less than .7 with the variables already in the equation. This seemed an unsatisfactory strategy because it would exclude in an arbitrary way many predictors of interest, and result in misspecificaiton of the model to be examined.

Another strategy frequently suggested to cope with multicollinearity is deliberately to introduce bias into the estimates of regression parameters in order to reduce the sampling uncertainly or instability associated with those estimates. The technique known as ridge regression (Hoerl & Kennard, 1970; Price, 1977) involves enhancing the diagonal elements of the correlation matrix. This procedure was eschewed precisely because the estimates it produces are not right—put more gently, they are biased (see Rozeboom 1979, for a comment on the uncritical use of ridge regression). When two variables are so highly correlated that they appear to be measuring the same underlying dimension, we have chosen to combine them.

The catch is that there exists no agreed upon rule for knowing when to combine predictors, or for knowing precisely when to regard multicollinearity as a problem. At one extreme, Rockwell (1975) has suggested regarding a matrix as a characterized by multicollinearity if one cannot reject the hypothesis of singularity according to the Hiatovsky (1969) test. This test is of limited usefulness because it depends on the number of cases in the sample, and because it focuses on the hypothesis that the matrix is singular. Even if the matrix is nonsingular, severe multicollinearity may still be present (Karweit, Fennessey, & Daiger, 1978). And, Hoerl and Kennard (1970) demonstrate that when the eigenvector contains values with a large variance, multicollinearity has a high probability of ravaging the precision of the beta weights, suggesting that one might gain some insight by inspecting the values of the eigenvector. Once a problem is identified, however, one still is faced with the question of what to do about it.

The approach adopted in the present research was to inspect the diagonal elements of the inverse correlation matrix.[8] This is valuable because these elements indicate which variables are most redundant (cf. Gordon, 1968; Karweit, Fennessey, & Daiger, 1978). When very large elements were found, indicating extreme redundancy, composites of closely related variables were formed, or when it appeared justified, a

---

[8]Because these values, C_{ii}, are related to the squared multiple correlation according to the identity $C_{ii} = 1/(1 - R^2)$, what we actually did was examine the squared multiple correlations using the BMD factor analysis program to produce these values (Dixon & Brown, 1977).

variable was dropped from consideration. Judgment is clearly involved in this strategy. More details are given in the chapters decribing the path analytical work.

Use of Rates in Aggregate Data

The second special problem posed when using aggregate data such as those in the present study involves the use of rates, ratios, or percentages. Rates are used because they are often the variables of interest. For example, we are interested in the proportion of teachers experiencing any victimization rather than the number of teachers victimized. The absolute number itself does not capture the essence or the meaning of the construct. Social statistics of this sort (infant mortality, accidents, etc.) are generally reported and interpreted as rates in part to convey the notion of relative risk. Similarly, in describing the social composition of a school, one is usually interested in the proportion of students who are of some ethnic group, not the absolute numbers. A clear consequence of the use of absolute numbers as measures in an ecological analysis is that most variables would measure primarily school size and would have high correlations with each other for that reason alone. For example, the number of white students, number of pop-tops found on the school grounds, and the number of rubber erasers consumed per school year would probably have substantial positive correlations with each other simply because they all would be related to school size.

Yet when rates are used, one runs the risk of introducing correlation among the items because of common elements in the denominators (Pearson, 1897). On the other hand, if the theoretical variables of interest are indeed rates, then the correlation among the raw numbers may also be spurious (Yule, 1910). Bollen and Ward (1979) have recently discussed these issues and some alternatives to the use of rates to avoid these problems.

Because the hypotheses examined in this research do involve rates as predictors and criteria (for example, we are interested in the *preponderance* of students expecting to go to college rather than the absolute number of such students) we have not avoided the use of rates. Instead, we adopt Yule's (1910) argument that the rates themselves *are* the important variable, but have taken additional steps to guard against spurious correlation to the extent possible. Specifically, we have avoided the use of common denominators in different ratio measures wherever feasible. For example, when examining the community variables, the measure of female-headed households used was the ratio of families with children under 16 headed by a female to families under 16 with both husband and wife present; in contrast, the measure of families with incomes 1.24 times the poverty level or below uses all families as the base. Similar approaches have been used throughout and may be expected to reduce spurious correlation due to the use of rates.

Alternative Measurement and Causal Models

Before drawing conclusions based on the Chapter 10 results, we perfomed the additional (rather technical) analyses for two reasons. First, multicollinearity remained problematic in our Chapter 10 results. The results of the path analyses reported in that chapter are in one sense highly conservative: they probably underestimate the influence of major dimensions of school organization on disorder simply because so many correlated predictors share the predictable variance. Second, there were strong hints in our examination of the victimization measures in Chapter 4 that alternative ways of measuring disorder could lead to different substantive interpretations. Accordingly, in Chapter 11 we assumed that a smaller number of underlying dimensions (or factors) characterize school organization. We abandoned the causal precedence assumed in Chapter 10 to arrive at a less conservative estimate of the influence of school characteristics on school disorder. In Chapter 11 we use maximum-likelihood techniques (Jöreskog & Sörbom, 1978) to estimate alternative structural and measurement models of student and teacher victimization. Chapter 11 is probably of most interest to social science methodologists, and many readers unfamiliar with recent statistical and psychometric developments (or who are anxious to get to the bottom line in Chapter 12) may want to skip this chapter. The methods used are described more fully in Chapter 11.

CHAPTER 4

The Measurement of School
Disorder

This chapter describes the research that went into developing measures of school disorder. The measures of disorder are limited largely to school rates of personal victimization. In other words, vandalism and property loss are excluded from the present focus. A sizable number of different items on the principal, teacher, and student questionnaires requested information about victimization experiences and school disruption. Information was requested about events that range in seriousness from remarks and gestures through rape and homicide. For the most part these items are specifically worded and refer to concrete experiences rather than to global reports of disorder. Exceptions exist. Principals were asked for their rating of the seriousness of the problem of "vandalism, personal attacks, and theft" during the 1975–1976 school year. And teachers reported on the frequency with which teachers "maintain control [keep order] in class."[1]

In general, we chose not to use the vaguer ratings of disorder as criteria, and instead restricted the analyses to the more concrete reports of personal victimization. Similarly, the many items in the teacher and student questionnaires requesting information about fear of crime or

---

[1]This item was treated as an independent rather than dependent measure in the NIE (1978) Safe School Study report. Because of the clear potential for this item to overlap with any dependent measure of student disruption we have avoided its use as a predictor in addition to excluding it from our criterion measures on the grounds of vagueness of wording.

fear for one's safety were excluded from these analyses. Fear is an important dependent variable in its own right, but fear may be the product of more than actual personal experiences (Antunes, Cook, Cook, & Skogan, undated; Cook & Cook, 1976).

Three exceptions were made to the selection of only concrete examples of personal victimization. The first of these was the question asked of principals that was mentioned earlier. It was included because it was the only item about recent school disruption asked of principals that had appreciable variance across schools. The second exception was the use of the item from the student questionnaire, "How often do you bring something to school to protect yourself?" (called "carry weapon" in the tables). This item was included because it appears to be the only self-reported misconduct item in the questionnaires. The third exception was teacher reports that they hesitated to confront misbehaving students for fear for their own safety. This item was included because of its relatively specific reference to concrete incidents.

The nature of these measures of school disorder requires some discussion. They are for the most part questionnaire reports of personal victimization of one sort or another. They differ from other frequently used measures of delinquency, such as self-reported delinquent activity of the sort studied by Gold and his colleagues (Gold & Moles, 1977; Gold & Reimer, 1975), interview-based victimization reports such as those conducted by the Census Bureau (1974), or officially reported crime (Kelley, 1976). Other types of data about school disorder were available for study. The first kind of such information is the set of incident reports submitted by principals as part of the Safe School Study. Many events, of course, never come to the attention of the principal, and this is one limitation of these incident reports. A second limitation that is more serious is that many schools did not return any incident reports, but it is not possible to discriminate between schools with no incidents and those which did not comply with the request. Additional information could be drawn from student interviews also conducted as part of the Safe School Study. These interviews, conducted with smaller samples of persons, generally resulted in lower rates of reported victimization than did the questionnaire reports (NIE, 1978, Vol. 1, p. 27; Vol. 2, Appendix C). Although there are reasons to prefer student interview reports to the student questionnaire reports for some purposes, we have opted to use student questionnaire reports because the larger number of responses makes for more reliable estimates in a study of variation across schools. The interview data may be superior for assessing the total amount of victimization or victimization rates for the entire population of students. The use of questionnaire data here focuses on variability in rates across school rather than in the central tendency estimates. The evidence suggesting that questionnaire estimates are too high is not necessarily a cause for great concern. The relations among alternative measures of school disorder are discussed in a technical note at the end of this chapter.

The student and teacher victimization reports involved a retrospective report for a 1-month recall period. The reports by principals refer to the most recent past school year. Although the use of victim surveys to estimate rates of offenses is a relatively recent development, considerable research has been performed to assess the characteristics of victim reports of personal victimization, and useful summaries of this research are presented by Biderman, Johnson, McIntyre, and Weir (1967), Ennis (1967), M. R. Gottfredson and Hindelang (1975, 1977), Hindelang and M. R. Gottfredson (1976), and the Law Enforcement Assistance Administration (1972). This prior research implies that victims fail to report a substantial number of crimes that are known to the police, especially crimes involving offenders related to the victim, and that substantial memory effects occur. These memory effects are of two types: forward telescoping of events transpiring before the recall period into the recall period (and to a lesser extent backwards telescoping) and decay of memory, or forgetting. The shorter the recall period the less reports are affected by forgetting, and the use of bounding (a technique used to raise the salience of the beginning of the recall period) decreases problems due to telescoping.

In the victimization reports examined here the recall period was short, but bounding was not used. The absence of bounding implies that a substantial amount of forward telescoping is to be expected. Some special checks based on a comparison of interview data from students and a small study involving bounded data collection from teachers reported by the NIE (1978, Vol. 2, Appendix C) suggest that time telescoping is not of major proportions in the teacher questionnaire data. At the same time, checks revealed major discrepancies between student interview and student questionnaire responses. The questionnaire method results in much higher estimates than does the interview method. A postinterview check suggested that serious recall problems ("I just didn't remember right"), misunderstanding ("I thought it meant the 80 cents I had stolen"), and telescoping ("When I thought about it I decided it was really in April or March") were the major sources of error. The foregoing implies that the questionnaire responses regarding victimization experiences may have problems if one wishes to make point estimates of the extent of victimization. It also implies that substantial noise or error variance, and indeed perhaps some systematic biases, exist in these data. A report by Decker (1977) implies that although rates for cities estimated using victimization data and official data are moderately correlated, these correlations are always far from perfect, and for some offenses are low. The extent to which these questionnaire measures covary with more objective but unavailable indexes of school disorder is a major problem for future research, and our lack of knowledge about this issue for these data is a limitation of the present research.

Table 2 shows the means and standard deviations for all school disorder items used in analyses in Chapters 5 through 11. (Refer to the questionnaires, shown in an appendix, for the exact wording of the items used.) Our initial expectation was that either a single general factor, or two broad groupings of items would emerge: personal victimizations such as attacks, rapes, and robberies; and property victimizations or theft. This expectation was based on earlier research which found such groupings (G. D. Gottfredson, 1975; D. M. Gottfredson, Neithercutt, Venezia, & Wenk, 1970; Sokal, 1974) using a variety of different types of data.

An inspection of Table 3 shows that this expectation was violated. This table shows the correlations among the items. One type of teacher report tends to correlate with another type of teacher report, one type of student report tends to correlate with another type of student report. The principal's overall assessment of the seriousness of problems of thefts, personal attack, and vandalism tended to correlate with teacher reports; and the principal's reports of homicide and rape, which had little variance (Table 2), were essentially unrelated to the other measures.

The structure of the items is clearer still in the factor analysis results shown in Tables 4 and 5 which show the one-factor and varimax rotated two- and three-factor solutions. All three solutions were inspected because a plot of the eigenvalues did not give a clear guide to the selection of the number of factors, and all three are shown here because of the central role of decisions about the dependent variable. Most of the

TABLE 2

Means and Standard Deviations for Measures of School Disruption
in Junior and Senior High Schools

Measure and source	Junior high			Senior high		
	M	SD	N	M	SD	N
Principal						
Seriousness of problem[a]	2.26	.90	305	2.41	.87	304
Any homicide[b]	.00	.06	308	.00	.06	311
Any rape[b]	.01	.08	308	.01	.10	308
Teacher						
Robbery[b]	.01	.01	311	.01	.02	312
Theft[b]	.22	.12	311	.20	.10	312
Rape or attempt[b]	.00	.00	311	.00	.00	312
Physical attack[b]	.01	.02	311	.00	.01	312
Remarks or gestures[b]	.87	.48	311	1.75	.39	312
Threats[b]	.22	.29	311	1.17	.20	312
Fear for safety[a]	1.18	.22	311	1.21	.23	312
Student						
Carry weapon[a]	3.61	.16	310	3.66	.18	311
Robbery less than $1[b]	.07	.05	310	.02	.03	311
Robbery, $1 or more[b]	.04	.04	310	.02	.02	311
Theft less than $1[b]	.31	.11	310	.18	.08	311
Theft, $1 or more[b]	.16	.07	310	.15	.07	311
Physical attack[b]	.07	.04	310	.03	.03	311
Overall disruption	−.04	7.24	296	−.17	6.98	295
Teacher victimization	−.07	4.55	301	−.16	4.45	304
Student victimization	−.02	3.63	301	.02	3.36	303

Note. Principals reported for a 12-month recall period. Teachers and students reported for a single month in an unbounded questionnaire.
[a]The mean reported for these measures is the mean (across schools) of the within-school mean report on Likert-type scales. The scale for principals' report of seriousness of problem ranged from 1 (no problem) to 5 (very serious problem). The scale for teachers' reports of how often they feared for their safety if they confronted misbehaving students ranged from 1 (never) to 4 (many times). The student reports of how often they carry something ("weapon") to protect themselves is scored in the reverse direction, ranging from 1 (most of the time) to 4 (never).
[b]The mean reported for these measures is the mean (across schools) proportion of respondents per school reporting that type of victimization.

variables load on a single factor shown by the one-factor solutions. At the same time clearly interpretable two-factor solutions emerge that are parallel for junior and senior high schools. The first factor may be labeled a Teacher-victimization factor, and the second factor a Student-victimization factor. An examination of the three-factor solutions shows that the third factor to emerge is not parallel for junior and senior high schools. In the junior high schools the third factor is a doublet factor

TABLE 3

Correlations among Measures of School Disruption in Junior and Senior High Schools

Measure and source[a]	1	2	3	4	5	6	7	8	9	10	11	12	13	14	15	16
1. Seriousness of problem, P	—	.04	.14	.10	.18	.11	.21	.36	.33	.34	.17	.08	.10	-.01	.16	-.03
2. Any homicide, P	.11	—	.00	-.02	-.05	-.01	-.02	-.10	-.04	-.05	.05	-.05	-.05	.01	.00	-.06
3. Any rape, P	.11	.70	—	.08	.01	-.01	-.02	.03	.02	.06	.02	.03	-.03	.05	.14	-.04
4. Robbery, T	.17	-.02	.16	—	.16	.28	.41	.28	.33	.34	.07	.14	.04	.04	.03	.10
5. Theft, T	.18	.08	.06	.28	—	.08	.24	.35	.33	.29	.14	.11	.04	.06	.07	.05
6. Rape or attempt, T	.05	-.01	-.01	.12	-.03	—	.34	.06	.06	.04	-.01	-.02	-.05	.02	-.01	.00
7. Physical attack, T	.20	-.02	-.04	.35	.26	.09	—	.40	.48	.35	.25	.21	.17	.04	.04	.16
8. Remarks or gestures, T	.33	-.03	-.03	.35	.49	.05	.49	—	.84	.76	.36	.27	.22	-.05	.06	.16
9. Threats, T	.30	-.04	-.03	.31	.36	.07	.47	.84	—	.80	.49	.32	.26	.03	.06	.16
10. Fear for safety, T	.31	-.03	-.03	.29	.35	.07	.41	.78	.85	—	.41	.21	.21	-.09	.12	.05
11. Carry weapon, S	.11	.05	.07	.09	.20	.08	.33	.38	.43	.41	—	.31	.31	.07	.11	.15
12. Robbery, less than $1, S	.21	.00	-.03	.17	.28	-.13	.20	.31	.24	.28	.40	—	.56	.24	.16	.45
13. Robbery, $1 or more, S	.16	.01	-.04	.10	.22	.01	.19	.24	.26	.26	.34	.63	—	.23	.17	.43
14. Theft, less than $1, S	.01	.19	.09	-.03	.12	-.08	-.10	-.16	-.18	-.18	.04	.25	.28	—	.48	.23
15. Theft, $1 or more, S	.02	.12	.03	-.01	.17	-.02	-.06	-.03	-.06	.03	.16	.39	.40	.58	—	.27
16. Physical attack, S	.08	-.10	-.10	.18	.29	-.08	.11	.23	.18	.17	.22	.48	.49	.30	.27	—

Note. Senior high schools ($N \geq 303$) above the diagonal, junior high schools ($N \geq 301$) below the diagonal. Signs have been reversed when appropriate so that high values reflect a greater degree of the characteristic in question.
[a]P = principal report, T = teacher report, S = student report.

TABLE 4

Varimax Rotated Principal Factor Analyses of School Disruption Measures in Junior (N≥ 301) and Senior (N ≥ 303) High Schools: One and Two Factor Solutions

| | Junior high | | | | Senior high | | | | |
| | One factor | | Two factor | | | One factor | | Two factor | | |
Measure and source	I	h^2	I	II	h^2	I	h^2	I	II	h^2
Principal										
Seriousness of problem	36	13	35	01	12	37	14	39	02	15
Any homocide	-02	00	-04	12	02	-06	00	-05	-04	00
Any rape	-02	00	-03	05	00	05	00	05	02	00
Teacher										
Robbery	40	16	40	-03	16	39	16	40	06	16
Theft	50	24	47	14	24	37	14	38	03	15
Rape or attempt	05	00	06	-12	02	13	02	16	-05	03
Physical attack	53	30	54	-10	30	54	29	52	14	29
Remarks or gestures	86	74	89	-18	83	83	69	86	11	75
Threats	83	69	88	-24	84	91	83	92	16	87
Fear for safety	80	65	84	-19	74	79	62	83	06	70
Student										
Weapon	51	26	49	16	27	50	26	42	30	27
Robbery, less than $1	51	26	48	57	56	43	19	23	70	54
Robbery, $1 or more	47	22	44	57	52	37	14	17	67	48
Theft, less than $1	01	00	-06	67	45	07	00	-10	46	22
Theft, $1 or more	14	02	08	69	48	16	03	04	34	11
Physical attack	39	15	36	47	35	26	07	07	57	33

Note. Decimals omitted. Variables are reflected when necessary so that higher values imply a greater degree of the characteristic in question.

TABLE 5

Varimax Rotated Principal Factor Analysis of School Disruption Measures in Junior (N ≥ 301) and Senior (N ≥ 303) High Schools: Three Factor Solutions

Measure and source	Junior high				Senior high			
	I	II	III	h^2	I	II	III	h^2
Principal								
Seriousness of problem	36	07	12	15	36	01	14	15
Any homicide	01	06	82	68	−05	−03	−01	00
Any rape	05	−03	84	72	04	02	03	00
Teacher								
Robbery	41	04	08	17	27	07	50	32
Theft	42	23	08	26	33	02	20	15
Rape or attempt	08	−10	00	02	−01	−04	54	29
Physical attack	44	01	−04	30	38	15	60	53
Remarks or gestures	91	01	−06	83	87	07	13	77
Threats	91	−05	−08	84	92	12	15	89
Fear for safety	86	−02	−07	74	85	02	11	73
Student								
Weapon	44	27	−11	28	45	28	01	28
Robbery, less than $1	35	66	−06	57	26	68	00	53
Robbery, $1 or more	31	66	−07	54	23	66	−08	50
Theft, less than $1	−18	62	18	46	−12	49	09	26
Theft, $1 or more	−06	68	10	47	03	34	06	12
Physical attack	24	56	−13	39	09	57	03	33

Note. Decimals omitted. Variables are reflected when necessary so that higher values imply a greater degree of the characteristic in question.

defined by the principals' reports of homicide and rape. These are items with very low means and little variance, suggesting that too many factors have been extracted. The third factor for senior high schools splits the Teacher factor into two separate factors: one defined by remarks, threats, and a hesitation to confront misbehaving students due to a fear for one's safety; and one defined by robbery, rape or attempted rape, and physical attack. The decision about the number of factors in this case was a difficult one, and no choice is clearly superior to the others. Our decision was to create measures representative of the two-factor solution factors as well as a (redundant) measure that represents the one-factor solution factor. A certain amount of judgment entered this decision and the selection of items. The Teacher factor appears attributable in part to the high correlations among three items of

TABLE 6

Correlations among the Composite Measures of School Disruption

Composite measure	Overall disruption	Teacher victimization	Student victimization
Overall disruption	—	.85	.67
Teacher victimization	.82	—	.21
Student victimization	.68	.19	—

Note. Senior high schools above the diagonal—N's range from 295 to 304; junior high schools below the diagonal—N's range from 296 to 301.

relatively minor seriousness (items 8, 9, and 10 in Table 2). An examination of alternative measures is presented in the technical note at the end of this chapter.

Three measures were created by assigning equal weight to each school disruption measure in the following composites:

1. *Overall Disruption.* High scoring schools on this scale are those where the principal reports a serious problem of thefts, attacks, and vandalism; teachers report being robbed, having students threaten to hurt them, hesitating to confront misbehaving students for fear of their own safety; students report bringing something to school to protect themselves, being robbed of small and larger amounts, having something worth more than a dollar stolen, and being attacked.

2. *Teacher Victimization.* High scoring schools on this scale are those in which teachers report robberies, rapes or attempted rapes, physical attacks, remarks or gestures, threats, and hesitating to confront misbehaving students for fear of their safety.

3. *Student Victimization.* High scoring schools on this scale are those in which students report small or slightly larger robberies, small or slightly larger thefts, and physical attacks.

Tables 6 and 7 provide crucial information about the criterion measures studied in Chapters 5 through 10. Table 6 shows the correlations among the measures of disorder. Overall disruption shows its expected substantial correlation with the other two measures. This is expected because of the part–whole relations among these measures: the overall disruption measure is largely redundant with the other two. It is used primarily because it provides a single summary index, and because it contains some items which it would have not made good sense to include in scales called "teacher victimization" or "student victimi-

TABLE 7
Alpha Reliability of School Disruption Scores

Measure	Junior high	Senior school	Number of items
Overall disruption	.79	.77	14
Teacher victimization	.77	.75	7
Student victimization	.78	.69	5

zation." These items are the principals' global reports and the students' reports that they carry something to school to protect themselves. The teacher victimization and student victimization reports are nearly independent, with only about 4% of their variance in common for either junior or senior high schools. Although this degree of association is significantly different from zero, the main thing to notice is that the size of the association is very small. We cannot expect the same variables that predict one of these criteria necessarily to predict the other.

Table 7 shows alpha reliability coefficients for the three measures. Alpha reliability is a measure of homogeneity or internal consistency of a measure. It ranges from 0.0 to 1.0 and is interpreted as the ratio of hypothetical "true score" variance to total score variance. These reliability estimates are important because unreliable measurement limits the extent to which the variable in question can be predicted (see Stanley, 1971, for an explanation). In the present case, Table 7 implies moderately high but not spectacular reliabilities.

Now that we have explained how the measures of school disorder were derived and provided some information on their characteristics, we go on in the remaining chapters to describe the search for reliable predictors of school rates of disruption. The technical note that follows provides some details of our examination of the convergent and discriminant validity of our victimization measures by comparing them to interview measures and by examining data aggregated in alternative ways. The next chapter describes work with the community variables, and some readers may want to skip ahead to that chapter.

TECHNICAL NOTE ON THE MEASUREMENT OF VICTIMIZATION

Interpretation of our research depends on an understanding of the victimization measures. Several considerations imply that this issue requires more careful scrutiny.

First, the victimization data collected in different ways in the Safe School Study resulted in discrepant estimates of the absolute levels of victimization in schools (NIE, 1978, Volume 2, Appendix C). The student-questionnaire method generally produced much higher estimates than the student interview. For teachers the discrepancies were smaller or not reliable for the more serious incidents, but were reliable and sizeable for the minor incidents (i.e., thefts of under $10). The NIE report (1978, p. 27) states that, although the levels of victimization derived from questionnaire and interview sources differ, variations among students and schools correspond more closely. This statement suggests that the two kinds of measures correlate highly with each other, although the evidence to support this conclusion is not presented. Careful examination of the correlations among measures of victimization based on alternative sources of information is required. Second, measures of school disorder derived from the student questionnaire victimization reports show low (positive) correlations with other measures of the level of school disorder. Specifically, the measures derived from aggregated teacher-questionnaire victimization reports or principal ratings of the seriousness of school theft, vandalism, and attacks show only low correlations with student victimization reports (Table 6). These correlations, which are much smaller than the reliabilities of the teacher and student victimization measures, imply that different things are being measured, and that the meaning of different measures of school disruption may be markedly different.

Third, boys and girls experience disparate rates of victimization. The percentage of boys attacked is 2.6 times greater than girls according to the student questionnaire reports, and 2.3 times greater according to the interview data, and results for robberies are also disparate (NIE, 1978, p. 100). Rates for boys and girls may vary in similar ways across schools, or they may not. This issue requires scrutiny.[2]

Fourth, despite some examination of cross-race victimization experiences in the NIE (1978) report, no thoroughgoing attempt to examine black and white school victimization rates has yet been made. Because of the central importance of race in American society, and because of concern about the quality of social interaction in desegregated schools, it is important to know if a single ecological measure adequately represents the experience of blacks and whites in schools.

[2]The possibility that pooling boys' and girls' reports in creating aggregate-level measures of victimization may create unclear criterion measures was suggested by Jackson Toby in personal communication.

Finally, several community and school characteristics examined later in Chapters 5 and 6 (percentage nonwhite, proportion of families on welfare, and teacher and principal estimates of student ability) that are closely linked to school racial composition are among the highest correlates of teacher (but not student) victimization rates. It is not clear why this pattern emerges, and it is a troublesome and difficult result to understand. Do students in predominantly black schools really victimize teachers more than do students in schools that are predominantly white? If so, why do the students not also inform us of more victimization? It is possible that poor measurement of the student victim experiences account for the pattern of results. Alternatively, white teachers may in certain circumstances perceive certain behavior as more offensive when performed by a black than the same behavior performed by a white.

One purpose of this technical note is to examine the reliability and construct validity of several alternative measures of school disruption available in the Safe School Study's data. The psychometric properties and degree of convergence of victim reports, aggregated separately by race and sex, are examined. And, measures based on interview and questionnaire data are examined to determine whether they show the same patterns of correlations across schools. Later, in Chapter 11, we put this work to a second purpose. There we explore some consequences of alternative victimization measures for the substantive interpretation of research results in the explanation of school disorder.

At the outset we assumed that the student-questionnaire data would provide a sounder basis for research on school disorder than would the interview data because the number of students responding to the questionnaire in a typical school was almost five times as large as the number of students responding to interviews. Large numbers mean more reliable means (Stanley, 1971) and therefore sounder ecological measures. The numbers of respondents in the average school to each potential data source are shown in Table 8.[3]

Analyses

In addition to the victimization measures described earlier in this chapter, several alternative indexes are examined here. The reports of

---

[3]No use was made of the principals' incident reports because those reports were collected in such a way that it is impossible to determine whether a school experienced no incidents or simply failed to send in the report, and too few teacher telephone interviews were conducted to enable useful school-level analyses.

TABLE 8

Response Rates for Questionnaires and Interviews for Schools in the Study

Instrument	Response rate	Avg. no. per school
Principal questionnaire	73[a]	1
Teacher questionnaire	76	37
Student questionnaire	81	49
Student interview	83	10

[a]623 of 851 schools in the sample. Of participating schools (642) the response rate is 97%.

personal victimization from the student interviews are aggregated to the school level. In addition, the teacher- and student-questionnaire reports of personal victimization are aggregated separately for males and females, and for blacks and whites. The correlations among various scales supposed to measure school disorder are examined, as are their reliabilities.[4] As one way to determine whether the various measures tap only a single construct, disattenuated correlations are computed for certain scales using Spearman's correction for unreliability. The patterns of correlation of the alternative victimization measures with other variables (shown in subsequent chapters to correlate with student or teacher victimization) are also examined.

Student Interview Measures

As shown in Table 8, few student interviews were conducted in the average school. In junior high schools, the number ranged from 7 to 17 (mean = 10.7), and in senior high schools the number ranged from 2 to 17 (mean = 9.6). These small n's imply that school-level aggregates are likely to have low reliability. Furthermore, the number of students interviewed per school is not independent of several school characteristics. Correlations of the number of students interviewed with several

---

[4]Scales are constructed by summing standard scores for the aggregated items. Because item variances therefore equal one, the reliability coefficients can be estimated by

$$\rho_{TX}^2 = \frac{I}{I-1} \frac{(1-I)}{\sigma_X^2}$$

where I is the number of items in the scale.

Table 9

Correlations of Number of Students Interviewed with
Other School Characteristics for Junior and Senior High Schools

School characteristic	Junior	Senior
Impoverished and disorganized community	−04	−19**
Affluent, educated community	13*	09
Percentage students white	10	23**
Parental SES and self-reported ability	13*	03
Social and educational disadvantage	−04	−20**
Percentage of teachers white	13*	18**
Number of different students taught	14*	06
School attachment	16**	00
Good race relations	18**	00
Mean grade point average	18**	02
Teacher victimization	01	−16**
Student victimization (questionnaire)	−06	−15**

Note. Decimals omitted. For junior highs, n's range from 256–307 schools. For senior highs, n's range from 254–311 schools.
*$p < .05$; **$p < .01$.

school characteristics are shown in Table 9. (The other variables in the table are discussed in Chapters 5–9). Taken together, the correlations shown here suggest that more interviews were conducted in schools that may be regarded as more pleasant places to conduct interviews. This would introduce some bias into these interview data.

The correlations (not shown) among the aggregated items from the student interviews are generally quite low. Nevertheless we attempted to create a scale by adding together the standard scores for the following aggregated student-interview victimization items: (a) In [the last two months] did anyone force you to hand over money or things *worth less than a dollar* while you were at school, going to or from school, or at a school event held off school grounds? (b) In [the last two months] did anyone take money or things worth a dollar or more directly from you by force, weapons, or threats while you were at school, or at a school event held off school grounds? (c) In the same two months, did anyone TRY to take anything directly from you by force, weapons, or threats without succeeding while you were at school, going to or from school, or at a school event held off school grounds? (d) Other than the incidents we have already talked about, did anyone attack you physically and hurt you in [the last two months] while you were at school, going to or from school, or at school events held off school grounds? (e) Other than the incidents we have already talked about, did anyone TRY to attack you physically without succeeding in [the last two months] while you were at school, going to or from school, or at a school event held off school grounds? (f) In [the last two months] did anyone steal anything of yours from your desk, locker, or other place at school?

Student- and Teacher-Questionnaire Measures

Scales were also created by aggregating the student- and teacher-questionnaire victimization items separately for males and females, and blacks and whites. These aggregates were used to create student and teacher victimization scales that paralleled the scales described earlier in this chapter. That is, the same items were used, but each scale only applies to the aggregated reports of white teachers, black teachers, and so on. In addition, because most victimization experienced by teachers is minor in nature (see Figure 1), and because of our concern that the teacher victimization scales would therefore be measuring mostly nuisance events or minor indignities, scales measuring only serious teacher victimization experiences were also constructed. Only robbery, theft, or physical attack were included. (Rape was so rare, it was not used as an item.) It is possible, of course, that many of these incidents were also relatively minor, but this does exclude the high frequency remarks or gestures, threats, and incidents where teachers feared for their safety.

Correlations among the alternative measures of victimization are shown in Table 10 for junior (above the diagonal) and senior (below) high schools. Note that many of the entries in this table are part–whole correlations—boys are a subset of all students, for example.

The student interview estimates (not aggregated for subgroups because of the small number of interviews per school) have low correlations with the other measures. Even though the students interviewed are a subset of those responding to the questionnaire, the correlations between the interview-based and questionnaire-based measures are only .42 and .30 for junior and senior high schools, respectively.

Other correlations in Table 10 are of special interest. However measured, student and teacher victimization measures have low or negligible correlations. Black student victimization has positive but tiny correlations with white student victimization, and boys' victimization

TABLE 10
Correlations among Alternative Measures of Student and

	Students					
	Questionnaire					
Group and method	All	Boys	Girls	Whites	Blacks	Interview
Student questionnaire						
All students	—	85**	79**	48**	35**	42**
Boys	84**	—	40**	40**	33**	36**
Girls	57**	15**	—	40**	24**	33**
Whites	66**	58**	38**	—	06	23**
Blacks	26**	17*	18**	03	—	06
Student interview						
All students	30**	29**	04	29**	−03	—
Teacher questionnaire						
Including indignities						
All	21**	18**	03	19**	−02	22**
Men	19**	19**	01	22**	−02	24**
Women	20**	14*	01	15*	−03	28**
Whites	22**	17**	03	21**	−01	29**
Blacks	14*	14*	05	24**	01	06
Serious events only						
Men	14*	15*	01	21**	01	16**
Women	15*	08	01	04	02	19**
Whites	20**	16**	02	18**	04	22**
Blacks	16*	19**	00	20**	−01	00

Note. Decimals omitted. Correlations above the diagonal are for junior high schools (N = 203–311); correlations below the diagonal are for senior high schools (N = 188–312).
*p < .05; **p < .01.

correlates only .40 and .15 with girls' victimization in junior and senior high schools, respectively. The correlations of black and white teacher victimization are only moderate.

Reliabilities

The Table 10 results are, of course, correlations among fallible measures. The measures are not perfectly reliable, and correlations less than 1.0 are to be expected. Even alternative measures of an identical construct do not correlate perfectly if they incorporate measurement error. Because all of these estimates are based on small numbers of teachers or students, especially for the subgroup measures, measurement error may be great.

Teacher Victimization for Junior and Senior High Schools

					Teachers			
	All types				Serious			
All	Men	Women	Whites	Blacks	Men	Women	Whites	Blacks
19**	19**	18**	23**	05	19**	23**	28**	−02
13*	13*	12*	15**	02	11*	15**	18**	−02
19**	18**	16**	21**	05	18**	21**	26**	−03
26**	29**	22**	28**	16*	14*	09	15**	03
01	00	−03	01	−05	04	00	07	−02
15**	17**	16**	18**	−04	18**	24**	23**	−06
—	87**	92**	95**	66**	65**	69**	76**	42**
86**	—	66**	82**	60**	83**	46**	68**	44**
88**	61**	—	88**	58**	44**	80**	70**	30**
95**	86**	84**	—	44**	62**	66**	84**	23**
57**	48**	46**	38**	—	44**	36**	27**	76**
66**	82**	42**	66**	39**	—	41**	70**	46**
65**	34**	82**	61**	29**	30**	—	77**	25**
81**	74**	71**	85**	31**	80**	69**	—	15**
39**	32**	25**	20**	76**	44**	24**	27**	—

Reliability estimates are shown in Table 11. None are high, and some are low. The reliabilities of the senior high school student measures are usually lower than for junior high schools. The relibility estimates for the interview-based measures are low, reliabilities for black teacher victimization are modest, and the reliabilities of the serious teacher victimization measures are also low.

Construct Validity

One way of assessing whether two alternative measures are measuring the same latent variable, or whether they are in part measuring more than one factor, is to estimate the correlations between

TABLE 11
Reliability Estimates for Victimization Measures

	Junior high		Senior high		
Group and method	α	Average persons per school	α	Average persons per school	Number of items
Student questionnaire					
All students	.78	53	.69	48	5
Boys	.70	26	.65	24	5
Girls	.77	26	.56	24	5
Whites	.73	35	.40	34	5
Blacks	.59	10	.68	11	5
Student interview					
All students	.46	11	.26	10	6
Teacher questionnaire					
Including indignities					
All teachers	.77	30	.75	46	7
Men	.69	14	.71	25	7
Women	.72	16	.73	21	7
Whites	.77	26	.78	39	7
Blacks	.63	6	.64	8	7
Serious events only					
Men	.45	14	.51	25	3
Women	.40	16	.37	21	3
Whites	.54	26	.51	39	3
Blacks	.39	6	.42	8	3

hypothetical underlying true scores. Classical true score theory postulates that a score is equal to the sum of two parts: true score and error.
The error is random and uncorrelated with the true scores. True scores
are systematic. The true score model is usually written

$$X_i = T_i + e_i$$

but it is possible to think of the true score as being composed of more
than one underlying construct or factor. The principal component
model can be written

$$X_i = \sum a_j T_{ij} + e_i$$

This model assumes that a variable may be composed of more than one
true score (shared with other observed variables) and error. When the
correlations between two variables—say male and female victimization

reports—are corrected for error, and are found to be substantially less than one, we may assume that each measures something other than what they measure in common. In other words, we may speculate that more than one underlying factor is responsible for the systematic variance in one or both of the measures.

Correlations that have been corrected for measurement error (when reliability is low, error is high) are shown in Table 12 for selected pairs of measures. With few exceptions, considering these pairs to be alternative measures of the same underlying variables would be unwise. It appears that, although they are highly unreliable, the student-interview measures do measure mostly the same thing(s) as the student-questionnaire measures, but it is highly likely that the interview and questionnaire measures each also systematically measure something that they do not measure in common. (The present results do not provide any particular clues about what those "somethings" may be.) In short, on the basis of the Table 12 results, the victimization measures appear factorially complex, and it appears that black and white student victimization measures, male and female victimization measures, and

TABLE 12

Disattenuated Correlations between Selected Measures
of Student and Teacher Victimization

Victimization measure	Junior high	Senior high
Student questionnaire		
Boys' with girls'	.54	.25
Whites' with blacks'	.09	.06
Student questionnaire and student interview		
All students'	.70	.71
Student and teacher questionnaires		
All teachers' with all students'	.24	.29
Student interview and teacher questionnaire		
All teachers' with all students'	.25	.50
Teacher questionnaire		
Including indignities		
Men's with women's	.94	.85
Black's with white's	.63	.54
Serious events only		
Men's with women's	.97	.69
Whites' with blacks'	.33	.58

Note. Correlations have been "corrected" for measurement error to estimate the correlations between hypothetical "true" scores, using homogeneity coefficients and Spearman's correction for attenuation.

black and white teacher victimization measures in part tap different underlying dimensions.

The assessment of the meaning of the alternative victimization measures is difficult using the Safe School Study data because essentially all of the measures of school disruption are self-reports of personal victimization. No good self-reported delinquency data were collected in the study, nor were direct observations of incidents in the school made.[5] As one means of determining the convergence of the various victimization measures being examined here with other measures of school disruption, however, the correlations of these measures with two other variables are of special interest. Table 13 shows correlations with an aggregated variable that comes close to being a self-report delinquency measure—students' reports that they bring something to school to protect themselves. And, Table 14 shows correlations with the principal's report about the seriousness of school vandalism, attacks, and thefts. These two variables tend to correlate most highly with the teacher measures, and there are some interesting patterns in the results for subgroups in Table 13. The most important of these is that black student victimization correlates .35 and .44 with black students' reports of carrying something to protect themselves, but that this latter measure has near zero correlations with white student victimization and all measures of teacher victimization. The highest correlations with all types of teacher victimization are girls' reports of carrying a weapon for self-defense. Attempts at interpretation of these results would necessarily be highly speculative, and we will resist the temptation.

The Table 13 and 14 results provide some evidence that the teacher victimization measures (especially) are related to some independent measures of school disruption. The evidence about the student victimization measures is more ambiguous.

One concern in assessing the meaning of the victimization measures is that they may be measuring not only victimization, but also differential social perception of victimization. For example, if white teachers perceive the same behavior as more serious or threatening when performed by black youth than when performed by white youth, then we may wish to regard the "victimization" measure as also partly a

---

[5]Principals' reports of incidents were collected. We have not used them here because the data were collected in such a way that distinguishing nonresponses from cases of no incidents to report is not possible, and we have not been able to figure out how to cope with that obstacle.

TABLE 13

Correlations Between Victimization Measures
and a Self-Report Misconduct Item

	How often do you bring something to school to protect yourself?							
	Junior				Senior			
Victimization measure	Boys	Girls	Whites	Blacks	Boys	Girls	Whites	Blacks
Student questionnaire								
All students	36**	10	17**	14*	20**	17**	17**	04
Boys	29**	03	10	15*	19**	13*	19**	04
Girls	31**	15**	20**	08	00	04	−02	−05
Whites	17**	09	16**	04	18**	15**	26**	01
Blacks	16*	−10	00	35**	05	−07	−02	44**
Student interview								
All students	19**	16**	06	13*	16**	16*	19**	06
Teacher questionnaire								
Including indignities								
All teachers	26**	39**	20**	07	20**	43**	26**	06
Men	26**	33**	21**	10	19**	40**	30**	11
Women	24**	36**	20**	04	22**	44**	23**	05
Whites	23**	39**	18**	07	25**	41**	33**	06
Blacks	15**	20**	12	02	−01	21**	−01	06
Serious events only								
Men	21**	15**	14*	06	12*	20**	22**	06
Women	16**	13*	13*	00	12*	31**	10	04
Whites	16**	18**	13*	03	21**	28**	26**	04
Blacks	12	02	09	−04	−03	09	−01	08
N's (range)	211– 310	211– 310	202– 301	188– 246	216– 307	217– 308	200– 291	191– 223

Note. Decimals omitted.
*p < .05; **p < .01.

measure of stereotyped social perceptions. The positive correlation between percentage of students black and teacher victimization (see Chapter 6) could be interpreted as reflecting social perception. Table 15, which documents levels of black and white reports of robbery and attack in schools of differing racial composition, implies that such an interpretation may be too facile. On the whole, both black and white teachers report more robbery and attack in predominantly black schools. (The anomolous bimodal distribution for black teachers' reports of attacks is an interesting puzzle.)

TABLE 14

Correlations between Victimization Measures and Principal's Report of Seriousness of the Problem of Vandalism, Personal Attack and Theft in the Past Year

Victimization measure	Junior	Senior
Student questionnaire		
All students	.13*	.09
Boys	.10	.02
Girls	.14*	.06
Whites	.09	.03
Blacks	−.05	−.06
Student interview		
All students	.14*	.02
Teacher questionnaire		
Including indignities		
All teachers	.33**	.35**
Men	.28**	.30**
Women	.32**	.38**
Whites	.31**	.31**
Blacks	.24**	.15*
Serious events only		
Men	.19**	.12*
Women	.21**	.32**
Whites	.24**	.20**
Blacks	.08	.05
N's (range)	202–296	207–296

$*p < .05; **p < .01.$

TABLE 15

Mean Percentage of White and Black Teachers Attacked and Robbed by Racial Composition of the Studentry

Percentage students white	Robbery				Attack			
	White	N	Black	N	White	N	Black	N
0–20	1.69	69	2.09	68	2.67	69	2.01	68
20–40	.66	34	1.57	33	2.14	34	.61	33
40–60	.43	80	.60	75	1.02	80	.68	75
60–80	.50	99	.61	95	.52	99	1.51	94
80–100	.43	331	.04	177	.27	331	.28	177

Note. Columns headed N indicate the number of schools on which the mean is based.

TABLE 16

Correlations between Black and White Teacher Reports about their Schools and Teacher Victimization Measures for Junior High Schools

Predictor and group	Junior			Senior		
	White	Black	All	White	Black	All
White teachers						
How well do students of different races get along	-.52**	-.35**	-.51**	-.35**	-.14**	-.36**
How well do students of different socioeconomic groups get along	-.41**	-.26**	-.39**	-.33**	-.20**	-.36**
How well do teachers and students get along	-.62**	-.40**	-.63**	-.63**	-.27**	-.60**
What percentage of the students you teach are black	.62**	.31**	.60**	.63**	.26**	.53**
What percentage of the students you teach are low ability	.48**	.34**	.50**	.67**	.33**	.63**
What percentage of the students you teach are underachievers	.44**	.30**	.45**	.62**	.31**	.58**
N's (range)	302–309	207–209	292–299	307–312	234–239	300–304
Black teachers						
How well do students of different races get along	-.30**	-.27**	-.31**	-.19**	-.14**	-.23**
How well do students of different socioeconomic groups get along	-.15*	-.21**	-.18**	-.05	-.09	-.11
How well do teachers and students get along	-.30**	-.23**	-.34**	-.24**	-.12	-.26**
What percentage of the students you teach are black	.51**	.26**	.49**	.58**	.23**	.49**
What percentage of the students you teach are low ability	.30**	.21**	.33**	.28**	.32**	.28**
What percentage of the students you teach are underachievers	.30**	.26**	.31**	.20**	.22**	.17**
N's (range)	198–210	198–209	192–204	216–239	216–238	211–233

*p < .05; **p < .01.

As we have already noted, no direct measures of actual behavior were made in the Safe School Study. In addition, no clear measures of stereotyped social perception are available. Yet the assessment of the possibility that stereotyped perception influences the victimization reports, especially for teachers, is important because the racial composition of the studentry is a strong correlate of teacher victimization reports. As one way of examining this issue, the correlations in Table 16 are presented. This table shows the correlations of white and black teacher victimization with teacher reports of school race relations, student ability and achievement, and racial composition. If white, but not black, teachers' reports of students of low ability correlated with victimization reports, then we would have evidence consistent with the social perception hypothesis. Or, if reports of school race or social relations were correlated with victimization reports only for white teachers, the social perception hypothesis would receive some support. Unfortunately, results are not clear-cut. The correlation of studentry racial composition with black teacher victimization is lower than for white teachers, but recall that the measures for black teachers are somewhat less reliable. And, although reports of school race relations are more strongly correlated with white than with black teacher victimization, differential reliability remains a potential explanation. These psychometric difficulties and the unavailability of needed additional data leave the important issue of the extent to which stereotyped perceptions influence teacher victimization reports unresolved.

In summary, regarding victimization in schools as a unitary construct is not the most productive way to proceed. The victimization measures for boys, girls, black students, white students, and male and female teachers appear to reliably measure distinct dimensions—at least in part.

In Chapters 5 through 10 we adopt the simplifying assumption that the student- and teacher-questionnaire victimization reports can be taken more or less at face value as indexes of school disorder. Then in Chapter 11 we will adopt an alternative perspective in which we assume that the reports of the different races and sexes are importantly different. This alternative analytical perspective provides a check on the more straightforward analyses in Chapters 5 through 10.

CHAPTER 5

The Community Context

> If certain deplorable facts present themselves with an
> alarming regularity, to whom is blame to be ascribed? Ought
> charges of materialism be brought against him who points
> out that regularity? What I have read and heard on the
> subject of my work, proves to me that I have not carried
> conviction to every mind, and that I have frequently been
> judged with prejudice. Judgments upon books are formed
> with even more haste and levity than judgments upon men.
> Writings are talked of without being known; and people
> take up an opinion for or against, in consequence of
> decisions of which it would cost them some trouble to
> determine the source. These are evils which must be borne
> with patience, and the more so because they are
> common. . . .
>   Could you possibly be afraid of applying the calculation
> of chances to moral phenomena, and of the afflicting
> consequences which may be inferred from that inquiry,
> when it is extended to crimes and to quarters the most
> disgraceful to society? "I should guard myself," said a
> scientific friend whose philanthropic views I otherwise re-
> spect--"I should guard myself, had I arrived at the afflicting
> results of which you speak, against grieving others with the
> relation of them. Draw a veil over the hideous spectacle;
> and if you believe that you possess the truth, imitate with
> respect to it the sage circumspection of Fontenelle."
>
> —Quetelet (1842/1969, pp. vii—viii)

Schools exist in communities that differ greatly in their characteristics.
The images conjured up by the communities surrounding a school in the
center of Newark, New Jersey, the college town of Storrs, Connecticut,
or a rural community such as Farmington, California, should be

sufficient to convince the reader that this community context will likely have great influence on what goes on within schools. It will largely determine the social composition of the studentry, have much to do with the kind of faculty that is recruited and retained, and the resources that are available or spent on education, among other things. In addition, a long history of research in criminology documents variations in crime rates among communities and strong associations between community characteristics and crime or victimization rates (Block, 1979; Harries, 1976; Pope, 1978; Quetelet, 1842/1969; Shaw & McKay, 1969). Block, for example, reports strong correlations at the census-tract level between log robbery rates and percentage black (.51), percentage high school graduates (−.54), percentage of families at 75% of the poverty level or below (.46), and percentage female-headed families (.53). Researchers in the human ecological tradition (Bordua, 1958; Chilton, 1964; Chilton & Dussich, 1974; Gordon, 1967; Lander, 1954; Shaw, 1929; Shaw & McKay, 1969; White, 1932; Wilkes, 1967) and social geographers (Hadden & Borgatta, 1965; Harries, 1976; Jonassen & Peres, 1960; Smith, 1973) have adduced incontrovertible evidence that delinquency rates vary in regular ways across social areas, and theorists (Kobrin, 1959; Kvaraceus & Miller, 1959; Mays, 1954; Miller, 1958; Shaw, 1929) have suggested some mechanisms through which these variations across social areas may come about. This tradition in social research has been neglected in recent years. For this reason, and because ecological community variables are regarded as important exogenous or control variables in the search for school characteristics related to disorder, a short description of the findings and perspectives of earlier researchers may be useful to many readers.

Research Traditions in Social Ecology

Researchers at the University of Chicago, headed by Shaw (1929), collected data about the spatial distribution of school truancy, delinquency, and adult crime in Chicago. They produced maps showing areas with high rates, and showed that high-rate areas tended to stay high-rate areas over the years. In contrast to the interpretations of other researchers (Ferguson, 1952) or commentators (National Conference on Prevention and Control of Juvenile Delinquency, 1946) who appear to have assumed that the deteriorated and substandard housing characteristic of these areas was to blame for their high delinquency rates, Shaw and his colleagues and followers began to suggest that the social disorganization characteristic of social areas determined the delinquency rates of the areas. In some areas the community as a unit of social control has disintegrated, leading to high delinquency rates.

A related theme was developed by Miller (1958) and Kobrin (1959), who described what they saw as important social organizational characteristics of "lower class culture." According to Miller (1958), youth living in areas where family life is characterized by female-headed households and "serial monogamy," where adult males contribute little to the support or stability of the family, tend to develop specific kinds of "focal concerns." More specifically, the concern of middle-class youth with "achievement" is said not to be a dominant concern in such social areas. Instead, boys are concerned with "trouble," "toughness," "smartness" (manipulative skill), "excitement," "fate" (explaining events by reference to chance or luck), and "autonomy" (characterized as an ambivalent relation to authority—overtly desiring on the one hand not to be pushed around but covertly harboring a desire to be cared for or controlled on the other).

The Shaw and McKay (1969) perspective differs from that of Kvareceus and Miller (1959) in that the latter assumes a *differential* organization of social areas. That is, Kvaraceus and Miller assume some social areas are *organized* in ways conducive to delinquency. In contrast, Shaw and McKay assume that some communities are *disorganized* and have lost control over youth behavior. Alinsky (1971) would say that little or no "community" exists in these disorganized areas.[1]

An empirical tradition of research in social ecology and social geography is also related to these social organization perspectives. Researchers have examined statistical regularities in the social and demographic characteristics of social areas and crime rates. This empirical work has attended little to interviews with or direct observation of inhabitants of a social area. Instead, it is purely "ecological," seldom attempting to explain how social processes may work in terms of the values or concerns of *individual* inhabitants of the social area.

Early social geographic research following the work of Shaw (1929) and his colleagues involved similar methods and produced similar results for other cities (White, 1932). More recently Beasley and

[1]The social organizational perspectives are discussed in more detail by G. D. Gottfredson (1981) and by Empey (1978).

Antunes (1974), Bordua (1958), Chilton (1964), Chilton and Dussich (1974), Gordon (1967), Harries (1976), and Lander (1954) have focused on the multivariate description of the geographical distribution of delinquency rates. And other researchers (Hadden & Borgatta, 1965; Jonassen & Peres, 1960; Smith, 1973) have produced factor-analytic examinations of the characteristics of communities. The 1954 multivariate study of Baltimore census tracts by Lander generated controversy. Lander studied juvenile court hearings and census data to describe the distribution of delinquency rates in Baltimore. Lander's specific conclusions (that deliquency rates are only superfically related to the socioeconomic status of the area and instead are related to race and home ownership) are less important than is the subsequent research he stimulated. Bordua (1958) and Chilton (1964) attempted replications and challenged Lander's methods and interpretations. Gordon (1967) pointed out methodological difficulties in Landers' work that make some of his specific conclusions misleading. A review of ecological studies of delinquency by Wilks appeared in 1967, and this area has recently been the topic of a tendentious review by Baldwin (1979), which is useful because it contains citations to British work.

Taken together, the empirical work on the social ecology or social geography of delinquency has established a clear and powerful association of social-area characteristics with delinquency rates. This work, despite differing levels of aggregation (Hadden & Borgatta, 1965; Harries, 1976; Jonassen & Peres, 1960; Smith, 1973), produces results showing delinquency rates to be related to urbanism, depressed economic conditions, and other indicators of social disorganization, such as a high proportion of female-headed families.

Critiques of the Ecological Traditions

The social disorganization perspective has been the subject of three kinds of criticism. In an influential paper, Mills (1943) discussed what he perceived as the "professional ideology of social pathologists." Mills made what was essentially a literary critique of the fuzzy presentation of "disorganization" or social "problems" in textbooks. Although Mills made no attempt to evaluate the worth of social disorganization concepts, he did portray the writers who popularized some ideas from this tradition in textbooks as academics of small town extraction—from "states not industrialized during the youth of the authors" (p. 167), who had parochial views of normal social organization. What these country boys saw as corrupt, pathological, or disorganized may have just been different. Although Mills is correct insofar as he discusses sloppy language of some early writers, the continuing influence of his nonsubstantive critique is amazing. Subsequent writers (Hawley, 1950) have sometimes been more explicit about what they meant by social organization than were the textbook writers who were the subject of Mill's critique.

A second line of criticism of the social disorganization (or ecological) perspective consists essentially of arguments that in so-called disorganized areas everyone does not "become dilinquent," and that some persons from low delinquency rate areas do engage in unlawful behavior. Some critics argue that the social disorganization perspective is overly deterministic for this reason. This argument does little justice to the data that Shaw and McKay (1969) and others have produced, or to their theorizing, which imply that *rates* of delinquency are associated with different social areas. The social organization perspectives do not attempt the explanation of isolated individual cases. Criticisms of this sort have been repeated and refuted with tedious frequency in the history of social science. When Quetelet (1842/1969) published his ecological studies of delinquency he was met with precisely the same criticisms as current texts make of more recent ecological or disorganization writing on delinquency. In response to such criticism Quetelet wondered whether his detractors would abandon life tables as a useful tool simply because one can find examples of individuals who live longer than expected. Regularities with respect to rates are useful objects of social inquiry.

A third line of criticism of the social disorganization perspective is advanced by Davis (1975), who argues that these theorists have overlooked the ways in which social areas come about as a result of political or economic influence. This is to some extent a valid criticism. Certainly, attempts at amelioration by workers in this tradition have focused on social work in the community rather than attempts to break down the system of political and economic constraints that cause disorganized areas to come about and be perpetuated. Yet this is not a limitation inherent in the ecological method, or even disorganization theory. Sophisticated social ecologists such as Hawley (1950) take the development and change of cultural areas as a topic of inquiry. And, an explicit purpose of the earliest systematic researcher in this area

(Quetelet, 1842/1969) was to search for appropriate methods to bring about amelioration of social ills. Quetelet was clear about his conviction that once one ascertained the causes of a given state of society, "that *society* may be ameliorated and reformed" (p. vii, emphasis added).

Implications

The social disorganization perspective on delinquency implies that careful assessment of the characteristics of the community in which a school is located is an essential first step in any attempt to unravel the sources of variation among schools in rates of disruption. Because the current research focuses on properties of schools and their potential role in delinquency rates, these community characteristics are here treated primarily as statistical controls or major exogenous variables. Eventually, it would be useful to explain the ways in which community structure influences school characteristics in a more explicit way than we shall in this book.

The Development of Community Measures

The following pages document our work to develop measures of community characteristics based on census data for the 642 schools in the Safe School Study. This work was made easier by the existence of several factor analyses of community characteristics available in the literature involving various levels of analysis.

Jonassen and Peres (1960) factor-analyzed data about the 88 Ohio counties. Despite some problems with multicollinearity and a large number of variables relative to geographical units studied, their results appear meaningful and instructive. They defined seven factors called urbanism, welfare, influx, poverty, magni-complexity, educational effort, and proletarianism. Crime, juvenile delinquency, and social control (a negative index of crime or deliquency) were associated with the first factor—urbanism. Hadden and Borgatta (1965) performed eight parallel factor analytic studies of all cities, town-cities, small cities, intermediate cities, large cities, central cities, suburbs, and cities of 25,000 or more outside of SMSA's, based on 1960 census data. They discovered a great deal of convergance in the results of the separate factor analyses, and described the following eight factors: socioeconomic status level, nonwhite, age composition, educational center, residential mobility, population density, foreign-born concentration, and total population. Finally, Richards (1978) factor-analyzed state characteristics, also identifying factors that resemble those found at lower levels of aggregation.

These earlier factor analyses guided the selection of variables for study in the present research.[2] We attempted to include measures of the most salient and relevant factors arising from the work of others. A major obstacle in doing so was the unavailability of clear, unequivocal measures of urbanism or central city location, and of racial composition of the community in the Safe School Study's community variable file.

The following list identifies the variables chosen for inclusion, and the abbreviations that appear in Table 17:

1. FEMHD Ratio of female-headed households with children under 16 to husband–wife-headed households with children under 16
2. DIVORC Proportion of persons ages 14 and over who are married with spouse absent, separated, or divorced
3. SSSSN Proportion of persons who are classified into any of the 1970 census' five Spanish categories in the question on "origin or descent"
4. STAB5YR Ratio of persons aged 5 years or older residing in the same house in 1965 and 1970 to persons residing in a different house
5. JHENROL Proportion of persons aged 7–13 years enrolled in school
6. HSENROLL Proportion of persons aged 14–17 years enrolled in school
7. EDUC Proportion of population 25 years or older who have completed four years of high school or more
8. NONPUB Nonpublic school enrollment relative to school enrollment
9. EMPLMTMA Male employment; number of males 16 or over employed or in the armed forces relative to total population of males excluding persons 65 or over who are not in the labor force

[2]After we had completed this portion of our research we discovered the excellent book by Smith (1973). Smith reviews a number of studies at various levels of analysis. His city-level and intracity analyses bear a strong resemblance to our own. The convergence in findings and interpretations made independently by Smith and ourselves is reassuring.

TABLE 17
Varimax Rotated Principal Factor Analysis of Community Indexes
for Entire Sample (N ≥ 635)

| | Factor | | | |
	I	II	III	h²
FEMHD	91	−08	04	83
DIVORC	75	−08	14	59
SSSSN	18	−24	07	09
STAB5YR	−18	−03	−38	17
JHENROL	−14	22	00	07
HSENROL	−03	36	−17	16
EDUC	−39	64	48	79
NONPUB	−05	38	−22	20
EMPLMTMA	−50	35	−12	39
UNEMPMA	53	−26	00	35
EMPLMTTFE	12	38	−21	21
UNEMPFE	13	−33	10	14
TEENEMPM	−23	12	−08	07
TEENEMPF	−04	07	03	01
PROFMGR	−32	55	50	65
FARMTOWS	−27	−38	−13	23
MEDINC	−38	73	30	76
WELFARE	74	−36	−01	68
POVERTY	48	−72	−01	75
SNOW	00	14	−46	23
TEMP	−03	−09	44	20
RAIN	−01	00	−09	01
UNEMP	27	03	−04	07
POPSIZ	−01	10	19	05
TEMPDIF	02	−04	13	02

Note. Indexes with a marked positive skew have been transformed. Decimals omitted.

10. UMEMPMA Proportion of males aged 16 or over who are in the labor force and unemployed relative to labor force
11. UNEMPLMTFE Female unemployment; number of females 16 or over employed or in the armed forces relative to total population of females exluding persons 65 or over who are not in the labor force
12. UNEMPFE Proportion of females aged 16 or over who are in the labor force and unemployed relative to labor force
13. TEENEMPM Proportion of males ages 14–15 who are employed

14. TEENEMPF Proportion of females ages 14–15 who are employed
15. PROFMGR Proportion of employed persons aged 16 and over employed in professional or managerial occupations
16. FARMTOWS Ratio of families with income from farm self-employment to families with wage and salary income
17. MEDINC Proportion of families with income of $12,000 or above[3]
18. WELFARE Proportion of families with income from public assistance or welfare
19. POVERTY Proportion of families with incomes 1.24 times the poverty level or below
20. SNOW Inches of snow or sleet
21. TEMP Average or median temperature
22. RAIN Number of days with .1 inches or more of precipitation
23. UNEMP Unemployment rate
24. POPSIZ Count of persons
25. TEMPDIF Difference from norm of average or median temperature

The first 19 variables and variable 24 in the preceding list are computed from fourth-count data from the 1970 census. Variables 20 through 23 and 25 are undocumented in the materials produced by NIE and Research Triangle Institute. Apparently they represent data obtained from noncensus sources that were produced by NIE staff.

Two notes about the way these data were treated are necessary. First, a number of the variables had a marked positive skew. These variables were log transformed to reduce the extent to which outliers influence the correlations among variables. Such transformations are common in this kind of ecological research (cf. Bidwell & Kasarda, 1975; Harries, 1976). We compared the pattern of correlations among the transformed and untransformed variables (not shown) and concluded that these transformations probably had little effect.

Second, the data in the Safe School Study's community variable file are not all based on the same type of geographical units. Instead, 155 are

[3]Median family income in 1970 was $12,531 (U.S. Department of Commerce, 1977).

for minor civil divisions (MCD's), 386 are census places, and 101 are for census tracts (for definitions of these census geoconcepts see U.S. Bureau of the Census, 1978). Because of a concern that the use of disparate kinds of geographical units might be an important consideration, some exploration of this issue was performed. Specifically, the factor structures of each type of unit were examined. These structures (not shown in a table) are largely similar. This does not imply that no problem exists, although it does provide some reassurance. In any event, the definition of the appropriate geographical unit is unclear, and is a fundamental problem in human ecology (Hawley, 1950).

The results of the factor analysis that defined most of our measures of community structure are shown in Table 17. The first factor is defined by a high proportion of families headed by females in the community, high rates of divorce or separation, high unemployment, and relatively many families on welfare. For convenience this factor will be called *poverty and disorganization*. It closely resembles the description of a disorganized social area provided by Miller (1958), and closely parallels Smith's (1973) Social Problems and Social Deprivation factors in his report on Tampa census tracts. It also resembles Hadden and Borgatta's (1965) Nonwhite factor; and Ross, Bluestone, and Hines's (1979) Family Status Factor. The second factor is defined by communities with high income and education, little poverty, and relatively many professional and managerial workers. This factor will be called *affluence and education*. It appears related to Smith's (1973) Socioeconomic Status factor. The third factor is defined by a negative loading for a community measure of residential stability, and moderately high loadings for measures of education and occupational status. It will be called *affluent mobility*. The loadings of the variables related to climate or the weather on this factor suggest that high scoring states may be located in the sunbelt, although we have not examined this possibility further. These climate variables have little of their variance in the factor space, and influence the results and the calculation of factor scores very little.

Using the factor solution summarized by Table 17, factor scores for communities were created. Because some information that earlier research had implied is important to characterize communities was not available in the community variable file, these factor scores were supplimented with other information about the community. First, information about a community's situation in the Safe School Study's

TABLE 18

Regression of Junior High School Disruption on
Exogenous Community Variables

Source and measure	Overall disruption		Teacher victimization		Student victimization	
	r	Beta	r	Beta	r	Beta
Census variable file						
Poverty and disorganization	.52**	.34**	.54**	.36**	.17**	.15
Affluence and education	−.02	−.04	.05	.03	−.05	−.04
Affluent mobility	−.02	.03	−.06	.00	.04	.06
Sample design						
Rural area	−.51**	−.25**	−.61**	−.37**	−.11	−.01
Principal report						
Distance from business district	.17*	.03	.21**	.06	.04	.02
Population of area	.48**	.13	.54**	.06	.12*	.04
R^2		.37**		.46**		.04

Note. N's range from 235 to 317. *$p < .05$; **$p < .01$.

sample design was used. This variable, called "rural area" in the tables, was coded as follows: 1 = SMSA central city with population of 500,000 or more, 2 = the remaining SMSA central cities, 3 = noncity portions of SMSA's, and 4 = non-SMSA counties or county groups. Second, two measures of community characteristics were obtained from the principal questionnaire. One of these was the principal's report of the distance of the school from the central business district if in a city or town, and the other was the principal's report of the population of the area in which the school is located (1 = town, place, or rural area under 2,500; 6 = city of 500,000 or more).

Tables 18 and 19 show results summarizing the associations of these community characteristics with the three criterion measures— overall disruption, teacher victimization, and student victimization. These tables show information about total associations icluding un- analyzed or spurious correlation. They show that 46% and 30% of the variance in rates of teacher victimization across junior and senior high schools, respectively, is predictable given this set of community characteristics. Only 4% of the variance in student victimizations is predictable. The results for overall disruption resemble the results for

TABLE 19
Regression of Senior High School Disruption on
Exogenous Community Variable

	Overall disruption		Teacher victimization		Student victimization	
Source and measure	r	Beta	r	Beta	r	Beta
Census variable file						
Poverty and disorganization	.35**	.18**	.37**	.18**	.10	.08
Affluence and education	.03	−.16*	.14*	−.08	−.14*	−.16*
Affluent mobility	−.13*	−.13*	−.12*	−.12*	−.08	−.08
Sample design						
Rural area	−.38**	−.20*	−.48**	−.28**	.00	.02
Principal report						
Distance from business						
district	.10	−.05	.12	−.07	.01	.01
Population of area	.37**	.24**	.46**	.22*	.00	.06
R^2		.24**		.30**		.04

Note. N's range from 239 to 311. *$p < .05$; **$p < .01$.

teacher victimization, which is far more predictable than is student victimization.[4]

The zero-order correlations imply that schools with high rates of teacher victimization are located in communities characterized by poverty and disorganization, and are in central cities rather than in non-SMSA counties. They also show a slight tendency to be located away from business districts, and are in high population areas. These same trends appear for student victimizations but are less marked and often nonsignificant. These results imply that the characterization of school disorder as not largely an urban phenomenon in the NIE (1978) Safe School Study report requires qualification. It is true that student victimization is fairly independent of these community characteristics, but teacher victimizations are strongly linked with the characteristics of the community. In addition, the results accord well with expectations derived from the social disorganization perspective. At the same time the divergent results for teacher and student victimization pose an interesting puzzle. These divergent results imply that additional attention to

[4]In subsequent chapters, results for overall disruption will be shown for completeness, but because of the redundancy of this measure with the other two, these results will seldom be commented on.

the measurement of school disruption, with a focus on alternative measures, is important. Chapter 11 examines alternative measures more closely.

Before leaving the initial exploration of community variables, we examine in Tables 20 and 21 the relations of school disruption to principal, teacher, and student reports regarding crime in the community. This is a set of predictors which the NIE (1978) Safe School Study report found to be related to student victimization. Tables 20 and 21 confirm this association. Seven percent and five percent of the variance in junior and senior high school student victimization, 54% and 49% of the variance in teacher victimization, and 46% and 47% of the variance in overall disruption is associated with these predictors. Notice that student reports of community crime show strong correlations with the teacher reports of victimization at school. This is important because the usefulness of these student reports to predict a criterion, the measurement of which is derived from teacher reports, lends confidence to the interpretation of these variables as measures of community crime rather than of generalized complaints that are correlated simply because they are based on reports from the same groups of people. Once again, the student victimization rate is less predictable than is the teacher victimization rate. The principal report is only weakly associated with any of the criteria, and is usually nonsignificant.

The results reported in this section have documented powerful links between the community context within which a school exists and

TABLE 20

Correlations of Junior High School Disruption with
Reports of Community Crime

Source and predictor	Overall disruption	Teacher victimization	Student victimization
Principal			
Crime problem in attendance area	.14*	.13**	.06
Teacher			
Crime problem in neighborhood	.61**	.69**	.12*
Student			
Parents robbed	.37**	.35**	.21**
House burgled	.36**	.31**	.20**
Fighting gangs in neighborhood	.54**	.56**	.18**
R^2	.46**	.54**	.07**

Note. N's range from 288 to 310. *$p < .05$; **$p < .01$.

TABLE 21

Correlations of Senior High School Disruption with
Reports of Community Crime

Source and predictor	Overall disruption	Teacher victimization	Student victimization
Principal			
Crime problem in attendance area	.01	.00	.02
Teacher			
Crime problem in neighborhood	.65**	.67**	.22**
Student			
Parents robbed	.48**	.45**	.18**
House burgled	.17**	.14*	.10
Fighting gangs in neighborhood	.51**	.52**	.15**
R^2	.47**	.49**	.05**

Note. N's range from 278 to 311. *$p < .05$; **$p < .01$.

disruption within the school. Although the reader should beware that the nature of these associations are essentially unanalyzed in these results, they accord with theory and earlier ecological research in implying that delinquency is related to community social organization as indexed by the census and location variables studied here. The next chapter examines the associations of school disruption with a variety of characteristics of schools' social and demographic composition—and to events, such as court-ordered desegregation, that may influence rates of disruption in the school but that may be largely beyond the control of the school.

CHAPTER 6

Demographic and Social Composition

This chapter explores the social and demographic composition of studentries, and several other characteristics of schools—tied primarily to desegregation efforts—that are plausibly related to school disruption. These seemingly diverse school characteristics are examined together because they may all be viewed as beyond the control of the school. This appears to be a tenable assumption at present, although one can imagine specific cases in which it might not be true. In general, schools must cope with, educate, manage, minister to, and interact with the kinds of students allocated to them; and desegregation and busing are also events that are in some sense imposed on the schools.

The school variables considered in this section and the zero-order correlations between each school characteristic and school disruption are shown in Table 22. Most of the variables in this list show substantial total associations with teacher victimization. The absolute values of these correlations with student victimizations are smaller, ranging in absolute value from .01 to .33. For teacher victimizations, the zero-order correlations for principal estimates of the percentage of students reading below grade level and children of persons on welfare, and student or teacher reports of percentage of students black indicate especially strong positive associations; and the zero-order correlations with percentage of students white based on either teacher or student reports, and aggregate student reports of a present father and parental discipline indicate especially strong negative associations. Various measures of desegre-

TABLE 22

Zero-Order Correlations of School Social Compositional Characteristics That are Externally Determined with the Three Measures of School Disruption

Source and predictor	Overall disruption		Teacher victimization		Student victimization	
	Jr.	Sr.	Jr.	Sr.	Jr.	Sr.
Principal						
Students reading below grade level	.42**	.36**	.47**	.37**	.07	.11
Children of persons on welfare	.43**	.42**	.47**	.49**	.10	.09
Court-ordered desegregation	.22**	.14*	.22**	.12*	.08	.06
Community desegregation plan	.23**	.14*	.22**	.10	.09	.06
Percentage students bussed	.31**	-.05	.22**	-.02	.23**	-.12
Recently started bussing[a]	.06	.18	.27	.34	-.21	-.05
Teacher						
Percentage students { white	-.54**	-.51**	-.65**	-.54**	-.07	-.12*
black	.52**	.52**	.59**	.53**	.10	.20**
Spanish	.19**	.14*	.29**	.19**	-.05	-.06
low ability	.46**	.56**	.50**	.61**	.11	.15*

Students						
female	-.05	-.16**	.02	-.04	-.08	-.19**
Percentage students { white	-.52**	-.53**	-.64**	-.56**	-.06	-.16**
black	.52**	.50**	.60**	.52**	.09	.18**
Spanish	.24**	.24**	.36**	.29**	-.06	-.02
Self-reported reading ability	-.04	-.18**	-.08	-.17**	.01	-.08
Father present	-.46**	-.51**	-.59**	-.56**	-.01	.12*
Mother present	-.15*	-.22**	-.13*	-.18**	-.05	-.10
Parents punish	-.16**	-.22**	-.24**	-.32**	.00	.12*
Father's education	-.08	-.14*	-.08	-.09	.00	-.07
Mother's education	-.04	-.11	-.05	-.10	.03	-.01
Racial imbalance^b	-.04	-.04	.03	.00	-.04	.01
Grade level	.04	-.20**	.09	-.07	-.08	-.33**

Note. N's range from 281 to 301 for junior high schools except for recent bussing—N = 42. for senior highs N's range from 274 to 303, except for recent bussing—N—s = 24 to 25.
^aVery small N.
^bAbsolute value of difference between 50% and percentage of students who report that they are white.
*p < .05; **p < .01.

gation activities show modest positive associations with student and especially teacher reports of victimization, particularly in junior high schools.

Few correlations even reach statistical significance for student victimizations. Those that do are percentage of students bused (junior high only), several measures of racial composition, parental discipline, and the average grade level in the school (senior high only).

Comments and Cautions

Some points require comment here. First, the large number of correlations involved implies that the nominal probability values for the significance tests shown may be slightly misleading. When many such tests are made, some values will be "significant" by chance alone. At the same time, the actual probability values are often much smaller than the values indicated in the footnote. In any event the size of the correlation is what should capture the reader's attention, not the stars on the table. Second, one may not always be able to take the meaning of a variable at face value. Most salient in this regard are the three measures of studentry ability. The principals' reports of students reading below grade level and teachers' reports of students of low ability are strongly positively correlated with each other, but are only weakly correlated with mean students' self-reported reading ability. Both of the teacher reports are much more strongly associated with a school's racial composition than with mean students' self-reported ability. In short, one does not know what these variables measure. No direct measures of student ability (such as standardized test scores) exist in the Safe School Study data. These direct measures were not included for fear that their inclusion would seriously deflate the response rate (D. Boesel, personal communication, October 1979). Third, correlation does not imply causation, and much of the association implied by the zero-order or multiple correlations reported in this chapter may be spurious.

Also requiring comment are the correlations of victimization rates with school racial composition and other indexes of studentry characteristics. Race, proportion on welfare, and teacher and principal estimates of ability are strongly associated with teacher, but not student, victimization reports. This is a troublesome and difficult-to-understand result. Students in schools that are largely black may actually victimize teachers more than do students in schools that are predominantly white. If so, why do not the students also inform us of more victimization?

Several potential difficulties with the criterion measures were discussed in Chapter 4, and it is possible that measurement difficulties inherent in the victim reports account for these results.

An alternative set of speculations about the results for racial composition is also plausible. Duncan (1977) has presented evidence that white subjects may in certain circumstances attribute more violence to a black than to a white performing the same behavior. He also provides a theoretical account of how the use of categories or personal constructs (in Kelly's, 1955, sense) may be involved in the generation of stereotyped perceptions. Similarly, Skolnick (1975) has suggested that control agents other than teachers—specifically, police—may also develop stereotypes of "offenders" that they apply in their work. Certainly no definitive evidence on the matter is available in the present results. The point is that the potential for informants' typical modes of perceiving social interaction may contribute to these results. This issue was examined in more detail in the technical note at the end of Chapter 4, and is taken up again in Chapter 11.

Finally, the NIE (1978) conclusion that racial composition is not systematically associated with *student* victimization is in accordance with our results. The NIE report did not examine teacher victimizations as we have, however, and the results are in stark contrast (also see Chapter 11). Teachers in the aggregate report more victimization in schools with proportionately many blacks.

A closer scrutiny of the other zero-order associations in Table 22 is deferred until later chapters when we make an attempt to apply appropriate statistical controls. Readers are reminded that controls for community variables may be expected to reduce or alter the portrait suggested by casual perusal of the uncontrolled associations.

Strength of Association

Table 23 summarizes evidence about the combined efficiency with which these demograpghic and social compositional characteristics and desegregation activities account (in a purely actuarial sense) for variance in disruption across schools. The total associations of the predictor set with the criteria ranges from 13% of the variance for junior high school student victimization to 53% of the variance for junior high school teacher victimization.

The list of predictors shown in Table 23 differs from the list shown in Table 22 because the difficulties associated with multicollinearity in

TABLE 23

Standardized Partial Regression Coefficients in the Regression of School Disruption Measures on School Compositional Characteristics That Are Externally Determined

Source and predictor	Overall disruption		Teacher victimization		Student victimization	
	Jr.	Sr.	Jr.	Sr.	Jr.	Sr.
Principal						
Children of persons on welfare	.05	.16*	-.01	.21**	.05	.04
Court-ordered desegregation	-.03	.03	.00	.00	-.03	.04
Community desegregation plan	.05	.04	.02	-.04	.06	.08
Percentage students bussed	.24**	-.12*	.12*	-.06	.25**	-.17**
Teacher–principal composite[a]						
Student ability-achievement	.11*	.00	.12**	.02	.05	-.01
Teacher–student composite[b]						
Percentage students { white	-.55**	-.32**	-.57**	-.29**	-.23	-.22*
Percentage students { Spanish	-.12	-.11	-.04	-.05	-.15	-.19**
Student						
Percentage female	-.05	-.21**	.02	-.08	-.09	-.21**
Self-reported reading ability	.05	-.06	.00	-.05	.06	-.06
Father present	.07	.19*	.24**	.23**	-.19	.02
Mother present	-.10	.00	-.17**	-.05	.03	.03
Parents punish	-.04	-.10	-.08	-.15**	.01	.03
Parents' education[c]	.08	.07	.10	.12*	.06	.08
Racial imbalance[d]	.10	-.01	.14**	.04	.07	.04
Grade level	.00	-.28**	.06	-.16**	-.12	-.33**
Parents talk about school	-.14*	.10	-.06	.06	-.21**	.06
R^2	.40**	.45**	.53**	.44**	.13**	.24**

Note. The N's on which the junior high correlations are based range from 273 to 310; N's for senior high range from 264 to 311.
[a] Equally weighted composite of closely related teacher and principal reports.
[b] Equally weighted composite of closely related student and teacher reports.
[c] Equally weighted composite of fathers' and mothers' education.
[d] Absolute value of the difference between 50% and percentage of students who report themselves to be white.
*$p < .05$; **$p < .01$.

these data (described in some detail in Chapter 3) made it necessary to form composites of some variables. Redundancy among predictors made it advisable to combine closely related sets of predictors into single measures. A composite was formed, for example, of teacher- and student-based estimates of racial composition. Similarly, because a school's percentage of black students will in general nearly equal 100 minus percentage white minus percentage Spanish origin, percentage black has been deleted from the regression equation. At this stage in the research it became obvious that the exploration of the data would be facilitated if each set of predictors were routinely factor analyzed to reduce the number and redundancy of the predictors prior to attempting to use multiple regression to assess the degree of association of the set with the criteria. Because considerable redundancy still exists in the variables included in Table 23—even though extreme multicollinearity does not exist—it would be risky to attempt to make much of the beta weights, even as measures of association with the other variables in the equation controlled.[1] These regression weights are subject to substantial sampling variability.

Table 24 shows the factor structures of the variables involved separately for junior and senior high schools. The results of this factor analysis were used to guide the development of composite measures for use in Chapter 10. An inspection of the factor loadings implies than an appropriate name for the first factor may be *social or educational disadvantage*.[2] The second factor appears defined by *parental education and self-reported ability*. And, the third factor is related to *school desegregation*.

Composite scales were formed by adding, with appropriate sign and unit weight, standardized values for variables representing each of these

---

[1]Note that community variables are not statistically controlled. These beta weights are shown only to illustrate the problem, not because they have any substantive meaning.

[2]We are aware that the words "social disadvantage" are considered by some persons (e.g., Kenneth B. Clark, remarks quoted in the *Education Daily*, October 2, 1979, p. 6) as euphemisms displaying an attitude that inner-city youngsters are inferior. We have no such intention here. But one would clearly not be justified in regarding black children of persons on welfare, who are reading behind grade level, judged to be of low ability, and residing in homes with the father absent was "advantaged." Our appellation for this scale does seem to summarize the characteristics of the studentry in a school scoring high on this factor. We use the word "disadvantage" literally (*Webster's New World Dictionary of the Engligh Language*, 1976).

TABLE 24

Varimax Rotated Factor Structure for School Social Compositional Characteristics

Source of information and predictor	Junior				Senior			
	I	II	III	h²	I	II	III	h²
Principal								
Children of persons on welfare	.73	-.17	.15	.58	.69	-.24	.02	.54
Court-ordered desegregation	.17	.00	.54	.32	.10	.03	.50	.26
Community desegregation plan	.19	-.02	.47	.26	.16	.04	.48	.26
Percentage students { bussed	.08	.09	.54	.31	-.08	-.02	.49	.24
reading one year below grade level	.66	-.23	.27	.56	.60	-.40	-.04	.52
Teacher								
Percentage students low ability	.65	-.36	.33	.66	.76	-.31	.06	.67
Teacher–student composite[a] Percentage students { white	-.90	.05	-.24	.88	-.85	.12	-.30	.84
Spanish	.50	-.19	.00	.28	.44	-.13	.05	.21
Student								
Percentage female	.01	.09	.03	.01	.07	.06	-.02	.01
Self-reported reading ability	-.14	.37	-.10	.16	-.28	.39	.03	.24
Father present	-.79	.05	-.26	.69	-.80	.09	-.24	.71
Mother present	-.44	.19	-.15	.25	-.35	.19	-.08	.17
Father's education	-.23	.88	-.06	.83	-.20	.93	.02	.90
Mother's education	-.20	.90	-.12	.87	-.24	.87	-.04	.82
Parent's punish	-.24	-.06	.10	.07	-.42	-.13	-.18	.23
Parents talk about school	-.09	.44	-.03	.20	-.05	.32	.00	.11
Grade level	.08	-.07	-.02	.01	.10	.10	.13	.04
Racial imbalance[b]	.07	.15	-.55	.33	-.06	.11	-.36	.15

[a] Equally weighted composite of closely related student and teacher reports.
[b] Absolute value of the difference between 50% and % students who report themselves to be white.

TABLE 25
Alpha Reliability Coefficients for Measures
of School Compositional Characteristics
That Are Externally Determined

	Junior high		Senior high	
Scale	Alpha	No. of items	Alpha	No. of items
Social disadvantage	.83	8	.81	8
Parental education and self-reported ability	.74	4	.74	4
Desegregation	.60	4	.71	4

factors. An appendix shows the item content of the scales, and Table 25 shows the reliability coefficients.

Table 26 summarizes the zero-order and multiple correlations of average grade level, percentage of students female, and the three composite measures of school demographic and social composition with the measures of school disorder. These results are in general accord with the results for individual items shown earlier in Table 23. As is to be expected when some highly specific information is lost as a result of using composite measures, the total association (R^2) for the entire set of predictors drops a little. The social and educational disadvantage characteristic of a school's studentry is strongly associated with teacher victimization rates, but not with student victimization rates. Even when taken all together, these social and demographic characteristics are associated with only 4% and 16% of the variance in student victimization rates in junior and senior high schools, respectively. This contrasts with the higher values—42% and 38%—for teacher victimizations. In short, these school compositional characteristics are strongly linked with school disorder only when our estimates are based on teacher rather than student reports.

This chapter has established that school demographic and social composition, and to a lesser extent desegregation activities are *associated* with rates of school disorder as assessed by the victimization measures used. It has also summarized information about three composite measures of school social composition that will be used in Chapter 10. The next chapter explores the relation of school size, staffing, and resources to school disruption.

TABLE 26

Regression of Composite Social Compositional Measures on
Measures of School Disruption

	Junior high		Senior high	
Measure of school social composition	r	Beta	r	Beta
Criterion is overall disruption				
Social and educational disadvantage	.54	.55**	.52**	.60**
Parental education and self-reported ability	−.09	.14*	−.13*	.14*
Desegregation	.29**	.12*	.14*	.03
Average grade level	.04	.01	−.20**	−.27**
Percentage female	−.05	−.07	−.16**	−.18**
R^2		.32**		.38**
Criterion is teacher victimization				
Social and educational disadvantage	.62**	.67**	.58**	.67**
Parental education and self-reported ability	−.07	.18**	−.12*	.18**
Desegregation	.24**	.03	.13*	−.01
Average grade level	.09	.06	−.07	−.14**
Percentage female	.02	.00	−.04	−.06
R^2		.42**		.38**
Criterion is student victimization				
Social and educational disadvantage	.09	.06	.08	.14*
Parental education and self-reported ability	−.03	.01	−.04	.03
Desegregation	.15**	.14*	.01	.00
Average grade level	−.08	−.10	−.33**	−.34**
Percentage female	−.08	−.10	−.19**	−.20**
R^2		.04*		.16**

*$p < .05$; **$p < .01$.

CHAPTER 7

School Size, Staffing, and Resources

School size, staffing patterns, and resources are school characteristics of importance because of the suggestions in the NIE (1978) and McPartland and McDill (1976) reports that school size, at least, may be an important determinant of school order, at least indirectly via negative consequences of large school size for the quality of teacher–student interaction. This suggestion is supported by Garbarino (1978). In addition, thorough examination of school size, staffing, and resources is a prerequisite to model testing at a later stage in the present research effort. Eventually, we will want to examine more explicitly hypotheses that these school characteristics influence other aspects of school climate, which in turn are related to delinquency. In this chapter we begin the task by examining correlations of school size, staffing patterns, and resources with our measures of school disorder.

Information about the school characteristics examined, their correlations with each of the measures of school disorder, and the proportion of variance in each criterion associated with the entire set of predictors is summarized for junior high schools in Table 27. Table 28 shows parallel information for the senior high schools. Once again, student victimization is less predictable using these predictors than is teacher victimization, with only 6% of the variance in student victimization predicted for junior high schools and 10% predicted for senior high schools. Interestingly, the teachers' aggregate reports about the extent to which the school supplies them with the materials and equipment they

TABLE 27
Correlations of Junior High School Disruption with Measures of
School Size, Staffing, and Resources

Predictor	Overall disruption	Teacher victimization	Student victimization
% of teachers white	−.38**	−.42**	−.10
Student–teacher ratio	−.12	−.16**	.02
Avg. years of teacher experience	−.09	−.04	−.10
% of teachers female	.04	.00	.04
Average educational level of teachers	.14*	.23**	−.02
Teaching resources	−.39**	−.40**	−.16**
Average no. of different students taught	.06	.04	.11
Average class size	.02	.08	−.06
School total enrollment	.30**	.36**	.08
R^2	.34**	.42**	.06*

Note. N's range from 290 to 311.
*$p < .05$; **$p < .01$.

need for teaching ("teaching resources") is weakly but significantly correlated with student victimizations in both groups of schools.

The number of different students taught was highlighted in the NIE (1978) report, where a claim was made that this variable contributed to the explanation of student victimizations. In fact, however, when one applies significance tests for the correlations shown in that report, this variable has a correlation significantly different from zero in only one of the groups of schools studied (suburban junior high schools). When the present measure of student victimizations is used, the number of different students taught correlates significantly with this criterion in senior but not junior high schools. The sign and magnitude of the correlation is consistent with that reported in NIE's (1978) report.

The NIE report also claimed that mean class size was related to student victimizations, although none of the correlations reported in their analyses is significant (significance levels were not reported in NIE's report). It appears unlikely that any of the partial regression coefficients could have been significant for these variables in the NIE report, although we have not attempted to determine these significance levels ourselves. The present results parallel the actual results in the NIE analysis: no significant association of class size with student victimization.

TABLE 28

Correlations of Senior High School Disruption with Measures of
School Size, Staffing, and Resources

Predictor	Overall disruption	Teacher victimization	Student victimization
% of teachers white	−.27**	−.29**	−.10
Student–teacher ratio	−.05	−.06	−.04
Avg. years of teacher experience	.01	.01	−.06
% of teachers female	−.04	.02	−.06
Average educational level of teachers	.16**	.24**	−.07
Teaching resources	−.39**	−.44**	−.14*
Average no. of different students taught	.28**	.26**	.18**
Average class size	.01	.06	−.06
School total enrollment	.22**	.25**	.02
R^2	.30**	.32**	.10**

Note. N's range from 286 to 312.
*$p < .05$, **$p < .01$.

Teacher victimizations are more strongly associated with several school characteristics in this set than are student victimizations. The squared multiple correlations for teacher victimization are .42 for junior and .32 for senior high schools. Percentage of teachers white and the availability of teaching resources are negatively correlated with teacher victimizations in both junior and senior high schools. Average level of educational attainment of the schools' teachers and school size (total enrollment) are positively correlated with teacher victimizations in both groups of schools.

All the results reported in this chapter refer to total associations of these measures of school size, staffing, and resources with school disruption. Because we have already shown that a number of other community and school characteristics that may be assumed to be causally prior to these measures are also associated with school disruption, and because those other factors are also undoubtedly not independent of the school characteristics examined here, some of the associations noted in this chapter are surely spurious. The decomposition of correlations into spurious components and contributions to the explanation of school disruption is attempted in Chapter 10.

The following chapter examines the structure of organizational climate characteristics including a variety of principal, teacher, and student attitudes; school governance styles and sanctioning practices; and school academic and social climate.

CHAPTER 8

School Climate
and Administration

Many of the strategies that have been suggested to help schools cope with school disorder have to do with how a school is run. The theoretical work done in preparation for the Safe School Study (Williams, Moles, & Boesel, 1975) implied that attitudes, beliefs, and values; school governance and administration; the ways in which rules are applied and formulated; school educational orientations; and grading practices are all potentially important. The development of the instruments used in the Safe School Study was guided by these speculations and by theoretical work by Spady (1974), Polk and Schafer (1972), and Hirschi (1969). As a consequence, the Safe School Study survey instruments collected a broad range of information pertinent to the evaluation of these speculations. This chapter summarizes research on the dimensions of school climate and administration, and it examines the relations of these dimensions to school disorder.

The extensive information collected in the Safe School Study relevant to school social organization, and the desire to efficiently analyze these data, led us to modify our initial plan for the research (Chapter 3) by breaking some large tasks up into smaller pieces. Because so much material is covered, the work is presented in segments. We first examine principal and teacher attitudes and styles for coping with or thinking about disruption. Second, we focus on school rules, sanctioning practices, control over decision making, parental and student involvement in school decision making, and principal and teacher reports on how equitably the school is run. Third, we examine other aspects of the schools' social climate, including academic climates according to reports from teachers and students, and several aspects of student social climate and peer culture.

Principal and Teacher Attitudes

The following paragraphs describe the development of measures of principal and teacher attitudes about school disruption, with a focus on how these groups believe school problems should be handled. We describe the meanings of these measures by showing their correlations with student reports about the teachers and principals, provide information about the reliability of the measures, and examine the association of these individual (principal) or group (teacher) attitudes with school disruption. Recall that we are not dealing with individual measures in the case of teachers, but with aggregate measures. Hence, although the word "attitude" with its individual-level connotation is used, we are really discussing group-level phenomena: group predispositions or typical group attitudes.

The blatant solicitation of attitudes was avoided in the principal questionnaire. Principals were asked, however, to express their recommendations to others about how school disruption should be dealt with, and their responses may be viewed as attitudinal measures. The attitude items considered and their factor structure are shown in Table 29. Based

TABLE 29

Varimax Rotated Factor Structure for Principal Attitude Items (N = 609)

Measure strongly recommended	Factor I	II	h^2
Provide security guards in school.	.04	.49[b]	.24
Have regular police stationed in school.	.02	.41[b]	.17
Suspend and/or expel discipline problem students.	−.06	.43[b]	.18
Put disruptive youngsters into separate schools or classes.	.03	.42[b]	.18
Get students more involved in the operation of the school.	.50[a]	−.09	.26
Draw up and enforce stricter rules of conduct.	−.04	.24[b]	.06
Provide more courses tailored to student needs, abilities and interests	.53[a]	.04	.28
Provide more counseling for students with problems	.47[a]	.12	.23
Get parents more involved in the operation of the school.	.35[a]	−.08	.13

[a]These items were added together to form the scale called *social approach*.
[b]These items were added together to form the scale called *enforcement approach*.

on this factor analysis (performed using data from junior and senior high principals combined) we formed two scales that are called *social approach* and *enforcement approach*. A principal who scores high on the social approach scale is one who recommends coping with disruption by trying to get students more involved in the operation of the school; providing courses tailored to the needs, abilities, and interests of the students; providing counseling; and involving parents. Such a principal apparently has an implicit social theory about the roots of disorder and seemingly would be predisposed to take action to remediate these problems at their source. A principal who scores high on the enforcement approach scale is concerned with rule enforcement and school security and tends to recommend the segregation or expulsion of problem students.

A variety of items intended to capture attitudes were included in the teacher questionnaire. The attitudinal items considered here, and the factor structure of the school-level correlations among the items, are shown in Table 30. Based on this factor analysis three scales were constructed that we call *teacher authority*, *democratic approach*, and *punitive approach*. In schools whose teachers in the aggregate score high on the teacher authority scale, teachers tend to believe schools should have rules about the ways students must dress, believe that beginning teachers tend not to be strict enough, eschew familiarity with students, and regard profanity as a moral offense. Although the interpretation of this scale as an authoritarianism measure occurred to us, the title we have chosen is less pejorative and has more justification because relatively few items would allow a clear tie-in with traditional measures of authoritarianism (Adorno, Frankel-Brunswick, Levinson, & Sanford, 1950). Also, the scale measures a group characteristic rather than a dimension of individual personality.

In schools that score high on the democratic approach scale, teachers tend to say that students and parents should have a say in the running of the school. In schools that score high on the scale called punitive approach, teachers typically say that some pupils are "just young hoodlums" who should be treated accordingly, and recommend severe punishments and summary suspensions.

As one way to assess the meaning of these principal and teacher attitude scales, we examined student ratings of principals and teachers. Our purpose was to determine whether the expressed attitudes of principals and teachers are related to student perceptions of their

TABLE 30

Varimax Rotated Factor Structure for Teacher Attitude Items (N = 623)

| Item | Factor | | | |
	I	II	III	h^2
Schools should have rules about the way students can dress.	$.53^a$	$-.29$	.03	.36
It is all right for schools to suspend students without a hearing.	.26	$-.28$	$.30^c$	.24
If students are in a fist fight, let them settle it themselves.	.12	.12	$-.04$	.03
If students use drugs around school, it is their own business.	.04	.23	.07	.06
Students should have a lot to say about how this school is run.	$-.24$	$.88^b$	$-.20$	.86
Parents should have a lot to say about how this school is run.	$-.18$	$.58^b$	$-.10$	.38
Pupils are usually not capable of solving their problems through logical reasoning.	$-.44^a$	.06	.32	.30
Beginning teachers are not likely to maintain strict enough control over their pupils.	.27	$-.03$	.23	.13
The best principal gives unquestioning support to teachers in disciplining pupils.	$.49^a$	.20	.14	.30
It is justifiable to have pupils learn many facts about subjects even if they have no immediate application.	.02	.01	.22	.05
Being friendly with pupils often leads them to become too familiar.	$.61^a$	$-.15$	.20	.44
Student governments are a good "safety valve" but should not have much influence on school policy.	$.49^a$	$-.48$	.17	.50
If a pupil uses obscene or profane language in school, it must be considered a moral offense.	$.66^a$	$-.14$	.02	.45
A few pupils are just young hoodlums and should be treated accordingly.	$-.03$	.04	$.99^c$	.99
A pupil who destroys school material or property should be severely punished.	.22	$-.15$	$.44^c$	.27
Pupils often misbehave in order to make the teacher look bad.	$.61^a$	.18	.05	.41

Note. The high h^2 estimates result from the inability to correctly invert the correlation matrix. See Chapter 3. Nevertheless, the solution appears easily interpretable.
[a]These items were scored in the appropriate direction and added together to form the scale called teacher authority.
[b]These items were added together to form the scale called democratic approach.
[c]These items were added together to form the scale called punitive approach.

TABLE 31

Varimax Rotated Factor Structure for Student Ratings of
Principal and Teacher Governance Styles (N = 621)

| Item | Factor | | | h^2 |
	I	II	III	
The principal is doing a good job.	.92[a]	.17	.10	.90
The teachers are friendly.	.03	.78[b]	−.07	.61
The principal runs the school with a firm hand.	.57	.22	.64[c]	.79
The teachers are doing a good job.	.33	.73[b]	.16	.67
The principal gets out of his office and talks with the students.	.72[a]	.09	.01	.53
The principal is tough and strict.	−.29	−.04	.80[c]	.72
The principal is fair.	.91[a]	.18	−.13	.88
The principal is friendly.	.89[a]	.15	−.24	.88

Note. The high communality estimates for some variables are a result of the high level of aggregation in these data. See Chapter 3.
[a] These Likert-type items were added together to form a scale called *good principal.*
[b] These Likert-type items were added together to form a scale called *good teachers.*
[c] These Likert-type items were added together to form a scale called *strict principal.*

behavior. The ratings examined and their factor structure are shown in Table 31. Three scales were constructed based on these factor analysis results, as indicated by the superscript letters in the table.

Evidence about the nature of the principal and teacher attitude scales is summarized in Table 32 by showing how they correlate with each other and with the student ratings of principal and teacher behavior. It also shows reliability estimates for all the measures. Although the two principal attitude scales are nearly orthogonal, the teacher scales show substantial overlap with each other, despite our use of factor analysis to build scales measuring distinct dimensions. The student ratings are sometimes significantly correlated with the attitude scales, but these correlations are small. If the attitudes tapped by these scales are translated into behavior by principals or teachers as a group, these behaviors do not result in clear-cut patterns of student perceptions of teacher or principal performance. Furthermore, the reliabilities of these scales are generally modest, implying that whatever they measure is in some cases not measured very well.

Principal and Teacher Attitudes and School Disruption. The zero-order correlations between the measures of principal and teacher

TABLE 32

Correlations among Principal and Teacher Attitude Scales, and Student Ratings of Principal and Teachers

Attitude or rating	Principal attitude		Student rating of principal		Teacher attitude			Student rating of teacher
	1	2	3	4	5	6	7	8
Principal attitude								
1. Social approach	(.52)							
2. Enforcement approach	.00	(.48)						
Student rating of principal								
3. Good principal	.02	-.17**	(.92)					
4. Strict principal	-.08	-.06	.10*	(.51)				
Teacher attitude								
5. Teacher control	-.15**	.03	.02	.23**	(.77)			
6. Democratic approach	.11*	.01	-.05	-.12**	-.41**	(.76)		
7. Punitive approach	-.04	.12**	-.06	-.08	.41**	-.30**	(.54)	
Student rating of teachers								
8. Good teachers	-.06	-.16**	.33**	.16**	-.10	-.04	-.23**	(.72)

Note. N's range from 578 to 623. Reliability coefficients (alpha) are shown on the diagonal.
*p < .05; **p < .01.

attitudes—and student rating—and the measures of school disruption are shown in Table 33. The principal attitude scales are sometimes significantly correlated with the criteria, but these correlations are small. The correlations between the student ratings and the three measures of school disruption imply moderate associations of student appraisals with all three measures of school disorder. Teacher attitudes are also often significantly related to the disorder measures, and except for the punitive approach scale, their size is also small. These correlations imply that disruption is greater in schools where teachers tend to express punitive views, and slightly greater in schools in which teachers express attitudes implying that students and parents should have a lot to say about how the school is run (democratic orientation). These correlations are descriptive, of course. Cause and effect inferences are inappropriate here.

The total associations of the entire set of attitude variables with the three measures of school disruption are summarized in Table 34. These results imply nonnegligible and significant associations.

School Governance and Sanctioning Practices

This section describes the development of measures of school governance—how principals, teachers, and students report that the school is run—and also examines sanctioning practices. After reporting on the characteristics of these measures, we examine their associations with school disorder.

Our exploration proceeded in several steps. First, the principals' reports of school rules, specific actions taken with respect to disruptive students, and the role of students in relation to rules and sanctions were examined. Table 35 describes the information obtained from principals and displays the factor structure of these pieces of information. A strong first factor is characterized by principal reports that relatively many students were put on probation, transferred, or dealt with via talks with parents. The second factor is difficult to interpret, with items regarding the enforcement of a dress code and paddling of students having high loadings.

Second, the structure of aggregated teacher reports about school governance, sanctions, and school administration or functioning were examined. Table 36 shows the variables considered and their factor structure. The second factor shown on this table is defined primarily by

TABLE 33

Zero-Order Correlations of Measures of Principal and Teacher Attitudes or Style with School Disruption

Attitude or style	Overall disruption		Teacher victimization		Student victimization	
	Jr.	Sr.	Jr.	Sr.	Jr.	Sr.
Principal attitude						
Social approach	.11	.10	.12*	.09	.04	.02
Enforcement approach	.14*	.16**	.16**	.17**	.01	.01
Teacher attitude						
Teacher authority	.07	.11	.08	.03	.01	.12*
Democractic orientation	.26**	.11	.18**	.15*	.22**	.03
Punitive approach	.30**	.33**	.34**	.35**	.05	.10
Student rating						
Good principal	-.26**	-.15**	-.22**	-.08	-.17**	-.17**
Strict principal	-.26**	-.13*	-.32**	-.18**	-.05	.03
Good teachers	-.47**	-.38**	-.39**	-.36**	-.33**	-.21**

Note. N's range from 287 to 312.
*p < .05; **p < .01.

TABLE 34
Squared Multiple Correlations of Principal and Teacher
Attitudes or Style, and Student Ratings, with Disruption Measures

Predictor set	Overall disruption	Teacher victimization	Student victimization
Junior high schools (N's = 291 to 311)			
Principal and teacher attitudes	.22**	.21**	.07**
Principal and teacher attitudes and student ratings	.36**	.33**	.15**
Senior high schools (N's = 287 to 312)			
Principal and teacher attitudes	.20**	.23**	.03
Principal and teacher attitudes and student ratings	.28**	.29**	.09**

**$p < .01$.

various sanctioning practices. Because we had difficulty in interpreting this factor, and because of the difficulty in making sense of the factor analysis of principal reports about school governance—most of which involved sanctioning practices—we deferred the interpretation of this teacher factor until we could examine both teacher and principal reports on sanctioning practices in a single factor analysis.

The interpretation of the remaining factors appears more straight-forward, and they were used to guide the construction of four scales. The first of these is called *teacher–administration cooperation*. In schools that score high on this scale, teachers typically report that all students are treated equally, they get help from counselors, teachers and administrators get along well, and teachers are kept informed about problem students by the school's administration. The high-scoring school seems to function smoothly and be well integrated. The second scale is called *student–parent influence*, and a high score means that teachers tend to report that students and parents have a say about how the school is run. The third scale is called *policy confusion*. In schools that score high on this scale, a large proportion of teachers replied that they could not say how policies relating to grading practices, controlling classroom disorder, dealing with problem students, or communicating with parents are set. In such schools, teachers may be somewhat disoriented about the proper way to deal with a variety of matters, and probably a clear set of policies is lacking. The fourth scale is called

TABLE 35

Varimax Rotated Factor Structure of Principal Governance Items

Item	Factor		
	I	II	h²
How strictly enforced is each of the following:[a]			
Students must comply with a dress code	−.02	.55	.30
Students must comply with smoking rules	−.06	.16	.03
Students who damage or destroy school property must repay the school	−.15	.23	.07
In [month] how many students were:[b]			
Put on school probation	.88	.08	.78
Paddled	.03	.40	.16
Suspended	.12	.19	.05
Expelled from your school	.04	.18	.03
Assigned to special day-long class in your school for disruptive students	.00	.18	.03
Transferred to special school for disruptive students	.70	.02	.49
Transferred to another regular school because of discipline problems here	.94	−.08	.90
Referred to a community mental health agency as disruptive student	.93	−.10	.87
Arrested by the police for incidents occurring at school	.23	.21	.10
You or assistant principal met with parents to discuss their children's behavior	.97	−.06	.94
Does your school have a discipline court with students on it?	.00	.02	.00
Does your school have a printed student rights and responsibilities code?[c]	.07	.12	.02

Note. The high communality estimates for some variables are a result of the high level of aggregation in these data. See Chapter 3.
[a]Coded as follows: 0 = no such regulation, 1 = little or no enforcement, 2 = moderately enforced, 3 = strictly enforced.
[b]Prior to analysis these variables were standardized by dividing them by the school's enrollment so that they do not simply measure the size of the school.
[c]Coded as follows: 1 = no; 2 = yes, not given to the students; 3 = yes, given to the students.

teacher culture. In high-scoring schools on this scale, teachers report that they learn about problem students from other teachers and have little personal discussion with students. This factor appears more problematic than the others. We examined the possibility that we had extracted too many factors, and that this factor would disappear in a four factor solution. It does not.

The third step in our exploration of school governance and sanctioning practices was to factor-analyze principal and teacher reports together. This was necessary because of the difficulties in interpreting

TABLE 36
Varimax Rotated Factor Structure of Teacher Governance Items

Item	Factor					h^2
	I	II	III	IV	V	
In dealing with misbehaving students, how often do you:						
Send them out of class?	.12	.53	.06	−.04	.15	.33
Give them additional school work?	.18	.09	−.36	.11	.24	.24
Use or threaten to use physical punishment?	.26	−.06	−.31	.07	.38	.32
Lower their grades if it is repeated?	−.16	.37	.06	−.03	−.12	.18
Give privileges to increase positive involvement?	.35	.47	−.11	.12	.26	.44
Ignore it when students talk back?	−.18	.48	.04	.13	−.10	.29
Percentage of teachers responding "Not possible to say" how policies regarding the following are set:						
Deciding on standards for passing and failing.	.05	−.04	−.12	.29[c]	.17	.13
Controlling classroom disorder.	−.16	.23	.04	.49[c]	−.11	.34
Dealing with serious behavior problems (e.g., fighting, etc.).	−.17	.11	.15	.68[c]	.01	.53
Discussing matters about students with parents.	−.10	−.07	−.11	.49[c]	−.08	.27
How much does each of the following describe your school?						
All students are treated equally.	.66[a]	−.21	−.04	−.19	−.24	.58
Students have a say about how this school is run.	.05	−.02	.71[b]	.02	−.20	.54
Parents have a say about how this school is run.	.13	.04	.76[b]	.03	.14	.61
Counselors give me advice about handling misbehaving students.	.43[a]	.15	.10	−.02	.04	.22
How well do teachers and administrators get along at your school?	.63[a]	−.20	−.03	−.19	−.13	.49
How many students discuss their personal problems with you each month?	.09	.05	−.07	.08	−.45[d]	.23
How many students do you send to the office for discipline each month?	.12	.60	−.22	.04	−.06	.43
Teachers are provided with up-to-date information about problem students by the school's administration.	.62[a]	−.07	−.02	−.12	.19	.43
Teachers hear about problem students from other teachers.	−.01	.09	−.18	.01	.61[d]	.42
Teachers maintain control in class.	.36	−.64	.01	−.07	−.10	.55

Note. Except for the items beginning with "how many" or where it is indicated that an item is a percentage, all are Likert-type items (aggregated, of course, to the school level). The "how many" items are standardized by dividing them by the average number of students taught each week prior to analysis.
[a] These items were added together to form the scale called *teacher–administration cooperation*.
[b] These items were added together to form the scale called *student–parent influence*.
[c] These items were added together to form the scale called *policy confusion*.
[d] These items were added together to form the scale called *teacher culture*.

the earlier factor analyses relating to sanctions. Table 37 shows the items involved and the resulting factor structure. Guided by these results, four scales were constructed. The first is called *isolation or referral* because it involves relocating the student or involving parents or another agency in coping with problem students. The second scale is called *principal intervention* because it involves such sanctions as suspension, sending students to the principal or vice-principal for discipline, or sending students out of the class (often, presumably, to the office). The third scale is called *clear sanctions*. In schools with high scores on this scale, both principal and teachers tend to report the use of corporal punishment, and teachers in the aggregate report the use of relatively specific, clear, or immediate sanctions, such as the assignment of additional schoolwork or the granting of special privileges. The fourth scale is called *ambiguous sanctions*. In high-scoring schools on this scale, teachers typically report that they lower students' grades as a response to misconduct and that they ignore misbehavior. The principal's report about the strictness of enforcement of a policy of requiring students to repay the school for damages done was not clearly associated with any factor. Because of the attention being given to restitution as a way of treating offenders in the criminological literature, however, we deemed this item to be important enough to be carefully examined. This single item is therefore included as a predictor in subsequent analyses.

Fourth, the student reports about school governance practices were examined. The aggregated student reports and their factor structure are described in Table 38. Based on these results, three scales were constructed. The first is called *perceived fairness and clarity*. High scoring schools on this scale are characterized by students as a group reporting that the rules, the teachers, and the principal are fair; they know what the school's rules are; punishments for rulebreaking are the same for everyone; and students are not treated like children. The second scale is called *student influence*. In a high-scoring school, students typically report that they have a say in how the school is run, they help to decide how courses are taught, they have a say in making the school's rules, and if the school does something wrong and a group of students complain, they can get a fair deal. The third scale is called *firm and clear rule enforcement*. In a high-scoring school, students typically report that the school rules are strictly enforced; if a rules is broken they know that punishment will follow; students need permission to do anything around the school; students are paddled for serious rule breaking; and the principal is firm, tough, and strict.

TABLE 37

Varimax Rotated Factor Structure of Principal and Teacher
Sanctioning Practices (N ≥ 574)

Item and source	Factor I	II	III	IV	h^2
Principal					
Students who damage or destroy school property must repay the school.	−.13	−.03	.10	−.19	.07
In [month] how many students were:[a]					
Put on school probation?	.87[c]	.07	.00	.02	.76
Paddled?	.03	.18	.38[e]	−.19	.22
Suspended?	.09	.43[d]	.01	.03	.20
Expelled from your school?	.02	.18	−.02	.00	.03
Assigned to special day-long class in your school for disruptive students?	−.01	.16	.05	.00	.03
Transferred to special school for disruptive students?	.69[c]	.02	−.05	.11	.49
Transferred to another regular school because of discipline problems here?	.95[c]	.00	−.04	.05	.90
Referred to a community mental health agency as disruptive student?	.93[c]	.00	.01	.08	.87
Arrested by the police for incidents occurring at school?	.21	.21	.00	.05	.09
You or assistant principal met with parents to discuss their children's behavior.	.96[c]	.12	−.02	.09	.94
Teacher					
In dealing with misbehaving students, how often do you do the following things:					
Send them out of class.	−.03	.51[d]	.07	.19	.30
Give additional school work.	−.04	−.03	.47[e]	.00	.23
Use or threaten to use physical punishment.	−.01	−.03	.65[e]	.28	.50
Lower their grades if it is repeated.	.03	.04	−.05	.54[f]	.30
Give privileges to increase positive involvement.	−.04	.19	.65[e]	.40	.61
Ignore it when students talk back.	.11	.22	−.02	.44[f]	.26
Each month, on the average, how many students do you send to the office for discipline?[b]	.04	.80[b]	.16	.12	.69

[a]Prior to analysis these variables were standardized by dividing them by the school's enrollment so that they do not simply measure the size of the school.
[b]Prior to analysis these variables were standardized by dividing them by the average number of students taught each week.
[c]These Likert-type items were added together to form a scale called *isolation or referral.*
[d]These Likert-type items were added together to form a scale called *principal intervention.*
[e]These Likert-type items were added together to form a scale called *clear sanctions.*
[f]These Likert-type items were added together to form a scale called *ambiguous sanctions.*

TABLE 38

Varimax Rotated Factor Structure of Student Reports of
School Governance Practices (N = 614 to 621)

Item	Factor			h^2
	I	II	III	
Everyone knows what the school rules are.	.48[a]	−.27	.14	.33
The school rules are fair.	.76[a]	.15	−.03	.61
The punishment for breaking school rules is the same no matter who you are.	.49[a]	.21	.30	.38
The school rules are strictly enforced.	.26	−.25	.59[c]	.48
If a school rule is broken, students know what kind of punishment will follow.	.17	.07	.48[c]	.26
Students can get an unfair rule changed.	.43	.50[b]	−.36	.57
Students need permission to do anything around here.	−.36	−.29	.48[c]	.44
Students are paddled for serious rule breaking.	−.04	.05	.45[c]	.21
Students are treated like children here.	−.69[a]	−.12	.26	.56
Students *do* have a lot to say about how this school is run.	.05	.66[b]	.04	.44
The teachers are fair.	.71[a]	.02	−.11	.52
They [teachers] let everyone know who gets high and low grades.	−.17	.21	.21	.12
[It is easy to] get an unfair grade changed.	.08	.38[b]	.03	.16
[It is easy to] talk over personal problems with a school counselor.	.28	.13	.03	.10
The principal runs the school with a firm hand.	.52	−.12	.55[c]	.59
The principal is tough and strict.	−.18	−.15	.48[c]	.28
The principal is fair.	.64[a]	.21	.08	.46
Students help decide how courses are taught.	.02	.62[b]	.05	.39
Students can rate the teachers.	.03	.41[b]	−.17	.20
If the school does something wrong and a group of students complain, they can get a fair deal.	.50	.59[b]	−.15	.62
Students have a say in making school rules.	.32	.61[b]	−.32	.58

[a]These Likert-type items were added together to form a scale called *perceived fairness and clarity*.
[b]These Likert-type items were added together to form a scale called *student influence*.
[c]These Likert-type items were added together to form a scale called *firm and clear rule enforcement*.

The correlations among the 11 scales just described are shown (for junior and senior high schools combined) in Table 39. The convergence of student and teacher reports of student influence (r = .25), and of student reports of firm and clear enforcement with principal and teacher reports of clear sanctions (r = .54) lends some support to the construct validity of these measures, even though the correlations are not large. Likewise, the small negative correlation between the scale for student–parent influence and student reports of firmness (-.35), and the small

TABLE 39

Correlations among Measures of School Governance

Measure and source	1	2	3	4	5	6	7	8	9	10	11
Teacher reports											
1. Teacher–administration cooperation	(68)										
2. Student–parent influence	06	(70)									
3. Policy confusion	-23**	-04	(52)								
4. Teacher culture	-03	-10**	01	(42)							
Teacher and principal reports of sanctioning practices											
5. Isolation or referral	-06	-01	00	-04	(54)						
6. Principal interventation	-04	-08	04	05	08	(54)					
7. Clear sanctions	18**	-24**	06	22**	-06	17**	(59)				
8. Ambiguous sanctions	-22**	03	06	-07	14**	19**	-04	(37)			
Student reports											
9. Perceived fairness and clarity	34**	11**	-16**	-12**	-03	-20**	-01	-15**	(78)		
10. Student influence	11**	25**	-06	-15**	10*	11**	-07	23**	35**	(79)	
11. Firm and clear enforcement	22**	-35**	-03	17**	-10*	11**	54**	-30**	05	24**	(56)

Note. Decimals omitted. N's range from 522 to 623. Homogeneity coefficients are shown on the diagonal.
*p < .05; **p < .01.

Table 40

Zero-Order and Multiple Correlations of Junior High School
Governance Measures with School Disruption

Measure and source	Overall disruption	Teacher victimization	Student victimization
Teacher reports			
Teacher–administration cooperation	−.36**	−.37**	−.15**
Student–parent influence	−.11*	−.10	−.03
Policy confusion	.18**	.12*	.18**
Teacher culture	−.05	−.05	.02
Teacher and principal reports of sanctioning practices			
Restitution enforced	−.24**	−.28**	−.03
Isolation or referral	.30**	.40**	.03
Principal intervention	.45**	.46**	.19**
Clear sanctions	.08	.01	.10
Ambiguous sanctions	.43**	.56**	.03
Student reports			
Perceived fairness and clarity	−.50**	−.36**	−.41**
Student influence	.22**	.31**	−.03
Firm and clear enforcement	−.14*	−.22**	.03
R^2 (all measures)	.49**	.55**	.20**

Note. N's range from 266 to 311.
*$p < .05$; **$p < .01$.

negative correlation between teacher culture and student influence (-.15) lends some support to the construct validity of the measures. The reliability coefficients shown in Table 39 imply that, in general, a moderate degree of internal consistency characterizes these scales.

School Governance and School Disruption. Table 40 summarizes for junior high schools the total associations of this set of measures of school governance and sanctioning practices with the three criterion measures—overall disruption, teacher victimization, and student victimization. Table 41 summarizes parallel results for high schools. Together, the school governance and sanctioning measures are associated with 55% and 40% of the variance in teacher victimization and 20% and 10% of the variance in student victimization in junior and senior high schools, respectively. The zero-order correlations imply substantial positive associations of teacher victimization with the use of isolation or referral and principal intervention, ambiguous sanctions, and the extent of student influence in school governance. They imply

TABLE 41
*Zero-Order and Multiple Correlations of Senior High School
Governance Measures with School Disruption*

Measure and source	Overall disruption	Teacher victimization	Student victimization
Teacher reports			
Teacher–administration			
cooperation	−.34**	−.40**	−.12*
Student–parent influence	−.14*	−.09	−.08
Policy confusion	.10	.11	.05
Teacher culture	.11	.09	.12*
Teacher and principal reports of			
sanctioning practices			
Restitution enforced	−.17**	−.26**	.08
Isolation or referral	.14*	.20**	−.09
Principal intervention	.15*	.24**	−.05
Clear sanctions	−.01	−.07	.11
Ambiguous sanctions	.35**	.44**	.02
Student reports			
Perceived fairness and clarity	−.29**	−.22**	−.25**
Student influence	−.04	.05	−.15**
Firm and clear enforcement	−.05	−.13*	.08
R^2 (all measures)	.29**	.40**	.10**

Note. N's range from 252 to 312.
*$p < .05$; **$p < .01$.

moderate to substantial negative associations with teacher–administration cooperation in governance, the use of restitution as a sanction, and student perceptions that the school rules are fair, clear, and firmly enforced.[1]

Although usually smaller in size, the zero-order correlations with student victimization imply a substantial negative link of this aspect of disorder with student perceptions of the fairness and clarity of rules, a smaller negative association with teacher–administration cooperation, and a small positive association with teachers' policy confusion in junior high schools and with teacher culture in high schools.

Readers are again cautioned against causal interpretations of these associations. At least part of the observed correlations are spurious in the sense that variables used here as predictors and criteria may be explained in part by other causes, not examined in this chapter, with

[1]The restitution item is the principal's report that students are required to repay the school for damages done.

which both predictors and criteria are correlated. These results should be regarded as descriptive. In Chapters 10 and 11 we probe some causal hypotheses by applying statistical controls before assessing the contributions of the school governance variables.

A second caution about some of the measures treated here as preditors is that some of these predictors look suspiciously like criteria. For example, sending students to the office suspending or transferring students, and the like are (at least partly) taken in *response* to instances of disruptive behavior. In short, disorder in the school may explain sanctioning practices as much as sanctioning practices explain disorder.

School Social and Educational Climate

The focus of the exploration of dimensions of school social organization now turns to school social and educational climate. In the present context, *climate* refers to hypothetical schoolwide predispositions to treat certain kinds of educational goals as important. Schools may be characterized by such dimensions as academic competitiveness; schoolwide peer influence on college or vocational expectations may exist; or teachers and administrators may favor one educational orientation over another. Thus conceived, educational climate has clear links with theorizing about schools and delinquency (G. D. Gottfredson, 1981; Hirschi, 1969; Polk & Schafer, 1972; Williams, Moles, & Boesel, 1975). It also has clear links with literature in the sociology of education that examines the relations of school social structure to more traditional educational outcomes such as achievement and educational and occupational attainment (Alwin, 1976; Bidwell & Kasarda, 1975; Coleman *et al.*, 1966; Feldman & Newcomb, 1969; McDill & Rigsby, 1973).

Explorations of the dimensions of school climate exist in the literature. Moos and Trickett (1974) have published a device to assess the social climates of classrooms. Their scales, which contain many items that resemble items of information collected in the Safe School Study, assess nine dimensions of classroom climate, including measures of relationships, personal development, system maintenance, and system change. Several of their subscales—especially the competition, order and organization, rule clarity, and teacher control subscales—seem relevant to classroom disorder, and one might expect dimensions resembling those Moos and Trickett have identified to emerge as predictors of school disruption in our research. In a study of the effects of schools on academic outcomes, McDill and Rigsby (1973) factor-analyzed a variety of measures of school climate and developed six factors to describe educational climate, but most of their factors are related to different aspects of academic climate rather than to broad dimensions of educational climate.

The Moos and Trickett and McDill and Rigsby research provides useful background information for our own exploration. Yet because of the classroom orientation of the former and the academic orientation of the latter, they do not enable us to bypass our own analyses of the dimensions of social and educational climate by simply seeking alternative measures of their dimensions in the Safe School Study data. Consequently, we have conducted research to develop measures of school educational and social climates. Because of the wide variety of information relevant to school educational and social climates, because of a desire to avoid factoring huge correlation matrices, and because we believed we could conceptually distinguish three broad categories of school climate variables, these explorations were conducted in three stages. The first stage involved the educational climate from the points of view of principals and teachers. The second stage involved student reports of general educational and social climate—aspects of climate that appeared to have broad relevance but that are not focused on or limited to the issue of school disruption. The third stage involved student reports of social climate that seemed especially relevant to delinquency and school disruption—aspects of social climate that are closely related to social control, subcultural, or opportunity theories of delinquency.

We decided in addition to construct separate scales measuring race relations and internal control of the studentry because of the general importance of race in American social relations, and because of the emphasis on internal control in the NIE (1978) study. This section also describes these measures.

Educational Climates from the Teacher and Principal Points of View. Tables 42 and 43 show the items and factor structure of variables presumed to be indicators of school climate based on principal and teacher reports for junior and senior high schools, respectively. Only two items from the principal questionnaire appeared appropriate to include in this set of variables for the senior high school sample, and at the junior high level these two items were not asked, apparently because they were not deemed relevant in junior high schools.

Table 42
Varimax Rotated Factor Structure of Junior High School Teacher Reports
of School Educational Climate (N ≥ 311)

	Factor		
Item	I	II	h^2
Teacher report on self			
Hours per month spent helping students out of class	−23	15	08
Class assignments at different levels for different students	25	−08	07
Justifiable to have students learn facts, even if no immediate application	−15	−02	02
Emphasis on { basic skills	−66	−20	48
job preparation	45	−05	21
college preparation	01	56	32
Teacher report on principal			
Emphasis on { basic skills	−54	−13	30
job preparation	31	−10	10
college preparation	01	60	36

Note. Decimals omitted. All data derived from teacher reports. Teachers reported on the principals' emphases.

Table 43
Varimax Rotated Factor Structure of High School Teacher
and Principal Reports of School Educational Climate (N ≥ 194)

	Factor		
Item	I	II	h^2
Teacher report on self			
Hours per month spent helping students out of class	−19	28	11
Class assignments at different levels for different students	38	−20	18
Justifiable to have students learn facts, even if no immediate application	−35	19	16
Emphasis on { basic skills	−63	−16	42
job preparation	86	−31	83
college preparation	02	82	67
Teacher report on principal			
Emphasis on { basic skills	−44	−18	22
job preparation	78	−26	68
college preparation	03	84	70
Principal report			
Relative number of students placed in jobs related to career planning	51	−17	29
Percentage of seniors applying to college	−30	54	39

Note. Decimals omitted. Information on the principals' educational emphases are derived from teacher reports.

Guided by the results of these factor analyses we constructed two scales. The first scale is called *vocational versus basic skills climate*. A high-scoring school is characterized by teachers typically reporting that they and the principal emphasize job preparation and not reporting that they emphasize basic skills. In high-scoring high schools, the principal also typically reported a relatively large number of students placed in jobs related to careers they are considering. The second scale is called *college preparation climate*. High scoring schools are characterized by teachers reporting that they and the principal emphasize college preparation and, in the case of high schools, the principal reports a high proportion of students applying to college.

School Social and Educational Climate from the Student Point of View. The student reports of school climate considered and their factor structure are shown in Tables 44 and 45. The results of these factor analyses guided the construction of three scales. The first scale is called *attachment to school*. In schools with high scores on this factor, students typically report that they like their school and their classes; their classes are interesting, not boring, and worth taking; the school is helping them to prepare for what they want to do after school; grades and their teachers' regard for them is important; and their school is better than other schools in the area. We have labeled this scale attachment to school because it resembles the group-level counterpart of Hirschi's (1969) construct of attachment. It also appears to be a general measure of liking for the school.

The second scale is called *college versus vocational orientation*. Its primary characteristic is that in high-scoring schools students plan and expect to go to college, and in low-scoring schools students plan and expect to get a job after high school. Because this scale is bipolar it is inappropriate to make a direct connection with Hirschi's (1969) construct of commitment. Students could conceivably be committed either to educational attainment or to jobs.

The third scale is called *peer and nonacademic orientation*. High-scoring schools are characterized by students reporting that what other students think of them is important; they do not know each others' grades; many have full- or part-time jobs; and relatively many are involved in extracurricular activities, such as athletics, band, or clubs. This scale resembles Hirschi's constructs of attachment (to peers) and involvement (in socially acceptable if not academic activities), and

TABLE 44

Varimax Rotated Factor Structure of Junior High Student Reports
of Educational and Social Climate (N ≥ 308)

Item	Factor			h^2
	I	II	III	
Do you take part in:				
Athletics outside of gym class.	−.02	−.07	.32	.11
Band, orchestra, or chorus.	.04	−.02	.32	.11
School clubs.	.13	−.03	.04	.02
Student government.	−.03	.11	−.07	.02
Other activities not part of class work.	.12	−.05	.35	.14
How good are your school's athletic teams compared to other schools' athletic teams in this area?	−.19	−.12	.00	.05
In other ways, how good is your school compared to other schools in this area?	.47	.12	.28	.32
How well do you like the following:				
This school.	.72	.00	.12	.54
The students.	.36	−.25	.33	.30
The principal.	.50	.14	−.03	.27
The classes you are taking.	.63	.13	−.29	.50
How many close friends do you have at this school?	.12	−.05	−.40	.18
Do you have a part-time or a full-time job?	−.22	−.23	.49	.35
In general, how often are teachers at your school like this:				
Teachers expect a lot of work from students.	−.34	.21	−.12	.17
They are teaching me what I want to learn.	.66	.01	−.38	.58
They are interested in the students.	.71	−.06	.14	.53
They let everyone know who gets high and low grades.	.00	−.08	−.51	.27
Teachers let students learn from each other in class.	.26	.03	.24	.12
How easy would it be to do the following things if you wanted to:				
Work faster or slower than the rest of the class.	.08	.04	−.30	.10
Have your ideas listened to in class.	.53	.10	.22	.34
Talk over school work problems with a teacher.	.58	.02	.15	.35
Most of the classes here are:				
Easy.	.08	−.15	−.20	.07
Interesting.	.72	−.10	−.14	.55
Hard.	.03	.12	.30	.10
Boring.	−.71	−.02	.21	.55
Worth taking.	.52	−.04	.44	.46
Which of these things should your teachers work hardest to do:				
Teach basic subjects and skills.	.10	.01	.14	.03
Prepare students for later jobs.	−.15	−.44	.12	.23
Prepare students for college.	.04	.33	−.33	.22
Is there a lot of competition for grades in this school?	.23	.11	−.09	.07
Do most of your friends think getting good grades is important?	.50	.18	.08	.29
Mean of course grades.	.27	.26	.25	.20

(Continued)

TABLE 44 (*Continued*)

Item	Factor			
	I	II	III	h²
Standard deviation of course grades.	−.06	−.01	−.30	−.09
How important is each of the following to you:				
What teachers think about you.	.50	−.06	.30	.34
The grade you get at school.	.45	.16	−.05	.23
Being a leader in school activities.	.32	.04	−.29	.18
What the other students at school think about you.	.14	−.21	.76	.64
What do you want to do most in the year after you leave high school:				
Go to college.	.21	.90	.10	.87
Get a job.	−.12	−.79	−.20	.68
How much is school helping you get ready for what you want to do after high school?	.49	.25	−.32	.41
What do you expect you will actually do in the year after high school:				
Go to college.	.18	.90	.23	.89
Go to business or trade school.	−.12	−.06	−.19	.05
Join the armed forces.	−.02	−.10	−.34	.13
Get a job.	−.10	−.75	.01	.58
Get married.	.06	−.36	−.03	.13

TABLE 45

Varimax Rotated Factor Structure of Senior High Student Reports of Educational and Social Climate (N ≥ 306)

Item	Factor			
	I	II	III	h²
Do you take part in:				
Athletics outside of gym class.	−.27	.17	.42	.28
Band, orchestra, or chorus.	.16	−.02	.43	.21
School clubs.	.22	.08	.35	.18
Student government.	.00	.24	.18	.09
Other activities not part of class work.	.06	.11	.46	.23
How good are your school's athletic teams compared to other schools' athletic teams in this area?	−.20	−.20	.01	.08
In other ways, how good is your school compared to other schools in this area?	.58	.23	.12	.41
How well do you like the following:				
This school.	.78	−.03	−.01	.60
The students.	.30	−.11	.45	.31
The principal.	.44	.10	−.18	.24
The classes you are taking.	.71	−.16	−.31	.62

TABLE 45 (*Continued*)

Item	Factor			h^2
	I	II	III	
How many close friends do you have at this school?	−.02	−.11	−.17	.04
Do you have a part-time or a full-time job?	−.08	−.16	.43	.21
In general, how often are teachers at your school like this:				
Teachers expect a lot of work from students.	.09	.30	−.07	.10
They are teaching me what I want to learn.	.76	−.19	−.25	.68
They are interested in the students.	.70	−.14	.11	.53
They let everyone know who gets high and low grades.	−.09	−.03	−.38	.16
Teachers let students learn from each other in class.	.53	−.17	.28	.39
How easy would it be to do the following things if you wanted to:				
Work faster or slower than the rest of the class.	.16	−.22	−.41	.24
Have your ideas listened to in class.	.49	.19	.28	.36
Talk over school work problems with a teacher.	.53	.11	.07	.30
Most of the classes here are:				
Easy.	−.20	−.20	−.14	.10
Interesting.	.70	−.08	−.22	.55
Hard.	.03	.34	.14	.14
Boring.	−.77	.18	.22	.68
Worth taking.	.63	.04	.23	.45
Which of these things should your teachers work hardest to do:				
Teach basic subjects and skills.	.00	−.10	.06	.01
Prepare students for later jobs.	.22	−.66	.07	.49
Prepare students for college.	.01	.67	−.15	.47
Is there a lot of competition for grades in this school?	.24	.44	.06	.26
Do most of your friends think getting good grades is important?	.47	.44	−.06	.42
Mean of course grades.	.10	.11	.37	.16
Standard deviation of course grades	−.15	.01	−.11	.04
How important is each of the following to you:				
What teachers think about you.	.53	.13	.16	.32
The grade you get at school.	.31	.41	−.52	.54
Being a leader in school activities.	.23	.16	−.02	.08
What the other students at school think about you.	.13	−.15	.75	.60
What do you want to do most in the year after you leave high school:				
Go to college.	.01	.92	.02	.85
Get a job.	.04	−.80	−.14	.67
How much is school helping you get ready for what you want to do after high school?	.65	.11	−.32	.54
What do you expect you will actually do in the year after high school:				
Go to college.	−.03	.91	.12	.84
Go to business or trade school.	.09	−.21	−.20	.09
Join the armed forces.	.13	−.12	−.16	.06
Get a job.	.00	−.77	−.03	.59
Get married.	.01	−.34	−.01	.12

tempts one to interpret it as the group-level counterpart of one or another of those constructs.

Student Reports of Aspects of Social Climate with Direct Relevance to Delinquency. We isolated for special scrutiny a set of student reports of social climate with special relevance to delinquency or student disruption. The set of items examined and their factor structure are displayed in Tables 46 and 47. Based on the factor analysis results, two scales were constructed. The first scale is called *delinquent youth culture.* In schools that score high on this scale, students as a group agree that if students use drugs at school it is their own business; alcohol, marijuana, herion, or stolen goods are easy to get at school; they would do nothing if they had information about an incident of vandalism, and would not tell a principal or a teacher; they would play hooky or cheat on a test if they could get away with it. This constellation resembles Hirschi's (1969) construct of belief in aggregate counterpart, but also resembles more closely some accounts of youth delinquent subcultures (England, 1960; Kvaraceus & Miller, 1959).

The second scale is called *belief in conventional social rules.* This scale characterizes schools in which many students reject the ideas that if people leave things around they deserve to have them taken, taking things from stores doesn't hurt anyone, people who get beat up usually asked for it, and if one wants to get ahead one cannot always be honest. In a high-scoring school, students report that they would not spray paint on walls or take money from others if they could get away with it. This constellation suggests that this scale measures the group-level counterpart of Hirschi's (1969) belief construct, or what amounts to nearly the same thing—Gough's (1964) empirically derived Socialization Scale.

Race Relations. Because of the central importance of race relations in our society, we singled out items related to race or ethnic relations for separate consideration when assessing a school's social climate. Several items that conceptually cohered and that had substantial positive interitem correlations were used to form a scale called *race-ethnic relations.* A high-scoring school is one in which teachers and students report that people of different races or nationalities get along well and that minorities are treated fairly in the schools.

Internal Control. To examine school average internal control, one of the cornerstones of the original Safe School Study report, we formed a composite of three items in the student questionnaire that apparently

TABLE 46

Varimax Rotated Factor Structure of Junior High Students' Reports of Belief
in Rules and Delinquent Youth Culture

	Factor		
Item	I	II	h²
How much do you agree with the following:			
Schools should have rules about the way a student can dress.	−39	−01	16
It is all right for schools to suspend students without a hearing.	−38	−18	18
If students are in a fist fight, let them settle it by themselves.	26	−32	17
If students use drugs around school, it is their own business.	61	−34	48
Students *should* have a lot to say about how this school is run.	57	06	33
How easy or hard is it for students to get the following things at your school:			
Beer or wine.	82	07	67
Marijuana.	81	−08	67
Heroin.	57	−22	38
Stolen things for sale.	62	01	38
If some other students here tore up things in a classroom at night and you knew who did it, what would you do:			
Tell your friends.	32	22	15
Tell your parents.	−28	26	15
Tell a teacher or the principal.	−76	17	60
Agree with the students who did it.	00	−32	10
Do nothing.	70	−27	56
How do you feel about each of the following ideas:			
People who leave things around deserve it if their things get taken.	−20	−32	15
Taking things from stores doesn't hurt anyone.	11	−72	54
People who get beat up usually asked for it.	−12	−50	27
If you want to get ahead, you can't always be honest.	01	−56	32
Would you do any of the following if you knew you could get away with it:			
Cheat on a test.	65	−12	44
Spray paint on school walls.	33	−58	44
Take money from other students.	44	−58	53
Skip school.	71	−14	53

Note. Decimals omitted. Smallest N = 308.

tapped this dimension. This is an *a priori* scale that shows low reliability.

Table 48 punctuates this description of the measures of school educational and social climate by summarizing the reliabilities of all the scales. The reliabilities of the scales based on teacher and principal reports are modest, and the reliabilities of the scales based on aggregated

TABLE 47

Varimax Rotated Factor Structure of Senior High Student Reports of Belief in Rules and Delinquent Youth Culture

| | Factor | | |
Item	I	II	h^2
How much do you agree with the following:			
Schools should have rules about the way a student can dress.	−50	15	27
It is all right for schools to suspend students without a hearing.	−32	−28	18
If students are in a fist fight, let them settle it by themselves.	16	−48	26
If students use drugs around school, it is their own business.	64	−34	53
Students *should* have a lot to say about how this school is run.	54	26	37
How easy or hard is it for students to get the following things at your school:			
Beer or wine.	73	16	56
Marijuana.	76	07	58
Heroin.	38	−08	15
Stolen things for sale.	49	−03	24
If some other students here tore up things in a classroom at night and you knew who did it, what would you do:			
Tell your friends.	29	23	14
Tell your parents.	−32	35	23
Tell a teacher or the principal.	−62	24	45
Agree with the students who did it.	−13	−36	15
Do nothing.	49	−34	40
How do you feel about each of the following ideas:			
People who leave things around deserve it if their things get taken.	−17	−58	37
Taking things from stores doesn't hurt anyone.	16	−72	54
People who get beat up usually asked for it.	−21	−56	36
If you want to get ahead, you can't always be honest.	09	−63	40
Would you do any of the following if you knew you could get away with it:			
Cheat on a test.	66	−06	44
Spray paint on school walls.	16	−49	27
Take money from other students.	28	−57	40
Skip school.	68	03	46

Note. Decimals omitted. Smallest N = 306.

student reports are moderately high-reflecting in part the lower standard errors of item means with greater aggregation and in part a larger number of items per scale.

Social Climate and School Disruption

This section reports the associations of our climate measures with the three criteria: overall disruption, teacher victimization, and student victimization. Table 49 shows the zero-order and squared multiple

TABLE 48

Alpha Reliability Coefficients for Measures of School Educational
and Social Climate

Scale and source of information	Junior high		Senior high	
	Alpha	No. of items	Alpha	No. of items
Principal and teacher				
Vocational vs. basic skills climate	.56	4	.57	7
College preparation climate	.53	2	.50	4
Student				
Attachment to school	.88	14	.90	14
College vs. vocational orientation	.82	7	.86	11
Peer and nonacademic ties	.69	7	.71	9
Delinquent youth culture	.90	9	.84	9
Belief in conventional social rules	.71	6	.77	6
Average internal control	.48	3	.32	3
Student and teacher				
Race/ethnic relations	.81	3	.81	3

correlations for junior and senior high schools. The school educational and social climate measures are associated with 40% and 35% of the variance in teacher victimization for junior and senior high schools, respectively; and with 17% and 12% of the variance in student victimizations.

The zero-order correlations imply that, in junior high schools, teacher victimizations are positively associated with an educational climate in which teachers and principals emphasize job versus college preparation—but, in senior high schools, this association is in the opposite direction. Teacher victimization is negatively associated with the studentry's attachment to the school, peer and nonacademic ties, belief in conventional rules, and good race relations. Teacher victimization is slightly positively associated with a college (rather than a job) orientation among students, and, at least for junior high schools, with the measure of delinquent youth culture. Although the correlations are small in size, the average grades students receive is negatively correlated with teacher victimization rates in senior high schools, and the dispersion of grades is positively correlated with teacher victimization.[2]

[2]Although measures of the mean and standard deviation of grades did not have substantial loadings on any of the factors derived from the educational and social climate items, these variables were included in the regressions of disruption on climate because their potential relevance was indicated by McPartland and McDill (1976).

TABLE 49

Zero-Order and Multiple Correlations of Measures of School Educational and Social Climate with Measures of School Disruption

Measure and source	Overall disruption		Teacher victimization		Student victimization	
	Jr.	Sr.	Jr.	Sr.	Jr.	Sr.
Teacher						
Job preparation vs. basic skills	.22**	−.19**	.27**	−.19**	.02	−.11
College preparation	.01	.04	−.03	.03	.07	.03
Student						
School attachment	−.32**	−.23**	−.20**	−.20**	−.31**	−.18**
College vs. job orientation	.12*	.11	.21**	.12*	−.05	.04
Peer and nonacademic ties	−.40**	−.42**	−.49**	−.48**	−.02	−.04
Average internal control	−.18**	−.08	−.04	−.01	−.28**	−.15**
Delinquent youth culture	.26**	.02	.20**	.09	.22**	−.10
Belief in conventional rules	−.43**	−.36**	−.41**	−.33**	−.21**	−.18**
Good race/ethnic relations	−.48**	−.33**	−.41**	−.29**	−.25**	−.18**
Mean grade average	−.09	−.25**	−.01	−.21**	−.10	−.17**
Dispersion (SD) of grades	.21**	.21**	.16**	.20**	.08	.11
R^2	.39**	.35**	.40**	.35**	.17**	.12**

Note. N's range from 296 to 311 for junior high schools, and from 260 to 311 for senior high schools.
*$p < .05$; **$p < .01$.

If grades are considered an indicator of status in an educational setting, then the latter result suggests a link between the degree of status differentiation characterizing a school and teacher victimizations. Alternatively, grade dispersion may reflect the tendency for some students to experience success, and other students to experience mostly failure. In schools with large grade dispersions, the reward structure may be "rigged" for failure for some students (Howard, 1978), resulting in low stakes in conformity for those students.

In keeping with the pattern in our previous analyses, the zero-order correlations imply generally lower associations of student victimizations with the predictors. Student victimization is somewhat lower in schools with a studentry characterized in the aggregate by attachment to school, high internal control scores, belief in conventional rules, and good race relations.

Again we emphasize that statistical association, as indexed by the zero-order and multiple correlations reported in this section, do not necessarily imply causation. We have now documented that a host of variables are related to school disruption. These include community social and demographic composition; community crime; school compositional characteristics; school size, resources, and staffing; school governance and sanctioning practices; and social climate. It would therefore be inappropriate to make any causal interpretations solely on the basis of the associations reported in this chapter.

This completes our initial exploration of school social climate. Before attempting to unravel the implications of all the associations between school characteristics and school disruption for potential school effects on disruption rates, we will briefly examine school security practices.

CHAPTER 9

School Security and Disruption

One may wish to gauge disruptive behavior for more than one reason. A first reason to measure disruption, victimization, vandalism, and the like is to assess damage. For example, one may wish to assess the cost of these activities in terms of dollars lost. A second reason to measure disruptive behavior is an interest in the moral and social status of the population in question.

We noted in an early chapter that it appears inappropriate to use simple counts of persons victimized as an index of school disorder because this would tend to measure school size as much as anything else. We have used *rates* of disruptive behavior because an index of disorder that measured mostly school size would be a poor index of the moral or social construct of interest.

For similar reasons, if an index of disruption were largely to measure the *opportunity* for disruption to occur, it would be a poor index of the moral or social construct of interest. A studentry that refrains from beating up on its members or on teachers because school security measures prevent it is not necessarily displaying more virtue than an unrestrained studentry characterized by mayhem. This same point was made by Boggs (1965) when she noted that "differing environmental opportunities should be reflected in . . . [crime] rates" (p. 899), and Cohen and Felson (1979) and Sparks (1981) have made related points.

The reason we seek to measure disorder in the present research is in part due to our desire to assess a moral construct—to make statements about the effectiveness or harmfulness of the school socialization process. Our research is ultimately concerned with testing hypotheses about the effects of school organizational properties, including governance, fairness, student–teacher interaction, and relevance of the curriculum on school disruption or delinquency. We are also interested in the practical issues of orderliness and safety, but we do not aim to focus on the ways in which security measures of serious sorts may promote safety. We are more concerned with the ways in which social control processes may lead to an orderly environment. Within the context of the theoretical rationale for these hypotheses, the criteria of interest must be regarded largely as moral constructs. If the dependent variables simply reflect opportunity for disruption to occur they are poor measures, and the link between the theoretical notions behind the research and the research itself is weakened.

For this reason we examine in this chapter the relations between victimization and measures of opportunity for disorder in schools, including decreases in opportunity due to security measures taken by the school. The existence of strong negative associations between security measures or other measures of the restriction of opportunity for disruption to occur (such as the shortness of the school day) and the victimization measures would undermine our confidence in the interpretation of the criterion measures as measures of a moral construct. In this section we report research which bears on the direction and size of this association.

A factor analysis (not shown) of school security measures implied that much of the common variance in these variables could be captured in a single factor. Consequently, we created a scale called *extensiveness of security* measures. The items included in this scale are displayed in an appendix, and the scale has a reliability (alpha) of .80 for junior and senior high schools combined. In addition to security measures, the opportunity for disruption to occur in school may be influenced by the total amount of time students spend at school during the day, the length of the lunch period, and the degree of freedom students have to do what they please during the lunch break. We have also examined indexes of these opportunities in the analyses.

Table 50 shows the results. There is a small negative association of length of school day with teacher victimization in junior but not in senior high schools; and a small positive association of length of the

TABLE 50

Regression of School Disruption on Measures of Opportunity for Disruption

Predictor	Junior high[a]		Senior high[b]	
	r	Beta	r	Beta
Criterion is overall disruption				
Length of school day	−.16**	−.09	−.01	.03
Length of lunch period	.09	.07	.04	.03
Students leave school during lunchtime	−.02	.03	.02	.01
Extensiveness of security measures	.34**	.32**	.32**	.32**
R^2		.13**		.11**
Criterion is teacher victimization				
Length of school day	−.18**	−.07	−.04	−.01
Length of lunch period	.13*	.08	.08	.06
Students leave school during lunchtime	−.10	−.03	−.01	−.01
Extensiveness of security measures	.48**	.45**	.38**	.38**
R^2		.24**		.15**
Criterion is student victimization				
Length of school day	−.05	−.08	.09	.10
Length of lunch period	−.02	.02	−.01	.01
Students leave school during lunchtime	.08	.10	.05	.06
Extensiveness of security measures	−.06	−.08	.00	.01
R_2		.02		.01

[a]N's range from 235 to 303.
[b]N's range from 238 to 304.

lunch period and teacher victimizations, again in junior high schools only. There is a more substantial positive association of the extensiveness of schools' security measures with teacher victimizations in both junior and senior high schools. Student victimization is essentially unrelated to the set of predictors examined here.

The results imply little reason to regard the dependent variables as measures of opportunity for disruption. The only sizable association with a measure of restricted opportunity is with the extensiveness of security measures, and this association has a sign *opposite* that expected. These results do not imply that increasing the extensiveness of school security may result in an increase in teacher victimization. These correlations do not necessarily imply causation. The difficulties inherent in trying to make any inferences about security measures and rates of school disruption from such results were summarized well in the NIE (1978, pp. 128—129) Safe School Study report, and interested readers should consult that discussion.

Because of the emphasis placed on the need for heightened school security in Congressional testimony (U.S. Senate, Committee on the Judiciary, 1976a, 1976b, 1977) and on the part of those who offer security services to schools, we are obliged to note that these results do *not* provide any support for suggestions that security measures increase safety. As a practical matter, schools adopting new security systems should do so with circumspection. To our knowledge no rigorous evaluations of such systems have been conducted. Therefore, school systems should approach the installation of security procedures and devices experimentally, and seek the assistance of impartial evaluators in the implementation of their experiment.

In the next chapter we explicitly state some assumptions about the appropriate application of statistical controls and seek evidence of nonspurious association between school characteritics and student and teacher victimization.

CHAPTER 10

School Contributions to School Disorder

In this chapter we make some conservative tests of the proposition that school social organization contributes to the explanation of the level of disorder the school experiences. This undertaking is a risky one: cross-sectional measurement-based research is a weak method for making causal inferences. Nevertheless, by carefully delineating the hypothetical causal model and assessing the implications of that model, we can sort hypotheses with merit from those with little support in the data.

Judgment is involved in the specification of the model, measurement is known to be imperfect, and no experimental manipulations have been made to enhance confidence that any observed effect is really due to any putative cause. Our judgment in the specification of a model may be wrong and an alternative specification may lead to quite different conclusions. The model presented here is the result of our most conservative judgment given the available data and what is known at present. In the next chapter we examine a less conservative model

Figure 3 shows the path model that has structured the application of statistical controls in this chapter. It is a fully recursive model. Each label in the figure stands for a group of blocked variables. Blocks at the left are regarded as causally prior to blocks at the right, and the model explicity excludes reverse or mutual causation among blocks. We have labeled the criterion measure in the Figure 3 model "teacher victimization" for convenience only. The same causal ordering is assumed for both student and teacher victimizations.

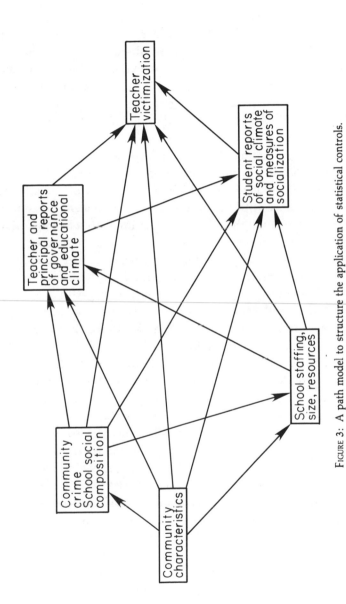

Figure 3: A path model to structure the application of statistical controls.

The selection of variables for inclusion in these analyses involved several steps. First, for each criterion variable (student or teacher victimizations) and for each type of school (junior or senior high), all predictors with a significant zero-order correlation with the criterion were identified. In other words, the results of the earlier chapters were used to identify four sets of predictor variables. Because problems of extreme multicollinearity (see Chapter 3) foreclosed the possibility of the straightforward procedure of regressing each criterion on all the predictors identified in the way just described, we examined the diagonal elements of the inverse correlation matrices based on each of these sets of predictors (excluding the criterion) to determine which predictors were most redundant with the others as a set. Our rule of thumb was to achieve a set of predictors in which no one predictor shared more than 70% of its variance with the others. This is equivalent to requiring that no diagonal element in the inverse correlation matrix be larger than 3.33. Predictors were dropped or, when combination seemed the most reasonable course, combined with other predictors with equal weighting. This procedure was followed in an iterative fashion until no diagonal element of the inverse correlation matrix was larger than 3.62 and 3.34 for the junior and senior high school teacher victimization models, respectively; and no larger than 3.03 and 2.19 for the junior and senior high school student victimization models.

As a result of this sequence of activities, certain highly redundant variables were dropped from one model or another. (For a comprehensive account of variables dropped in this way for a given model, a reader may review the significant correlations reported in earlier chapters and compare the predictors involved with the detailed list of variables employed in each model.) In addition, in the model developed for teacher victimizations in the junior high schools, a composite was formed involving the first community factor (poverty and disorganization) and one measure of school composition (social and educational disadvantage). The consequence of combining these two variables is that this aspect of the schools' social composition must be treated as an exogenous variable in the same way as the community characteristics. In addition to these steps, we also reconstructed our measure of community crime to guard against criterion contamination. In models involving teacher victimization as the criterion, no item based on a teacher report was used in our community crime index. In models where student victimization was the criterion, no item based on student reports was used in the community crime measure.

The following subsections provide results and more details of the models developed, first for teacher and then for student victimizations.

Teacher Victimizations

Table 51 shows for teacher victimizations the total associations and net contributions for *blocks* of predictors according to the path model specified earlier. The total associations shown parallel those shown for blocks of predictors in earlier chapters. The differences between the values in this table and in earlier chapters arise because they have been recomputed here using only those variables used to evaluate the path model. The results imply that once community characteristics are statistically controlled, the net contribution is much smaller than the total associations for remaining groups of variables. The large total associations summarized here and in earlier chapters may thus be interpreted as due in large part to the redundancy of school variables with variables that measure the characteristics of the communities where the schools are located. The hypothetical model, and the results it produces, imply that knowledge of school characteristics increases only modestly our ability to account for variance in teacher victimizations once community characteristics are taken into account.

With one exception, however, each block of predictors does make a noticeable increment in the amount of variance in teacher victimization explained by the model (all increments in R^2 are significant for both junior and senior high schools except for that due to student reports of social climate in the senior high schools). The major implication of these results is that, provided one regards the model as well specified, school characteristics including staffing, size, and resources; governance and educational climate; and social climate make a difference in the amount of teacher victimization in the school. At the same time, the net contributions due to school social organizational characteristics are modest, not large, in size.

Finer grained versions of the results for teacher victimization are presented in Tables 52 and 53. These tables show for junior and senior high school respectively, the total associations, total contributions (effects), and direct contributions (effects) *according to the path model* for specific variables in each block. Table 52 implies that, for junior high schools, the following school characteristics influence the level of

TABLE 51

*Total Associations and Net Contributions of Blocks of Predictors
in the Model for School Rates of Teacher Victimization*

Predictor set	R^2 for this block	R^2 at this stage in the model	Net contribution
Junior high schools			
Exogenous community characteristics	.52	.52	.52**
Community crime and characteristics of the studentry that are externally determined	.29	.54	.02*
Staffing, size, and resources	.36	.57	.03**
Teacher and principal reports of governance and educational climate	.45	.63	.06**
Student reports of social climate and measures of socialization	.44	.66	.03*
Senior high schools			
Exogenous community characteristics	.28	.28	.28**
Community crime and characteristics of the studentry that are externally determined	.37	.44	.15**
Staffing, size, and resources	.24	.52	.09**
Teacher and principal reports of governance and educational climate	.42	.60	.07**
Student reports of social climate, measures of socialization, and grades	.32	.62	.02

Note. The total association is the squared multiple correlation of all the predictors in a particular block with the criterion. In the context of the path model it includes spurious correlation for endogenous variables and unanalyzed correlation for the exogenous variables. All these SMC's are significantly different form zero.

The column headed "R^2 at this stage in the model" gives the proportion of variance in the criterion accounted for by all predictors up to and including the block of predictors in question, but no predictors that are assumed to be sequiturs to this block according to the path model.

Net contribution is the increase in R^2 that results when these variables are added to the equation at the appropriate stage according to the path model.

*Increase in R^2 significant at the $p < .05$ level.
**Increase in R^2 significant at the $p < .01$ level.

TABLE 52

Total Association, Total Contribution, and Direct Contribution to Rates of Teacher Victimization in Junior High Schools

Predictor and block	Total association	Total contribution	Direct contribution
Exogenous community characteristics			
Poverty and disorganization (including measures of studentry racial composition and educational disadvantage)	.64**	.45**	26**
Rural (vs. urban location)	−.61**	−.38**	−.13*
Community crime and characteristics of the studentry that are externally determined			
Community crime	.53**	.17**	.11*
Desegregation	.24**	.00	.02
Staffing, size, and resources			
Percentage of teachers white	−.42**	.01	−.07
Student–teacher ratio	−.16**	−.03	−.02
Teaching resources	−.40**	−.16**	−.09
Total enrollment	.36**	.11*	.11*
Teacher and principal reports of governance and educational climate			
Principal social approach	.12*	−.01	−.02
Principal enforcement approach	.16**	−.03	−.03
Teacher democratic orientation	.18**	.10*	.06
Teacher punitive approach	.34**	.12*	.11*
Teacher–administration cooperation	−.37**	−.06	−.06
Policy confusion	.12*	.04	.03
Restitution enforced	−.28**	−.05	−.05
Ambiguous sanctions	.56**	.20**	.13*
Emphasis on job preparation (vs. basic skills)	.27**	.06	.06
Student reports of social climate, measures of socialization, and grades			
Perceived fairness and clarity of rules	−.36**	−.05	−.05
Student influence	.31**	.02	.02
Firm and clear enforcement	−.22**	−.09*	−.09*
Peer and nonacademic ties	−.49**	.09	.09
Delinquent youth culture	.20**	.04	.04
Belief in conventional rules	−.41**	−.08	−.08
College vs. job orientation	.21**	.05	.05
Good race/ethnic relations	−.41**	−.07	−.07
Grade dispersion (standard deviation)	.16**	−.05	−.05

Note. All N's ≥ 247.
*p < .05; **p < .01.

TABLE 53
Total Association, Total Contribution, and Direct Contribution to
Rates of Teacher Victimization in Senior High Schools

Predictor and block	Total association	Total contribution	Direct contribution
Exogenous community characteristics			
Poverty and disorganization	.37**	.22**	.00
Affluence and education	.14*	−.04	.05
Affluent mobility	−.12*	−.10	−.05
Rural (vs. urban location)	−.48**	−.41**	−.08
Community crime and characteristics of the studentry that are externally determined			
Community crime	.46**	.16**	.04
Social and educational disadvantage	.58**	.42**	.36**
Desegregation	.13*	−.05	−.01
Staffing, size, and resources			
Number of different students taught	.26**	.22**	.18**
Teaching resources	−.44**	−.15**	−.06
Total enrollment	.25**	.02	.00
Teacher and principal reports of governance and educational climate			
Principal enforcement approach	.17**	.01	.00
Teacher punitive approach	.35**	.15**	.14*
Teacher democratic orientation	.15*	.07	.08
Teacher–administration cooperation	−.40**	−.19**	−.18**
Restitution enforced	−.26**	−.02	−.03
Ambiguous sanctions	.44**	.15**	.13*
Emphasis on job preparation (vs. basic skills)	−.19**	−.03	−.02
Student reports of social climate, measures of socialization, and grades			
Perceived fairness and clarity of rules	−.22**	−.11	−.11
Perceived firm and clear rule enforcement	−.13*	−.02	−.02
Peer and nonacademic ties	−.48**	−.04	−.04
School attachment	−.20**	.07	.07
Belief in conventional rules	−.33**	−.11*	−.11*
Good race/ethnic relations	−.28**	.04	.04
Mean grade received	−.21**	.00	.00
Grade dispersion (standard deviation)	.20**	.06	.06

Note. All N's ≥ 225 schools.
*$p < .05$; **$p < .01$.

teacher victimization experienced in the school. All these contributions are relatively small.

1. The greater the teaching resources, the less the teacher victimization.
2. The larger the school, the more the teacher victimization.
3. The more ambiguous the sanctions used (lowering grades as a disciplinary practice and ignoring misconduct), the more the teacher victimization.
4. The more democratic the attitudes of teachers in a school (saying that students and parents should have a say in how the school is run), the greater the teacher victimization.
5. The more punitive the attitudes of teachers in a school, the greater the teacher victimization.
6. The more studentries perceive the rule enforcement as firm and clear, the less the teacher victimization.

Table 53 implies that, for senior high schools, the following school characteristics influence the level of teacher victimization experienced in the school. All influences are modest in size.

1. The larger the number of different students taught by the average teacher, the greater the teacher victimization.
2. The greater the teaching resources, the less the teacher victimization.
3. The better the teacher–administration cooperation, the less the teacher victimization.
4. The more ambiguous the sanctions used (lowering grades as a disciplinary practice and ignoring misconduct), the more the teacher victimization.
5. The more punitive the attitudes of teachers in a school, the more the teacher victimization.
6. The more the students as a group believe in conventional social rules, the less the teacher victimization.

Student Victimizations

Table 54 shows, for student victimization, the total associations and net contributions for blocks of predictors *according to the model specified earlier*. In contrast to the results for teacher victimizations, the

TABLE 54

Total Associations and Net Contributions of Blocks of Predictors
in the Model for School Rates of Student Victimization

Predictor set	R^2 for this block	R^2 at this stage in the model	Net contribution
Junior high schools			
Exogenous community characteristics	.03	.03	.03*
Community crime and characteristics of the studentry that are externally determined	.04	.05	.02
Staffing, size, and resources	.03	.06	.01
Teacher and principal reports of governance and educational climate	.09	.12	.06**
Student reports of social climate and measures of socialization	.19	.24	.12**
Senior high schools			
Exogenous community characteristics	.02	.02	.02*
Community crime and characteristics of the studentry that are externally determined	.19	.19	.17**
Staffing, size, and resources	.04	.19	.00
Teacher and principal reports of governance and educational climate	.03	.20	.01
Student reports of social climate, measures of socialization, and grades	.12	.25	.05*

Note. The total association is the squared multiple correlation of all the predictors in a particular block with the criterion. In the context of the path model it includes spurious correlation for endogenous variables and unanalyzed correlation for the exogenous variables. All these SMC's are significantly different form zero.

The column headed "R^2 at this stage in the model" gives the proportion of variance in the criterion accounted for by all predictors up to and including the block of predictors in question, but no predictors that are assumed to be sequiturs to this block according to the path model.

Total contribution is the increase in R^2 that results when these variables are added to the equation at the appropriate stage according to the path model.

*Increase in R^2 significant at the $p < .05$ level.
**Increase in R^2 significant at the $p < .01$ level.

community characteristics are only weakly associated with aggregated student victimization reports. Indeed, again in contrast to the analyses for teacher victimizations, *all* predictors combined are weakly associated with student victimizations—accounting for less than one-fourth of the variance, versus well over three-fifths for teacher victimizations. More-

TABLE 55

Total Associations, Total Contributions, and Direct Contributions
to Rates of Student Victimization in Junior High Schools

Predictor and block	Total association	Total contribution	Direct contribution
Exogenous community characteristics			
Poverty and disorganization	.17**	.16*	.12
Rural (vs. urban) location	−.11*	−.04	.03
Community crime and characteristics of the studentry that are externally determined			
Community crime	.14*	.06	−.01
Desegregation	.15**	.12*	.06
Staffing, size, and resources			
Teaching resources	−.16**	−.11	−.03
Teacher and principal reports of governance and educational climate			
Policy confusion	.18**	.14*	.09
Teacher democratic orientation	.22**	.18**	.14*
Teacher–administration cooperation	−.15**	−.05	.07
Student reports of social climate and measures of socialization			
Perceived fairness and clarity of rules	−.41**	−.28**	−.28**
School attachment	−.31**	.04	.04
Average internal control	−.28**	−.12	−.12
Delinquent youth culture	.22**	.11	.11
Belief in conventional rules	−.21**	.04	.04
Good race/ethnic relations	−.25**	−.06	−.06

Note. All N's ≥ 247.
*$p < .05$; **$p < .01$.

over, the increment in predictive power that is obtained when community crime or characteristics of the school are used in addition to exogenous community characteristics is also modest. Significant increments in predictive efficiency are made only with the block of predictors involving student reports of social climate, measures of socialization and grades, teacher and principal reports of school governance and educational climate (junior high schools only), and characteristics of the community that are determined outside the school (senior high schools only).

Finer grained versions of the results for student victimization are provided in Tables 55 and 56. These tables show, for junior and senior high schools, respectively, the toal associations, total contributions

TABLE 56

Total Associations, Total Contributions, and Direct Contributions to
Rates of Student Victimization in Senior High Schools

Predictor and block	Total association	Total contribution	Direct contribution
Exogenous community characteristics			
Affluence and education	−.14*	−.14*	−.07
Community crime and characteristics of the studentry that are externally determined			
Community crime	.18**	.21**	.16*
Mean grade level	−.33**	−.33**	−.32**
Percentage of students female	−.19**	−.17**	−.19**
Staffing, size, and resources			
Number of different students taught	.18**	.10	.01
Teaching resources	−.14*	−.02	.02
Teacher and principal reports of governance and educational climate			
Teacher authority	.12*	.06	.01
Teacher–administration cooperation	−.12**	−.05	.00
Student reports of social climate, measures of socialization, and grades			
Good race/ethnic relations	−.18**	−.09	−.09
Perceived fairness and clarity of rules	−.25**	−.16*	−.16*
Student influence	−.15**	−.02	−.02
Average internal control	−.15**	−.02	−.02
Belief in conventional rules	−.18**	.06	.06
Mean grade received	−.17**	−.10	−.10

Note. All N's $\geq$ 225.
*$p < .05$; **$p < .01$.

(effects), and direct contributions (effects) of specific variables within each block *according to the path model.* Table 55 implies that for junior high schools the following characteristics influence the level of student victimization experienced in the school. Nearly all influences are small in size.

1. The more confused teachers are about the ways school policies are determined, the more students report being victimized.
2. The more democratic the attitudes of the average teacher (e.g., teachers' indicating that students should have a say in how the school is run), the *more* students report victimization.

3. The more students on the average report that school rules are fair and clear, the less they report being victimized.

Table 56 implies that, for senior high schools, the more students on the average report that school rules are fair and clear, the less they also report being victimized.

Influences Beyond the School's Control

The foregoing lists enumerate contributions of school organizational characteristics that contribute to the explanation of school disruption when extrinsic community characteristics and school social compositional characteristics that are largely beyond the control of school administration and staff are statistically controlled. To gain further insight into the distribution of school disruption, we now focus our attention on these extrinsic variables and their contributions to school disruption.

Teacher Victimization. Tables 52 and 53 imply that teachers on the average report more victimization in the following kinds of schools:

1. Schools located in areas characterized by poverty, unemployment, and a high proportion of female-headed families.
2. Urban schools.
3. Schools located in high crime communities.
4. Schools where large proportions of the students are black, rated as low in ability, and come from families on welfare.

The foregoing list is consistent with the result for both junior and senior high school teacher victimization.

Student Victimization. Students on the average report more victimization in the following kinds of schools.

1. Schools located in areas characterized by poverty, unemployment, and high proportion of female-headed families. (Junior high schools only.)
2. Schools located in areas where the general population has little education and is not affluent. (Senior high schools only.)
3. Schools located in high crime communities. (Senior high schools only.)

4. Schools in which most students are at the lower grade levels. (Senior high schools only.)
5. Schools where a large proportion of students are male. (Senior high schools only.)
6. Schools where desegregation programs exist (e.g., busing or court-ordered desegregation programs). (Junior high schools only.)

This last result that junior high schools undergoing desegregation experience more student victimization appears inconsistent with the National Institute of Education's (1978) report. That report summarized its results as follows:

> The statistical analysis shows that a school's being under court order to desegregate is associated with only a slight increase in the amount of student violence when other factors are taken into account. It shows further that there is no consistent association between *number* of students bused and school violence, controlling for other factors. Finally, there is a weak association between student violence and the *recentness* of initial desegregation efforts at a school. Together these findings suggest that some violence may be due to the initiation of mandatory desegregation, but that as time goes on and larger numbers of students are bused to achieve racial balance the desegregation process ceases to be a factor. (p. 132)

Their statistical results (National Institute of Education, 1978, Appendix A, pp. 17–19), however, are in greater agreement with our results than is their verbal summary. In their results for urban junior high schools, percentage of students bused did make a moderate direct contribution to school violent crime level. (Their measure is closely related to our student victimization measure. Suburban and rural junior high schools did not produce this result.) In short, their results for the junior high schools in which desegregation programs may be expected to be a major issue parallel our results closely. Neither their results nor ours directly address the recentness of desegregation efforts. Their evidence is indirect and unclear on this issue, and we were unable to examine it carefully. In our research we did briefly examine the recentness of busing, but discovered that the skip pattern of principal questionnaire was such that information about recentness was available for so few schools that no confident statements are possible (see our Table 22).

Limitations

These conclusions require qualification. First, we have already noted that one may question the model guiding the application of statistical controls and elsewhere (Chapter 3; G. D. Gottfredson, 1979) we discuss the difficulties in interpreting path models involving ecological data. More research examining alternative models is required. Chapter 11 examines some alternatives. Second, although we have taken extraordinary care in the development of the measures used, they are known to be subject to substantial measurement error, and they are also potentially subject to misinterpretation in terms of the constructs they measure. Third, one does not know what consequences would really ensue if one were to deliberately alter some school characteristic, and it is not at all clear how these characteristics could be successfully altered. Fourth, despite our efforts to avoid criterion contamination in selecting predictors—omitting from consideration any predictors that obviously overlapped the criterion—nagging doubts persist that criterion contamination exists or that some global positive attitude toward the school may have influenced both predictors and criterion in these analyses. It is often difficult to decide whether one should consider a variable a predictor, an alternative measure of the criterion, or a consequence of the criterion. In the present research we have not, as did NIE (1978), used reports of the extent to which teachers maintain order in the classroom as a predictor. Although one certainly may expect that teachers manage classes differently—some maintaining order better than others—reports that classrooms are disorderly can equally well be construed as a criterion measure. Other variables included here are problematical as well. The ambiguous sanctions scale includes reports by teachers that they lower grades in response to repeated misconduct, and that they ignore the misconduct. These items presume some misconduct, and it may be that this measure represents a consequence of school disruption as much as it represents a cause. A similar argument could be made about punitive teacher attitudes. These are pervasive flaws which will accompany all cross-sectional survey research in this area.

In short, these data should be further explored using alternative models and techniques. The next chapter examines some alternative causal models to probe (a) the consequences of assuming that the diverse and particular measures of school characteristics examined in this chapter may more appropriately be viewed as indicators of a smaller number of underlying dimensions of school organization, and (b) the consequences of using alternative methods of measuring school disorder.

CHAPTER 11

Alternative Models of School Disorder

Here we stand back from the research reported in Chapters 5 through 10 to approach the explanation of school disorder from another perspective. In this chapter we bring together two strands of doubt about the utility of the model examined in Chapter 10.

First, and most important, the fine-grained decomposition of the contributions of particular school characteristics to victimization leads in our opinion to an excessively conservative conclusion about the ways schools create (or fail to prevent) disorder. In Chapter 10 we used multiple regression analysis to determine whether there was evidence that school practices contribute to the explanation of victimization rates. We decided that the evidence was persuasive that they do. That approach, although useful for providing conservative tests of the independent contribution of sets of predictors, is less useful for learning about the underlying structure of school organization and the global effects of the major dimensions of school structure on school orderliness. The regression approach can be misleadingly conservative and even confusing because extreme multicollinearity (see Chapter 3) makes regression coefficients unstable and difficult to interpret. The relative contributions of highly correlated school characteristics, in particular, are difficult to sort out.

Second, in Chapter 4 we described a number of reservations about the principal measures of school disorder—student and teacher victimization—used in the following six chapters. Concerns persist that racial stereotypes or sex differences in the experiences of students or teachers becloud those measures. Attempts to understand the causes of school disorder should take account of the factorial complexity of victimization reports discovered in the final section of Chapter 4, because different causal processes may determine the reports of victimization by different social groups in schools.

Accordingly, in this chapter we (a) examine alternative models for the measurement of victimization and (b) probe the implications of structural models of school disorder that involve a small number of global dimensions on which schools differ. We use confirmatory factor analysis in the context of linear structural equations models as our research vehicle. Exploratory factor analyses guide the specification of measurement models for school organizational characteristics, and exploratory factor analyses also guide the specification of alternative measurement models for school disorder. First one and then another measurement model for school victimization is specified and the alternative models compared with respect to their fit to the data. This examination of models with different assumptions about the underlying structure of victimization is intended (a) to determine whether the data accord with the assumption that school victimization is a unitary construct that may be explained by a single explanatory model, and (b) to provide insight into the ways major dimensions of school environments are related to school victimization.

Guided by exploratory factor analyses of school and community characteristics, we have specified models of victimization that postulate that a small number of underlying factors or "latent variables" cause a larger number of observed measures. Then we postulate that these same latent variables determine school victimization rates. We attempt to estimate the contribution of each of these hypothesized underlying causal variables to school victimization, and we do this making different assumptions about the appropriate measurement model for victimization. We use maximum likelihood estimates for parameters in these models and test the "goodness of fit" for alternative models using LISREL IV (Jöreskog & Sörbom, 1978). If a model that postulates more than one latent victimization variable fits the data better than does a model that postulates only a single latent variable, then any model that treats victimization as a single construct may be misspecified and therefore misleading.

To provide some structure for the reader, and as a preview of the subsequent subsections, the measurement and structural models con-

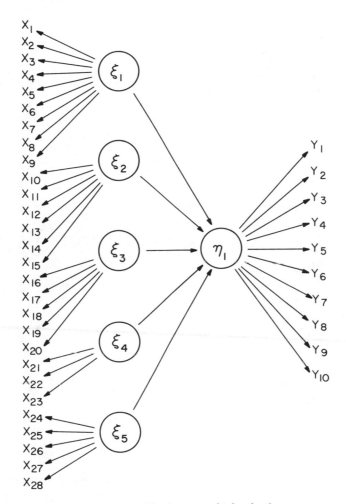

FIGURE 4: Model 1 for senior high schools.

sidered here are shown in Figures 4 through 11. Figures 4, 6, 8, and 10 refer to senior high schools, and Figures 5, 7, 9, and 11 refer to junior high schools. Tables 57 and 58 supplement these figures by describing the observed variables postulated to measure the several latent variables in these models. With one exception these measures have been described earlier in this report.

The exception is *Principal Rating.* This is a composite of five Likert-type items from the teacher questionnaire in which teachers were asked

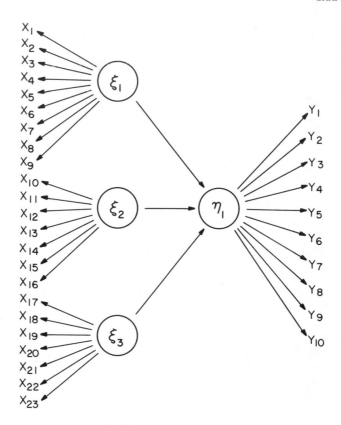

FIGURE 5: Model 2 for junior high schools.

to describe how friendly, fair, permissive, and informal the principal is, and whether he or she shares decision making (these are components of question 29 in the Phase II teacher questionnaire).

In the figures the ξ_n refer to postulated latent variables that, according to the model, cause both the observed variables taken as measures of them, which are represented as X_p, and the latent variables that underlie the observed measures of victimization. The latent victimization variables are represented as η_m and the measures of them as Y_q.

The indicators X_p and Y_q for the ξ_n and η_m are selected after performing a series of exploratory factor analyses of victimization measures and school and community characteristics. All but one of the measures considered in earlier chapters are considered here. Teacher

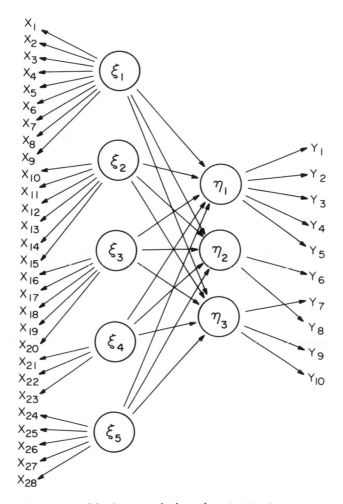

FIGURE 6: Model 3 for senior high teacher victimization.

reports of threats were not used to avoid loading up the analysis with a large number of trivial incidents. Plots of eigenvalues and judgments about the substantive interpretability of alternative varimax rotated principal factor solutions guided the specification of these measurement models.

These exploratory factor analyses were followed by confirmatory factor analyses in order to enable the specification of measurement models for victimization and school and community characteristics. Because of the unreliability of the student interview data (Chapter 4),

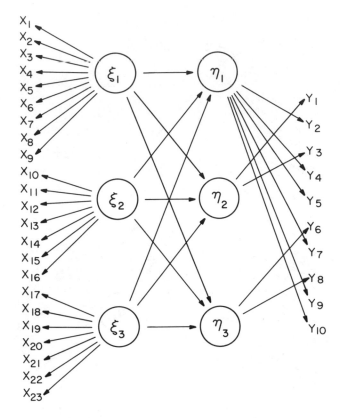

FIGURE 7: Model 4 for junior high teacher victimization.

TABLE 57

Observed Variable for the Measurement Components of the Two Models for Senior High School Characteristics

X_1 Community poverty and unemployment (factor score based on 1970 census data).
X_2 Rural (vs. urban) location.
X_3 Community crime (principal and student reports).
X_4 % of students from families on welfare or unemployed (principal's report).
X_5 % of students white.
X_6 % of teachers white.
X_7 Peer and nonacademic ties (9-item scale based on student reports).
X_8 % of students behind grade level (principal's report).
X_9 % of students who have never repeated a year of school because of failure.
X_{10} Community affluence and education (factor score based on 1970 census data).
X_{11} Educational level of teachers.
X_{12} Clear sanctions (principal's and teachers' report).

TABLE 57 (*Continued*)

X_{13} Teacher authority (7-item scale based on teachers' attitudes).
X_{14} Firm and clear enforcement of rules (6-item scale based on students' reports).
X_{15} Delinquent youth culture (9-item scale based on student reports).
X_{16} Parental education and students' self-reported ability (4-item scale based on students' reports).
X_{17} College preparation emphasis (5-item scale based on teachers' and principal's reports).
X_{18} Belief in conventional social rules (6-item scale based on students' reports).
X_{19} College vs. job orientation of the studentry (11-item scale based on students' reports).
X_{20} Internal control (3-item scale based on students' reports).
X_{21} Number of different students taught by the average teacher.
X_{22} Vocational vs. basic skills climate (7-item scale based on teachers' and principal's report).
X_{23} Percentage of teachers who teach mostly industrial arts.
X_{24} Teacher–administration cooperation (4-item scale based on teachers' reports).
X_{25} Principal rating (5-item scale based on teachers' reports).
X_{26} Perceived fairness and clarity of rules (6-item scale based on students' reports).
X_{27} Student influence (7-item scale based on student reports).
X_{28} School attachment (14-item scale based on students' reports).

TABLE 58

Observed Variables for the Measurement Components of the Two Models for Junior High School Characteristics

X_1 Community poverty and unemployment (factor score based on 1970 census data).
X_2 Rural (vs. urban) location.
X_3 Community crime (principal and student reports).
X_4 Percentage of students from families on welfare or unemployed (principal's report).
X_5 Percentage of students white.
X_6 Percentage of teachers white.
X_7 Peer and nonacademic ties (7-item scale based on student reports).
X_8 Percentage of students behind grade level (principal's report).
X_9 Percentage of students who have never repeated a year of school because of failure.
X_{10} Community affluence and education (factor score based on 1970 census data).
X_{11} Educational level of teachers.
X_{12} Clear sanctions (principal's and teachers' report).
X_{13} Teacher authority (7-item scale based on teachers' attitudes).
X_{14} Firm and clear enforcement of rules (6-item scale based on students' reports).
X_{15} Parental education and students' self-reported ability (4-item scale based on students' reports).
X_{16} College vs. job orientation of the studentry (11-item scale based on students' reports).

(*Continued*)

TABLE 58 (*Continued*)

X_{17} Belief in conventional social rules (6-item scale based on students' reports).
X_{18} Teacher–administration cooperation (4-item scale based on teachers' reports).
X_{19} Principal rating (5-item scale based on teachers' reports).
X_{20} Perceived fairness and clarity of rules (6-item scale based on students' reports).
X_{21} School attachment (15-item scale based on students' reports).
X_{22} Internal control (3-item scale based on students' reports).
X_{23} Delinquent youth culture (9-item scale based on student reports).

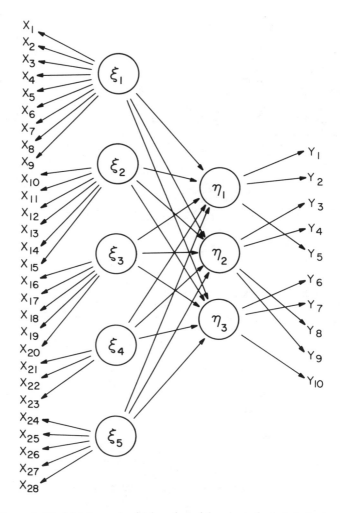

FIGURE 8: Model 5 for senior high male and female student victimization.

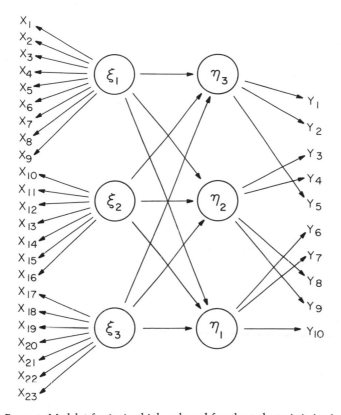

FIGURE 9: Model 6 for junior high male and female student victimization.

they were not included in these analyses. The following analyses are restricted to principal, teacher, and student questionnaire measures.

MEASUREMENT MODELS

Teacher Victimization. Because the Chapter 4 analyses suggested that the victimization reports of black and white teachers may not be alternative measures of the same underlying factor, the factor analyses involved teacher victimization reports aggregated separately for blacks and whites. In the exploratory factor analyses for senior high teacher victimization measures, all variables have positive loading on the first unrotated factor (not shown). Several varimax rotations were examined.

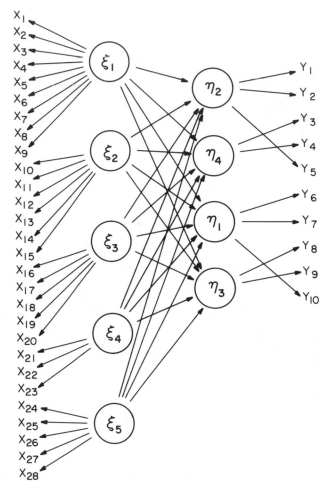

FIGURE 10: Model 7 for senior high black and white student victimization.

The clearest structure emerged from the three-factor varimax rotation shown in Table 59. The first factor might be called *white teacher victimization*, the second is dominated by *serious teacher victimization*, especially as reported by black teachers, and the third is dominated by less serious measures of victimization reported by black teachers.

Two confirmatory factor analyses were then performed. In the first, all observed variables Y were assumed to be indicators of a single underlying factor (η), and factor loadings (λ_Y) were estimated using maximum likelihood procedures. In the second, guided by the results of the exploratory factor analysis, the Y's were assumed to be indicators of

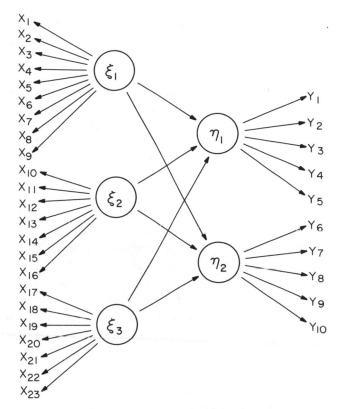

FIGURE 11: Model 8 for junior high black and white student victimization.

TABLE 59

Exploratory Factor Analysis of Senior High Teacher Victimization Measures

		Factor			
Observed variable		1	2	3	h^2
Y_1	White teachers' robbery	41	40	−02	32
Y_2	White teachers' theft	40	01	05	16
Y_3	White teachers' physical attack	47	22	09	28
Y_4	White teachers' remarks, gestures	84	03	28	79
Y_5	White teachers' fear for safety	86	05	14	77
Y_6	Black teachers' robbery	09	84	−04	72
Y_7	Black teachers' theft	02	07	55	31
Y_8	Black teachers' physical attack	01	49	19	28
Y_9	Black teachers' remarks, gestures	14	08	68	49
Y_{10}	Black teachers' fear for safety	34	00	49	36

Note. Varimax rotation of principal factor solution with iterated communalities. Decimals omitted.

three underlying factors. The solution was constrained by fixing some factor loadings at zero, and allowing others to vary freely—except that the η_n were constrained to be orthogonal ($\Phi = I$).

Table 60 shows the results for senior high schools. As anticipated, the three-factor model fits the data much better than the one-factor model [χ^2 ($df = 3$) = 157.9, $p < .001$]. Despite the restrictions on the analysis, introduced to provide for interpretive clarity and which account for the fairly large chi-square values, the simplified three-factor model appears to reproduce the inter-item correlations reasonably well (36 out of the 45 off-diagonal elements of the residual matrix are less than .11). These results accord with the Chapter 4 suggestion that more than a single underlying factor is being represented by the victimization measures for senior high school teachers.

The results of the exploratory analysis for junior high school teacher victimization measures are shown in Table 61. The exploratory results were difficult to interpret, and we examined several alternative confirmatory analyses. The best of the confirmatory analyses is shown in Table 62. This three-factor model fits the data much better than the single-factor model [χ^2 ($df = 3$) = 32.9, $p < .001$]. The first factor, η_1,

TABLE 60

Standardized λ_Y for Two Models of Senior High Teacher Victimization

		Model 1	Model 3		
Observed variable		η_1	η_1	η_2	η_3
Y_1	White teachers' robbery	.391	.349	.351	—
Y_2	White teachers' theft	.404	.399	—	—
Y_3	White teachers' physical attack	.470	.461	—	—
Y_4	White teachers' remarks, gestures	.925	.827	—	.232
Y_5	White teachers' fear for safety	.869	.897	—	—
Y_6	Black teachers' robbery	.156	—	.960	—
Y_7	Black teachers' theft	.160	—	—	.393
Y_8	Black teachers' physical attack	.122	—	.428	—
Y_9	Black teachers' remarks, gestures	.367	—	—	.957
Y_{10}	Black teachers' fear for safety	.469	.354	—	.316
χ^2		258.6	100.7		
v		35	32		

Note. The factors (ξ_n) are relabeled η_m in this table because in subsequent models estimating structural parameters these factors are endogenous variables. Dashes indicate parameters fixed at zero. The three-factor model provides a better fit to the data than the one-factor model ($\chi^2 = 157.9$, $v = 3$, $p < .001$). Notice that the structure shown here for "model 3" does not exactly match the model 3 diagram shown in Figure 5. See the text for the explanation.

TABLE 61

Exploratory Factor Analysis of Junior High Teacher Victimization Measures

		Factor			
Observed variable		1	2	3	h^2
Y_1	White teachers' robbery	05	41	02	11
Y_2	White teachers' theft	42	43	02	37
Y_3	White teachers' physical attack	12	65	05	28
Y_4	White teachers' remarks, gestures	62	63	17	83
Y_5	White teachers' fear for safety	67	38	06	54
Y_6	Black teachers' robbery	14	20	44	20
Y_7	Black teachers' theft	32	−04	13	08
Y_8	Black teachers' physical attack	09	−10	69	43
Y_9	Black teachers' remarks, gestures	57	18	08	29
Y_{10}	Black teachers' fear for safety	45	16	35	35

Note. Decimals omitted. Varimax rotation of principal factor solution with iterated communalities.

might be interpreted as an *overall victimization* measure—dominated somewhat by incidents of minor seriousness. The second, η_2, might be interpreted as *serious victimization reports for white teachers.* The third, η_3, parallels η_2 for black teachers, *serious victimization reports for Black teachers.*

TABLE 62

Standardized λ_Y for Two Models of Junior High Teacher Victimization

		Model 2	Model 4		
Observed variable		η_1	η_1	η_2	η_3
Y_1	White teachers' robbery	.293	—	.402	—
Y_2	White teachers' theft	.621	.595	—	—
Y_3	White teachers' physical attack	.521	—	.742	—
Y_4	White teachers' remarks, gestures	.942	.918	—	—
Y_5	White teachers' fear for safety	.763	.744	—	—
Y_6	Black teachers' robbery	.330	—	—	.829
Y_7	Black teachers' theft	.202	.196	—	—
Y_8	Black teachers' physical attack	.142	—	—	.352
Y_9	Black teachers' remarks, gestures	.552	.537	—	—
Y_{10}	Black teachers' fear for safety	.507	.490	—	—
χ^2		118.1	85.2		
ν		35	32		

Note. Dashes indicate parameters fixed at zero. Model 4 fits the data better than does model 1 ($\chi^2 = 32.9$, $\nu = 3$, $p < .001$).

Student Victimization. Whereas Chapter 4 suggested that male and female teacher reports measure the same phenomena, but that black and white teacher reports do not, it suggested that both sex and race of respondent are problematical for student reports. First we report results for boys versus girls, and then we report results for blacks versus whites.

The exploratory factor analysis results for senior high male and female student victimization reports are shown in Table 63, and the results of the confirmatory analyses for one- and three-factor models are shown in Table 64. The first factor in Table 64 might be called *boys' personal victimization.* The second might be called *student theft.* And the third might be called *girls' personal victimization.* The three-factor model fits the data much better than the single-factor model (χ^2 = 82.3 and 238.1, respectively, each with v = 35).

Results of the exploratory analysis of junior high student victimization reports are shown in Table 65, and confirmatory results are shown in Table 66. Although the fit of the junior high models to the data is not as good as was the case for the senior high analyses, the three-factor model is superior to the one-factor model (χ^2 = 207.2 and 353.3, respectively, with 35 degrees of freedom for each). It again appears appropriate to label the factors *girls' personal victimization, student theft,* and *boys' personal victimization.*

TABLE 63
*Exploratory Factor Analysis of Senior High
Male and Female Student Victimization Measures*

Observed variable		Factor 1	2	3	h^2
Y_1	Boys' robbery, less than $1	71	−06	15	54
Y_2	Boys' robbery, $1 or more	72	−04	00	52
Y_3	Boys' theft, less than $1	36	20	02	17
Y_4	Boys' theft, $1 or more	25	15	00	09
Y_5	Boys' physical attack	57	−01	09	34
Y_6	Girls' robbery, less than $1	08	11	59	36
Y_7	Girls' robbery, $1 or more	−05	02	67	45
Y_8	Girls' theft, less than $1	07	71	13	53
Y_9	Girls' theft, $1 or more	00	74	05	56
Y_{10}	Girls' physical attack	11	03	42	19

Note. Decimals omitted. Varimax rotation of principal factor solution with iterated communalities.

TABLE 64

Standardized λ_Y for Two Models of Senior High Male and Female Reports of Student Victimization

		Model 1	Model 5		
Observed variable		η_1	η_1	η_2	η_3
Y_1	Boys' robbery, less than $1	.737	.738	—	—
Y_2	Boys' robbery, $1 or more	.689	.704	—	—
Y_3	Boys' theft, less than $1	.339	—	.227	—
Y_4	Boys' theft, $1 or more	.238	—	.154	—
Y_5	Boys' physical attack	.591	.595	—	—
Y_6	Girls' robbery, less than $1	.178	—	—	.585
Y_7	Girls' robbery, $1 or more	.070	—	—	.674
Y_8	Girls' theft, less than $1	.097	—	.803	—
Y_9	Girls' theft, $1 or more	.030	—	.743	—
Y_{10}	Girls' physical attack	.181	—	—	.424
χ^2		238.1	82.3		
ν		35	35		

Note. Dashes indicate parameters fixed at zero. Model 5 fits the data better than does model 1 (for two models with the same number of degrees of freedom, the difference in χ^2 is 155.8).

TABLE 65

Exploratory Factor Analysis of Junior High Male and Female Student Victimization Measures

		Factor			
Observed variable		1	2	3	h^2
Y_1	Boys' robbery, less than $1	14	09	74	57
Y_2	Boys' robbery, $1 or more	24	14	61	45
Y_3	Boys' theft, less than $1	01	65	18	45
Y_4	Boys' theft, $1 or more	−01	57	35	45
Y_5	Boys' physical attack	05	14	51	28
Y_6	Girls' robbery, less than $1	77	07	14	62
Y_7	Girls' robbery, $1 or more	76	13	11	60
Y_8	Girls' theft, less than $1	27	65	03	50
Y_9	Girls' theft, $1 or more	42	53	06	47
Y_{10}	Girls' physical attack	63	12	17	44

Note. Decimals omitted. Varimax rotation of principal factor solution with iterated communalities.

TABLE 66

Standardized λ_Y for Two Models of Junior High Male and Female Reports of Student Victimization

		Model 1	Model 5		
Observed variable		η_1	η_1	η_2	η_3
Y_1	Boys' robbery, less than $1	.415	—	—	.772
Y_2	Boys' robbery, $1 or more	.478	—	—	.645
Y_3	Boys' theft, less than $1	.370	—	.628	—
Y_4	Boys' theft, $1 or more	.383	—	.565	—
Y_5	Boys' physical attack	.299	—	—	.519
Y_6	Girls' robbery, less than $1	.655	.801	—	—
Y_7	Girls' robbery, $1 or more	.668	.782	—	—
Y_8	Girls' theft, less than $1	.509	—	.731	—
Y_9	Girls' theft, $1 or more	.599	—	.644	—
Y_{10}	Girls' physical attack	.616	.624	—	—
χ^2		353.3	207.2		
ν		35	35		

Note. Dashes indicate parameters fixed at zero. Model 6 fits the data better than does model 2 (for two models with the same number of degrees of freedom, the difference in χ^2 is 146.1).

The results of the exploratory factor analysis for senior high school black and white student victimization reports appear in Table 67, and the corresponding confirmatory factor analyses are presented in Table 68. (In contrast to our other exploratory factor analyses that use iterated communality estimates, Table 67 is a principal components solution because the factor analysis program we were using [SPSS, PA2] gave implausible communality estimates.) The four factors might be described as follows: the first is *black student attack and robbery*, the second is *white student attack and robbery*, and the third is *black student theft*, and the fourth is *white student theft*. The four-factor model fits the data much better than the one-factor model [χ^2 $(df = 4) = 620.7, p < .001$]. Some anomalies in Table 68 require explanation. The correlation matrix was predominated by very small values. In order to expedite the confirmatory analyses, the λ_Y corresponding to the largest loadings in the exploratory factor analysis for each factor were fixed at 1.0. Consequently, all other λ_Y are interpretable only relative to those fixed parameters. The confirmatory analyses were performed solely to test the goodness-of-fit of alternative models.

Results of the exploratory and confirmatory factor analyses for

TABLE 67

Exploratory Factor Analysis of Senior High Black and White Student Victimization Measures

			Factor			
Observed variable		1	2	3	4	h^2
Y_1	Whites' robbery, less than $1	00	96	00	−02	92
Y_2	Whites' robbery, $1 or more	−05	93	06	−02	87
Y_3	Whites' theft, less than $1	00	−03	02	84	71
Y_4	Whites' theft, $1 or more	−01	−04	01	84	71
Y_5	Whites' physical attack	23	28	−18	−08	17
Y_6	Black's robbery, less than $1	86	01	16	−05	78
Y_7	Blacks' robbery, $1 or more	79	04	08	04	64
Y_8	Blacks' theft, less than $1	24	−02	84	01	76
Y_9	Blacks' theft, $1 or more	13	00	87	02	78
Y_{10}	Blacks' physical attack	71	−02	17	−01	54

Note. Decimals omitted. Principal component solution.

TABLE 68

Standardized λ_Y for Two Models of Senior High Black and White Reports of Student Victimization

		Model 1	Model 7			
Observed variable		η_1	η_1	η_2	η_3	η_4
Y_1	Whites' robbery, less than $1	1.000	—	1.000	—	—
Y_2	Whites' robbery, $1 or more	.172	—	.721	—	—
Y_3	Whites' theft, less than $1	−.026	—	—	—	1.000
Y_4	Whites' theft, $1 or more	−.060	—	—	—	.428
Y_5	Whites' physical attack	.137	—	.243	—	—
Y_6	Blacks' robbery, less than $1	1.026	1.000	—	—	—
Y_7	Blacks' robbery, $1 or more	.834	.616	—	—	—
Y_8	Blacks' theft, less than $1	.555	—	—	1.000	—
Y_9	Blacks' theft, $1 or more	.426	—	—	.564	—
Y_{10}	Blacks' physical attack	.732	.535	—	—	—
χ^2		731.4		110.7		
ν		36		39		

Note. Dashes indicate parameters fixed at zero. Model 7 fits the data better than does Model 1 ($\chi^2 = 620.7$, nu = 3, $p < .001$). One loading in each column is constrained to equal 1 to identify the model.

junior high school black and white student victimization reports are shown in Tables 69 and 70. The two factors are readily interpretable as white students' reports and black students' reports. The two-factor model provides a much better fit to the data than a one-factor model $\chi^2 = 103.5$ and 372.7, each with 35 degrees of freedom).

School Organization and Community Characteristics. Earlier research (Chapters 5 through 10; NIE, 1978; Wiatrowski, Roberts, & G. D. Gottfredson, 1983) provided a basis for choosing school organizational and community characteristics useful for describing schools. The goal of the research in this chapter is to parsimoniously characterize schools in terms of the major dimensions along which they vary. Exploratory and confirmatory factor analyses were performed to specify parsimonious measurement models for school and community variables.

An exploratory factor analysis for senior high school and community characteristics is presented in Table 71, and the corresponding confirmatory factor analysis is shown in Table 72. The first latent variable, ξ_1 might be called *social disorganization.* A school with a high score on ξ_1 is in a high crime community, with many female-headed families, high unemployment, a high percentage of persons on welfare, and is predominantly nonwhite. A high proportion of students are a year behind grade level in reading and have repeated a year in school.

TABLE 69

Exploratory Factor Analysis of Junior High Black and White Student Victimization Measures

Observed variable		Factor 1	2	h^2
Y_1	Whites' robbery, less than $1	58	02	34
Y_2	Whites' robbery, $1 or more	94	−01	88
Y_3	Whites' theft, less than $1	52	06	27
Y_4	Whites' theft, $1 or more	65	05	43
Y_5	Whites' physical attack	66	−02	44
Y_6	Blacks' robbery, less than $1	08	62	39
Y_7	Blacks' robbery, $1 or more	02	76	58
Y_8	Blacks' theft, less than $1	01	39	15
Y_9	Blacks' theft, $1 or more	−01	64	42
Y_{10}	Blacks' physical attack	01	49	24

Note. Decimals omitted. Varimax rotation of principal factor solution with iterated communalities.

TABLE 70

Standardized λ_Y for Two Models of Junior High Black and White
Reports of Student Victimization

Observed variable		Model 2 η_1	Model 8 η_1	η_2
Y_1	Whites' robbery, less than $1	.566	.565	—
Y_2	Whites' robbery, $1 or more	.966	.966	—
Y_3	Whites' theft, less than $1	.443	.442	—
Y_4	Whites' theft, $1 or more	.606	.606	—
Y_5	Whites' physical attack	.722	.722	—
Y_6	Blacks' robbery, less than $1	.077	—	.658
Y_7	Blacks' robbery, $1 or more	.023	—	.784
Y_8	Blacks' theft, less than $1	−.001	—	.371
Y_9	Blacks' theft, $1 or more	−.020	—	.596
Y_{10}	Blacks' physical attack	.037	—	.494
χ^2		372.7		103.5
v		35		35

Note. Dashes indicate parameters fixed at zero. Model 8 fits the data better than does Model 2 (for two models with the same number of degrees of freedom, the difference in χ^2 is 269.2).

The second latent variable, ξ_2, might be called *permissive middle-class affluence*. A high-scoring school on this factor is located in an affluent and highly educated community and has relatively many teachers with advanced degrees. Corporal punishment for misconduct or explicit special privileges for good behavior are seldom employed, students tend not to report that rules are clear and firmly enforced, and the teachers tends to reject attitude items such as, "If a pupil uses obscene or profane language in school, it must be considered a moral offense." Finally, in such a school students tend to report that alcohol and marijuana are available, that they would cheat on a test or skip school if they could get away with it, and that they would not "rat" on another person.

The third latent variable, ξ_3, might be called *conventional academic orientation*. In a high-scoring school on this variable, students report that they have highly educated parents, and they rate their own ability as high. Students and faculty are oriented towards college preparation, and students tend to score high on measures of internal control and belief in conventional social rules.

The fourth latent variable, ξ_4, might be called *vocational training*. In a high-scoring school the teachers tend to emphasize job preparation

TABLE 71

*Exploratory Factor Analysis of Senior High School
and Community Characteristics*

Observed variable		Factor					
		1	2	3	4	5	h^2
X_1	Community poverty and unemployment	62	00	08	−01	07	40
X_2	Rural (vs. urban) location	−58	−33	−27	−05	27	59
X_3	Community Crime	54	13	−04	−10	−22	36
X_4	Student families on welfare	66	−09	−16	03	03	47
X_5	Percentage students white	−92	10	−09	10	−02	88
X_6	Percentage teachers white	−62	25	−23	10	−04	51
X_7	Peer and nonacademic ties	−72	−16	−03	−09	13	58
X_8	Students reading behind grade level	60	−21	−26	15	04	50
X_9	Percentage students never repeated year	−54	30	19	−10	14	44
W_1	Dropouts relative to enrollment	18	06	−08	−02	05	04
W_2	School total enrollment	25	33	33	−14	−22	35
X_{10}	Community affluence and education	01	61	41	08	−21	59
X_{11}	Teacher educational level	11	57	28	−44	−07	62
X_{12}	Clear sanctions	−09	−59	−17	−02	07	40
X_{13}	Teacher authority	16	−65	−09	16	−18	51
X_{14}	Firm and clear enforcement	06	−75	−02	04	−06	57
X_{15}	Delinquent youth culture	−17	66	−05	09	−40	63
X_{16}	Parental SES and self-reported ability	−38	33	67	−16	−02	73
X_{17}	College prep. orientation (teacher & prin.)	−09	32	63	−26	−11	59
X_{18}	Belief in conventional social rules	−29	−03	44	03	28	35
X_{19}	Student college prep. orientation	12	09	79	−34	−02	76
X_{20}	Internal control	04	13	46	−05	27	31
X_{21}	Number of different students taught	04	−03	12	−61	−10	40
X_{22}	Vocational vs. basic skills climate	−02	−11	−13	70	14	53
X_{23}	Industrial arts	10	00	−15	88	09	82
X_{24}	Teacher–administration cooperation	−15	−12	−12	13	37	20
X_{25}	Principal rating	−13	−08	−08	04	42	21
X_{26}	Perceived fair and clear rules	04	−08	24	19	72	62
X_{27}	Student influence	22	33	06	−02	67	61
X_{28}	School attachment	09	−12	35	49	65	81

Note. Decimals omitted. Varimax rotated principal factor solution with iterated communalities. Variables W_1 and W_2 are not represented in the confirmatory analysis. When the number of factors is increased to 7, the communality of W_1 increases only to .46, and it still has loadings on several factors. No clear school size factor emerges in any solution examined.

rather than basic skills, a relatively high proportion of the faculty teach mostly industrial arts, and each teacher teaches relatively few students.

The fifth latent variable, ξ_5, appears to be related to *sound school*

TABLE 72

Standardized λ_X for All Senior High School Models

Observed variable		ξ_1	ξ_2	ξ_3	ξ_4	ξ_5
X_1	Community poverty and unemployment	.612	—	—	—	—
X_2	Rural (vs. urban) location	−.512	—	—	—	—
X_3	Community crime	.519	—	—	—	—
X_4	Student families on welfare	−.645	—	—	—	—
X_5	Percentage students white	−.958	—	—	—	—
X_6	Percentage teachers white	−.731	—	—	—	—
X_7	Peer and nonacademic ties	−.666	—	—	—	—
X_8	Students reading behind grade level	.566	—	—	—	—
X_9	Percentage students never repeated year	.491	—	—	—	—
X_{10}	Community affluence and education	—	.678	—	—	—
X_{11}	Teacher educational level	—	.626	—	—	—
X_{12}	Clear sanctions	—	−.645	—	—	—
X_{13}	Teacher authority	—	−.648	—	—	—
X_{14}	Firm and clear enforcement	—	−.719	—	—	—
X_{15}	Delinquent youth culture	—	.615	—	—	—
X_{16}	Parental education and self-reported ability	—	—	.741	—	—
X_{17}	College prep. orientation (tch., prn.)	—	—	.851	—	—
X_{18}	Belief in conventional social rules	—	—	.315	—	—
X_{19}	Student college prep. orientation	—	—	.858	—	—
X_{20}	Internal control	—	—	.402	—	—
X_{21}	Number of different students taught	—	—	—	−.641	—
X_{22}	Vocational vs. basic skills climate	—	—	—	.772	—
X_{23}	Industrial arts	—	—	—	.868	—
X_{24}	Teacher–administration cooperation	—	—	—	—	.329
X_{25}	Principal rating	—	—	—	—	.376
X_{26}	Perceived fair and clear rules	—	—	—	—	.907
X_{27}	Student influence	—	—	—	—	.541
X_{28}	School attachment	—	—	—	—	.782

Note. Dashes indicate parameters fixed at zero.

administration. In a high-scoring school, teacher–administration co-operation is high, the principal is highly regarded by the teachers, students tend to perceive the rules as clear and fairly enforced, and they tend to be strongly attached to their school.

The results of the exploratory and confirmatory factor analyses for junior high school and community characteristics are shown in Tables 73 and 74. The first latent variable for the junior high school model, ξ_1, appears to be the same as for senior high schools, and could be called *social disorganization.*

The second latent variable, ξ_2, resembles a composite of the senior

TABLE 73

Exploratory Factor Analysis of Junior High School
and Community Characteristics

		Factor			
Observed variable		1	2	3	h^2
X_1	Community poverty and unemployment	72	−03	−04	52
X_2	Rural (vs. urban) location	−66	−34	16	57
X_3	Community crime	59	01	−28	42
X_4	Student families on welfare	71	−23	−03	56
X_5	Percentage students white	−93	13	02	89
X_6	Percentage teachers white	−70	15	−02	51
X_7	Peer and nonacademic ties	−71	00	19	54
X_8	Students reading behind grade level	70	−28	−08	57
X_9	Percentage students never repeated year	−41	46	11	39
W_1	Dropouts relative to enrollment	14	−32	−06	12
W_2	School total enrollment	40	35	−10	29
X_{10}	Community affluence and education	−14	75	−04	58
X_{11}	Teacher educational level	21	58	04	39
X_{12}	Clear sanctions	13	−55	02	32
X_{13}	Teacher authority	13	−48	−11	26
X_{14}	Firm and clear enforcement	−06	−49	08	25
X_{15}	Parental education and self-reported ability	−22	65	27	54
X_{16}	Student college prep. orientation	28	47	26	36
X_{17}	Belief in conventional social rules	−38	05	43	33
X_{18}	Teacher–administration cooperation	−23	−01	46	26
X_{19}	Principal rating	−12	−08	32	12
X_{20}	Perceived fair and clear rules	−16	02	81	69
X_{21}	School attachment	07	02	88	78
X_{22}	Internal control	08	29	52	36
X_{23}	Delinquent youth culture	−07	39	−61	53
W_3	Student influence	47	14	28	32
W_4	College prep. orientation (tch., prn.)	−03	13	−02	02
W_5	Number of different students taught	−01	26	−07	07
W_6	Vocational vs. basic skills climate	27	−19	−08	12
W_7	Industrial arts	18	29	−13	14

Note. Decimals omitted. Varimax rotated principal factor solution with iterated communalities.
Variables labeled W_i are omitted from the confirmatory factor analysis.

high school latent variables ξ_2 and ξ_3, implying less differentiation
among junior high schools than senior high schools. A high-scoring
school on this latent variable is in an affluent and educated community,
has relatively many teachers with advanced degrees, and has a college-
oriented studentry with students who rate themselves high in ability.
Teachers reject items in the teacher authority scale, paddling and special

TABLE 74
Standardized λ_x for All Junior High School Models

Observed variable		ξ_1	ξ_2	ξ_3
X_1	Community poverty and unemployment	.717	—	—
X_2	Rural (vs. urban) location	−.573	—	—
X_3	Community crime	.560	—	—
X_4	Student families on welfare	.731	—	—
X_5	Percentage students white	−.950	—	—
X_6	Percentage teachers white	−.777	—	—
X_7	Peer and nonacademic ties	−.683	—	—
X_8	Students reading behind grade level	.718	—	—
X_9	Percentage students never repeated year	−.449	—	—
X_{10}	Community affluence and education	—	.713	—
X_{11}	Teacher educational level	—	.539	—
X_{12}	Clear sanctions	—	−.557	—
X_{13}	Teacher authority	—	−.492	—
X_{14}	Firm and clear enforcement	—	−.474	—
X_{15}	Parental education and self-reported ability	—	.709	—
X_{16}	Student college prep. orientation	—	.521	—
X_{17}	Belief in conventional social rules	—	—	.315
X_{18}	Teacher–administration cooperation	—	—	.440
X_{19}	Principal rating	—	—	.280
X_{20}	Perceived fair and clear rules	—	—	.879
X_{21}	School attachment	—	—	.865
X_{22}	Internal control	—	—	.521
X_{23}	Delinquent youth culture	—	—	−.581

Note. Dashes indicate parameters fixed at zero.

privileges are rarely used as sanctions, and students tend not to report that rule enforcement is firm. This latent variable might be called *permissive affluence and academic orientation.*

The third latent variable, ξ_3, closely resembles ξ_5 for senior high schools. Belief in conventional social rules, internal control, and low delinquent youth culture also index this factor. Consequently, it might be called *prosocial school organization.*

COMBINING STRUCTURAL AND MEASUREMENT MODELS

It is evident from results presented earlier that student and teacher victimization are best treated as distinct constructs, and that senior high schools are factorially more complex than junior high schools. Therefore student and teacher victimization are examined separately for junior and senior high schools in the next set of analyses. Results for teacher victimization are described first, followed by results for student victimization. Because male and female teacher victimization measures are so closely related (see discussion in Chapter 4) we have focused the analyses of teacher victimization on white and black teacher victimization.

In this section, the concern is with the explanation of school victimization in terms of the characteristics of the schools and their communities. Here, the measurement and structural components of the models diagramed in Figures 4 through 11 are combined in an effort to estimate the structural components of the models. Guided by the confirmatory factor analyses just described, the parameters of the measurement models for the latent predictors are fixed. Specifically, the λ_X matrices are fixed at the values shown in Tables 72 and 74. The contraints on the variances of the η_m are relaxed, so they are no longer completely orthogonal as they were in the comfirmatory factor analyses. In each model, one λ_Y for each latent variable is fixed at 1.0 to identify the model. In each set of analyses, a model postulating that victimization is a unitary construct is contrasted with a model postulating that it is a multifactorial to illustrate practical differences in the substantive interpretations implied by the results.

Models of Teacher Victimization

Results for two models of senior high teacher victimization—corresponding to models 1 and 3 of Figures 4 and 6—are presented in Table 75. Note that the structure for the victimization measures shown in model 3 differs slightly from the structure tested earlier with the confirmatory factor analysis (Table 62). The structure used in Table 75 is intuitively more appealing and, although it was too restrictive to yield a sensible solution in the confirmatory factor analysis, this structure seemed to produce sensible results for the present analysis. Model 3 yields a much better fit to the data than does model 1 ($\chi^2 = 110.2$, $p < .001$). White teacher victimization is well accounted for by model 3 ($\psi = .20$). According to model 3, the largest standardized contribution to white teacher victimization (η_1) is the social disorganization characteristic of the school and its community (ξ_1). Permissive middle-class affluence (ξ_2) makes a moderate positive contribution, and sound school administration (ξ_5) makes a moderate negative contribution to white

TABLE 75

Structural Parameters (γ) in the Two Models of
Senior High Teacher Victimization

Latent variable and label	Model 1	Model 3		
	η_1	η_1^a	η_2^b	η_3^c
ξ_1 Social disorganization	.772**	.783**	.222**	.371**
ξ_2 Permissive middle-class affluence	.311**	.314**	−.048	.391**
ξ_3 Conventional and academic orientation	−.111**	−.106*	−.036	−.216**
ξ_4 Vocational training	−.120**	−.130**	−.028	.023
ξ_5 Sound school administration	−.243**	−.244**	−.016	−.135
Residual (ψ)	.222	.200	.946	.644
χ^2	2,942		2,831	
ν	716		706	

Note. Model 3 provides a better fit to the data than does model 1 (χ^2 = 110.2, ν = 10, $p < .001$). Because the ξ_n are uncorrelated ($\Phi = I$), the γ_{nm} equal the corresponding zero-order correlations. In the results for model 3 the η_m are moderately correlated: ρ_{12} = .170, ρ_{13} = .466, ρ_{23} = .073.
[a]White teacher victimization
[b]Black teacher robbery and attack
[c]Black teacher theft
*$p < .05$; **$p < .01$.

teacher victimization. The other two school factors (ξ_3) and (ξ_4) make significant but small contributions to white teacher victimization.

According to model 3, the pattern of effects is different for black teacher reports of robbery and attack (η_2). η_2 is poorly explained. The only significant predictor is ξ_1, social disorganization.

Finally, black teachers report more theft (η_3) in schools located in disorganized social areas and in schools characterized by permissive middle-class affluence, but less theft in schools high in conventional academic orientation.

Models 1 and 3 lead to some differing implications. Were it assumed that only a single factor underlies victimization reports, one might conclude that social disorganization is of overwhelming importance in determining teacher victimization. Model 3, in contrast, suggests that social disorganization is much more important in determining white teacher victimization reports than Black teacher victimization reports. Some other differences in Table 75 suggest that minor but not major victimization experiences for blacks tend to occur in permissive, affluent schools, and occur less in conventional, academic schools. Vocational training is associated negatively only with white teacher reports.

TABLE 76
Structural Parameters (γ) in the Two Models of
Junior High Teacher Victimization

		Model 2	Model 4		
Latent variable and label		η_1	η_1^a	η_2^b	η_3^c
ξ_1	Social disorganization	.756**	.760**	.587**	.276**
ξ_2	Permissive affluence and academic orientation	.324**	.335**	.228**	.127
ξ_3	Prosocial school organization	−.337**	−.342**	−.200*	−.111
Residual (ψ)		.209	.193	.563	.895
χ^2		1,839	1,817		
ν		538	532		

Note. Model 4 provides a better fit to the data than does model 2 ($\chi^2 = 17.8$, $\nu = 6$, $p < .01$). Because the ξ_n are uncorrelated ($\Phi = I$), the γ_{nm} equal the corresponding zero-order correlations. In the results for model 4 the η_m are moderately correlated: $\rho_{12} = .591$, $\rho_{13} = .290$, $\rho_{23} = .213$.
[a]Overall teacher victimization (Minor)
[b]White teacher robbery and attack
[c]Black teacher robbery and attack
*$p < .05$; **$p < .01$.

Results for the two models of junior high teacher victimization—corresponding to models 2 and 4 of Figures 5 and 7—are shown in Table 76. The three-factor model provides a significantly [χ^2 ($df = 6$) = 17.8] but only slightly better fit to the data. The results for the first factor for model 4 resemble closely the results for the single-factor model. According to either model, overall teacher victimization is influenced most by social disorganization (ξ_1), with permissive affluence and academic orientation having a moderate positive influence, and prosocial school organization having a moderate negative influence on overall victimization. The results for white teacher robbery and attack parallel those for overall victimization, but black teacher reports of robbery and attack are related only to social disorganization and are poorly explained ($\Psi = .90$).

Models of Student Victimization

First we show results of models involving the reports of boys and girls, regardless of race; and then we show results of models for blacks and whites, regardless of sex. This form of analysis (pooling across race when analyzing for sex, and vice versa) is necessary because of the small number of students per school that would be involved in analysis for nonoverlapping subgroups. The results for two models of senior high student victimization—corresponding to models 1 and 5 of Figures 4 and 8—are shown in Table 77. The three-factor model fits the data much better than the single-factor model [χ^2 ($df = 10$) = 181.1], and it has some interesting implications. The first factor (η_1), boys' robbery and attack, is moderately influenced by social disorganization, and sound school administration negatively influences this factor. The second factor (η_2), theft, is *unrelated* to social disorganization, but is negatively influenced by permissive middle-class affluence (ξ_2) and sound school administration, and *positively* influenced by school conventional and academic orientation (ξ_3). The last factor (η_3) is essentially unrelated to the school and community characteristics. No ξ_n has a significant gamma, and only 4% the variance in η_3 is explained. The differential pattern of influences on different types of victimization suggested by model 5 is masked in the single-factor model.

Results of the two models for junior high student victimization are shown in Table 78. Again, the three-factor model yields an interesting pattern of results, and it fits the data much better than the single-factor model [χ^2 ($df = 6$) = 239.8, $p < .001$]. According to model 6, girls' robbery and attack (η_1) is moderately positively influenced by social disorganization and negatively influenced by prosocial school organ-

TABLE 77

Structural Parameters (γ) in the Two Models of Male and Female Reports of Victimization in Senior High Schools

		Model 1	Model 5		
Latent variable and label		η_1	η_1^a	η_2^b	η_3^c
ξ_1	Social disorganization	.239**	.270**	−.065	.104
ξ_2	Permissive middle-class affluence	−.150*	−.087	−.279**	−.008
ξ_3	Conventional and academic orientation	−.031	−.067	.289**	−.124
ξ_4	Vocational training	−.046	−.038	.044	−.097
ξ_5	Sound school administration	−.249**	−.208**	−.231**	−.077
Residual (ψ)		.855	.870	.779	.959
χ^2		2,679		2,497	
v		716		706	

Note. Model 5 provides a better fit to the data than does model 1 (χ^2 = 181.1, v = 10, $p < .001$). Because the ξ_n are uncorrelated ($\Phi = I$), the γ_{nm} equal the corresponding zero-order correlations. In model 5 the η_m are slightly correlated: $\rho_{12} = .057$, $\rho_{13} = .034$, $\rho_{23} = −.027$.
[a]Boys' robbery and attack
[b]Students' theft
[c]Girls' robbery and attack
**$p < .01$.

Table 78

Structural Parameters (γ) in the Two Models of Male and Female Reports of Student Victimization for Junior High Schools

Latent variable and label		Model 2	Model 6		
		η_1	η_1^a	η_2^b	η_3^c
ξ_1	Social disorganization	.151*	.315**	−.292**	.191**
ξ_2	Permissive affluence and academic orientation	−.073	−.089	−.164*	.104
ξ_3	Prosocial school organization	−.359**	−.248**	−.346**	−.425**
Residual (ψ)		.843	.831	.768	.772
χ^2		1,965		1,725	
v		538		532	

Note. Model 6 provides a better fit to the data than does model 2 (χ^3 = 239.8, v = 6, p < .001). Because the ξ_n are uncorrelated (Φ = I), the γ_{nm} equal the corresponding zero-order correlations. The η_m in model 6 are modestly correlated: ρ_{12} = .156, ρ_{13} = .074, ρ_{23} = .008.
[a]Girls' robbery and attack
[b]Student theft
[c]Boys' robbery and attack
*p < .05; **p < .01.

ization. Student theft (η_2) is negatively influenced by all three latent predictors, with prosocial school organization making the largest contribution. Finally, boys' robbery and attack (η_3) is moderately positively influenced by social disorganization, and more strongly negatively influenced by prosocial school organization. Girls' personal victimization is less well explained than either student theft or boys' personal victimization—17% vs. 23% and 23% of the variance in η_1, η_2, and η_3, respectively, accounted for by the ξ_n.

In contrast to the three-factor model, the one-factor model makes social disorganization appear less important, partly because it has effects with different signs on the different η_m. And it fails to suggest an influence of permissive affluence and academic orientation, which is suggested in the more complex model for student theft.

Results for models predicting black and white students' reports of victimization appear in Tables 79 and 80. Two models for senior high schools—corresponding to models 1 and 7 of Figures 4 and 10—were estimated. Table 79 shows that the four-factor model fits the data better than the one-factor model [χ^2 (df = 15) = 562.8, p < .001]. Caution should be exercised in interpreting the coefficients reported in this table

TABLE 79

Structural Parameters (γ) in the Two Models of Black and White Reports
of Student Victimization in Senior High Schools

Latent variable and label	Model 1	Model 7			
	η_1	η_1^a	η_2^b	η_3^c	η_4^d
ξ_1 Social disorganization	−.146	−.137*	.128**	−.146*	−.025
ξ_2 Permissive middle-class affluence	−.077	−.064	.017	−.273**	.013
ξ_3 Conventional and academic orientation	−.044	−.051	−.071	.145*	.107
ξ_4 Vocational training	−.024	−.030	−.018	.014	.068
ξ_5 Sound school administration	−.185	−.171**	−.013	−.175*	−.082
Residual (ψ)	.936	.945	.978	.853	.976
χ^2	3,135.9	2,573.1			
ν	716	701			

Note. Estimates reported in this table are from solutions that did not reach convergence after 250 iterations. Model 7 provides a better fit to the data than does model 1 ($\chi^2 = 562.8$, $\nu = 15$, $p < .001$). Because the ξ_n are uncorrelated ($\Phi = I$), the γ_{nm} equal the corresponding zero-order correlations. The correlations among η_m in model 7 range from .009 to .06.
[a]Black attack and robbery
[b]White attack and robbery
[c]Black theft
[d]White theft
*$p < .05$; **$p < .01$.

TABLE 80

Structural Parameters (γ) in the Two Models of Black and White
Student Reports of Victimization in Junior High Schools

Latent variable and label	Model 2	Model 8	
	η_1	η_1^a	η_2^b
ξ_1 Social disorganization	.345**	.346**	−.135
ξ_2 Permissive affluence and academic orientation	−.033	−.032	−.126
ξ_3 Prosocial school organization	−.063	−.061	−.192**
Residual (ψ)	.876	.876	.929
χ^2	2,089.1	1,804.5	
ν	538	530	

Note. Model 8 provides a better fit to the data than does model 2 ($\chi^2 = 284.5$, $\nu = 8$, $p < .001$). Because the ξ_n are uncorrelated ($\Phi = I$), the γ_{nm} equal the corresponding zero-order correlations. The η_m in model 8 are slightly correlated: $\rho_{12} = -.031$.
[a]White students' victimization
[b]Black students' victimization
**$p < .01$.

because the fit of both models to the data are poor, and the residual variances are high. In fact, the computer algorithm used in LISREL failed to converge on an acceptable solution after 250 iterations. We can conclude on the basis of this solution that the one-factor model does not do justice to the complexity of student victimizations in senior high schools. The black reports are predicted better than are white reports, and the influence of being located in a socially disorganized area seems to run in different directions for blacks and whites.

Results for junior high school models of black and white student reports—Models 2 and 8 of Figures 5 and 11—are more straight-forward. Again, the two-factor model fits the data better than the single-factor model [X^2 (df = 8) = 284.5, p < .001]. The results for model 8 imply that social disorganization makes a moderate contribution to white students' reports of victimization (η_1), but that neither of the factors representing school characteristics influences these reports. Conversely, only prosocial school organization influences black students' reports (η_2) according to the two-factor model.

The solution based on the one-factor model closely parallels the results for white students' victimization. Hence, it is partly misleading in light of the differing pattern of predictors for black and white reports. (Note that the first latent endogenous variables (the η_1) in the "model 2" on Tables 78 and 80 are quite different. See Tables 66 and 70.)

The Need for Better Measures

One reasonably clear implication of the research reported here (and in Chapter 4) is that better measures of school disruption are required. Because there are few independent benchmarks in the Safe School Study data against which to assess the meaning of the victimization reports, their meaning remains unclear. We have adduced evidence that reports by black teachers and white teachers may have different meanings and different causes, and that boys' and girls' victimization experiences may also have different meanings and different causes. Furthermore, the evidence implies that teacher and student victimization reports measure different phenomena. In planning future surveys, victimization reports must be supplemented by self-reported delinquent and disruptive behavior, and wherever possible by other objective evidence about the amount of victimization and disorder occurring in the school. In addition, because differential social perception may provide an explanation for the differences in the patterns of correlates of reports by different racial groups, information about racial attitudes and perceptions would also be a useful supplement to victimization reports in future surveys.

A second implication can be drawn from the Chapter 4 estimates of reliabilities for the various measures. Many more persons per school must be involved in reporting their experiences if adequately reliable measures are to be obtained. Much of the "victimization" that occurs in schools involves minor indignities: smartass remarks or gestures, one boy forcefully asking another for a quarter, a notebook lifted from someone's desk. More serious victimizations are relatively rare. This makes the task of measuring them difficult, and it implies that many more persons must be surveyed per school to gain reliable estimates. The increase in reliability that can be gained by increasing the number of persons reporting is illustrated in research by Burack and Downing (1980), who aggregated reports for 100 to 200 students per school and obtained estimated reliability coefficients in the .80's and .90's. Another illustration of the benefits of larger samples in reliably measuring school climate are provided G. D. Gottfredson (1985).

Implications of the Models

Limitations. The construct validity of the victimization reports, and the cross-sectional, measurement-based nature of the research are serious limitations. Despite these inherent limitations, we have extended the Chapter 5 through 10 research on the correlates of school victimization in important ways in this chapter. We have used more sophisticated, but less conservative, modeling techniques to provide an alternative view of school social organization and victimization.

These models assume that it is useful to think of a small number of underlying factors of school organization that account for a larger number of observed variables. This contrasts with Chapter 10, where we built statistical models of delinquency using a large number of rather specific characteristics of schools, many of which were higly correlated with each other. Those high correlations among predictors make discerning the relative relations of major underlying dimensions (or second-order factors) of school characteristics with victimization reports difficult. These relations are easier to see in the results presented in this chapter.

As in other research using statistical models to understand or explain social phenomena, the structure of the results depends in large part on the specification of the model. These models *postulate* certain causal structures, and examine the consequences of those structures. The results are constrained by the data, to be sure. But the results depend strongly on the judgments made in constructing the models. In constructing these models we have assumed that mutual causation (such as victimization causing school administration and vice versa) does not exist. Although we regard this assumption as reasonable, it may be false. These and other details of the models examined, and the passive analysis of data in which no experimental manipulation of independent variables occurred, make the research subject to speculations about other statistical models that may also fit the data reasonably well. Our best current judgments about model specification are incorporated in the present research, but because judgment has been involved, these results must be interpreted cautiously.

Interpretations.   With these limitations in mind, the models used here have several important implications, including the following:

1. Social disorganization—measured by such school characteristics as a high proportion of students behind grade level in reading, many students from families on welfare, a high proportion of minority students; and such community characteristics as high unemployment, high crime, much poverty and unemployment, and many female-headed households—is strongly linked to the victimization reports of white teachers, and is the only dependable predictor of serious teacher victimization. Although the link is not as strong as for white teachers, social disorganization is also a fairly potent predictor of black teacher victimization, and of the personal victimization (robberies and attacks) of male and female students. Social disorganization *negatively* influences student experiences of theft. The Chapter 10 results, which did not suggest much influence of social disorganization on student victimization, are probably due to the use of a single measure of victimization reports, which combined kinds of victimization that are related to social disorganization in different ways.

2. The soundness of a school's administration—indexed by measures of teacher–administration cooperation, ratings of the principal's behavior, the perceived fairness and clarity of the school rules, and student influence on the way the school is run and their attachment to the school—is linked to teacher reports of victimization in both junior

and senior high schools (and to the reports of both black and white teachers in the senior high analyses). Furthermore, the soundness of school administration is linked with all measures of student victimization in both junior and senior high schools, except for robberies and attacks of senior high school girls, which are relatively unpredictable using any of the school or community characteristics. The models always imply that the better administration, the less the victimization. The models evaluated in this chapter imply a strong effect of the way a school is run on victimization rates that was obscured in the Chapter 10 results.

3. Middle-class affluence (for senior high schools) and affluence and academic orientation (for junior high schools) *positively* influence teacher victimization reports (except for serious victimization in high schools and white victimization reports in junior high schools). These same factors *negatively* influence student reports of theft in both junior and senior high schools.

4. In academically oriented (or college preparatory emphasis) high schools, teachers report less victimization, but students report more theft.

5. A vocational training emphasis appears essentially unrelated to victimization reports.

School disruption is not a unidimensional construct. Several distinct dimensions of victimization can be measured, and these different dimensions are not all related to community and school characteristics in the same way.

Our results strengthen the suggestion of earlier research (Burack & Downing, 1980; Grant, Daniels, Neto, & Yamasaki, 1979; NIE, 1978), reviews (Johnson, Bird, & Little, 1979; G. D. Gottfredson, 1981; Weis & Hawkins, 1980), and practical experience (Howard, 1978; Woodall, 1979) that school administrative practices contribute to the level of disruption a school experiences even though a host of studentry characteristics and the community environment are also major determinants of disruption in a school. The contribution of these practices may be large.

CHAPTER 12

Advice for Policymakers

In the preceding chapters we have described a complex, highly technical research effort based on a large scale survey of disorder in the nation's public schools. Those data are the best data currently available to bring to bear on this problem. The earlier chapters summarize our best efforts, and although we regard the results as sometimes confusing or inconsistent, in this chapter we explain in direct language what we believe to be the major implications of the research to date.

These implications are of three types. First, school management and broader social policies make a difference. The research bears most directly on school management, and this conclusion is drawn with considerable confidence. We describe the promising leads: the strategies to decrease school disruption that merit attention by administrators, teachers, funding agencies, legislators, and citizens. These strategies, on the basis of the evidence, deserve discussion, and they deserve to be implemented, monitored, and evaluated to learn whether they really do prevent school disorder in practical application. Second, we discuss ways to achieve better, more trustworthy knowledge about prevention strategies. Gaining this knowledge will involve not only researchers but also committed and courageous school officials, teachers, and funding agencies. Third, we suggest a policymaker's guide to learning to reduce school disorder. We try to spell out how legislators, administrators, teachers, and the public can learn to cope with school disruption. Our advice is that to do better we must adopt new strategies for learning what works, and we must make realistic attempts to bring about desirable social change.

PROMISING STRATEGIES

Our research leads to the conclusion that schools may be able to reduce the levels of disorder they experience by taking some specific actions to alter their own practices. None of these steps will be particularly easy to implement: some are costly, others require the exercise of leadership and commitment. Furthermore, none of these strategies is a surefire remedy or prevention technique, but they are approaches to the reduction of school disorder that merit the careful consideration of school administrators, teachers, school boards, and community organizations.

School Size and Resources

The results accord closely with those of earlier research that suggests that large schools with limited resources experience more problems. A constellation of related school characteristics—total enrollment, number of different students taught by the typical teacher in a school, and the extent to which teachers are provided with the materials and equipment they need to teach—is implicated in those aspects of school disorder that affect teachers personally. School size is very likely related to the availability of opportunities for students to engage in a variety of roles that provide a stake in conformity. Manning theory (Barker, 1968; Bechtel, 1974; Pence & Taylor, 1978) may provide an explanation of the role school size plays in school disorder. According to this perspective, inhabitants of an environment exert social control when the number of inhabitants is so small that the conforming behavior of all persons is required to conduct ordinary activities. When an environment is "undermanned," its inhabitants will attempt to control or restrain deviant behavior. In contrast, when an environment is "overmanned," persons who deviate from conforming behavior are not needed, and may be rejected.

The results, and manning theory, suggest that consideration be given to changes in schools that would result in schools of smaller size, where teachers have extensive responsibility for and contact with a limited number of students in several aspects of their education, and where steps are taken to ensure adequate resources for instruction.

To the extent that small schools may be more costly to operate than larger schools, and to the extent to which supplying teachers with teaching tools is costly, these strategies will, of course, cost money. Yet, for junior high schools in particular, small schools have fewer problems of teacher victimization. The increase in cost should be considered in relation to the cost of teacher victimization. To some extent this is a matter of judgment about relative costs, and to some extent it is a matter that can be properly addressed by more careful studies of changes in school size in which differences in cost, disruption, and perhaps other consequences are examined.

A useful alternative to schools of smaller size may be to compose multiple, socially discrete environments within a single large school. This approach—schools-within-a-school—has been suggested by the Carnegie Council on Policy Studies in Higher Education (1979). Schools-within-a-school may be a useful alternative to smaller schools because it seems unlikely that size *per se* is the actual causal variable. Structural arrangements that accomplish the same effects as smaller schools can perhaps be created.

The Organization of Instruction

In senior high schools, especially, consideration should be given to reorganizing instruction so that each teacher has greater contact with a more limited number of students. By this we do *not* mean smaller class sizes. Our analyses do not suggest that smaller classes would decrease school disruption, but do suggest that the rotation of students through classes taught by different teachers influences levels of teacher victimization in high schools. We have not determined how or why this happens. Perhaps the mere exposure of teachers to a large number of different students increases the chance that they wil be exposed to a large number of potential perpetrators. Perhaps, as others have suggested (NIE, 1978), when teachers are involved in the education of large numbers of different students, the educational climate is impersonal and leads to disruption.

Reducing the number of different students taught by the typical teacher would necessarily require a reorganization of instructional practices so that teachers teach more than one subject to a group of students, and may call for a greater range of teaching competencies for individual teachers and more instructional preparation. Again, a trade-off of alternatives is involved.

School Climate and Disciplinary Practices

Some other strategies for preventing school disruption implied by our research are more closely tied to social processes within the school—what we have called school governance and social climate. These strategies would require school administrators and teachers to alter their operating procedures, and would depend for their implementation on the leadership, commitment, and social competencies of these personnel. A constellation of school characteristics is involved in these strategies, all related to a central theme. The more clear, explicit, and firm the running of the school, the less the disorder—in terms of both teacher and student victimizations—that the school experiences. When a school is characterized by a high degree of cooperation between teachers and administration, teachers are victimized less. In such a school teachers report that they get along well with the administration, that they are provided with up-to-date information about problem students by the administration, that all students are treated equally in the school, and that they get advice about handling misbehaving students from the counselors. When, however, teachers are confused about how school policies are set, or when the teachers provide students with ambiguous sanctions by lowering grades as a response to misconduct or by ignoring misbehavior, disruption either in the form of student or teacher victimizations is relatively high.

Additional evidence in our analyses suggests that when schools are run in clear, explicit ways, disruption is lower. When students report that rule enforcement is firm and clear, or that the rules are fair and clear, their schools experience less disruption. Little evidence suggests that student participation in the generation of these rules is a necessary ingredient. The essential elements appear to be firm, clear, persistent, and evenhanded application of rules. The results suggest, in short, that misconduct should not be ignored but should be responded to in ways that students can anticipate, and in a way that separates responses to academic performance from responses to misconduct. By this we do not mean that schools should be run in authoritarian ways, or in ways that deny students their dignity; rather we mean that responses to behavior should be predictable, consistent, and fair. Ample experience with behavioral technologies implies that sanctions need not be harsh to be effective, and that rewards (not just punishments) are valuable in creating conformity.

Implementing the strategy suggested here would involve the concerted effort of administrators and teachers to formulate explicit rules and disciplinary policies, to make these rules and policies known, and to ensure that these policies are adhered to. The rules must not only be clear, firmly enforced, and equitably administered, but they must also appear to be so to students.

Community Influences and Social Policy

Our research also implies that community and governmental action that alters the conditions in which schools operate may influence levels of school disruption. Teacher victimization rates are high in schools located in areas characterized by much poverty, unemployment, and a high proportion of female-headed families; or in schools where large proportions of the students are black, rated by teachers and principals as low in ability, and come from families on welfare. This constellation resembles a community-organization factor that may be referred to as social problems or social disorganization. Although we go beyond our data in suggesting this strategy, the perpetuation of areas characterized by social disorganization may be halted by removing policies or practices (Polikoff, 1978) that result in the concentration of disadvantaged or poor people in certain sections of large urban areas (for example, locating low cost housing projects only in urban slums rather than in more widely dispersed locations). We have used community variables primarily as statistical controls in our attempt to identify school variables related to levels of school disruption. We note, however, that housing segregation, poverty, and unemployment are major problems that are tied to disruption in schools, and remedying these social ills may have major consequences for school disruption, especially in terms of rates of teacher victimization.

Because housing is segregated, schools are segregated, and many communities have implemented school desegregation programs. In junior high schools desegregation programs are associated with somewhat higher rates of student victimization. Schools where many students are bused, which are under court order to desegregate, which have a local desegregation plan, or which are characterized by racial imbalance have slightly higher rates of student victimizations. The major variable appears to be the percentage of a school's students that is bused to achieve racial balance.[1]This outcome was not replicated for senior high schools.

If the racial and economic segregation of neighborhoods that characterizes American society did not exist, busing students to achieve racial balance would not be an issue. If it is true that busing to desegregate junior high schools slightly increases student victimization, then the strategy suggested earlier of decreasing residential segregation, and avoiding the concentration of poor families only in certain areas of cities, takes on increased importance. At the same time, we reiterate that our suggestion of this strategy is based on reasonable speculation rather than on firm evidence.

We do not suggest that consideration be given to halting desegregation programs. Even were it true, as the evidence suggests, that junior high schools with high proportions of students bused for racial balance experience slightly more student victimizations than similar schools without such busing, busing is less objectionable than the alternative of providing some groups of citizens with inferior schooling. In addition, the contribution of desegregation to student victimization suggested by our analyses is smaller than the contributions of school administrative and governance styles that could presumably be altered to reduce disruption in junior high schools.

An interpretation of our results is that social policies influence the orderliness of schools, and indeed the quality of education more broadly, in profound ways. Current social policies serve to perpetuate segregation of the poor from the rich. These policies range from zoning ordinances to mortgage interest deductions on income taxes. New potentially destructive policies or actions are proposed from time to time. One such policy, in our opinion, is the proposal for tuition tax credits now before the Congress. A foreseeable consequence of tuition tax credits is the increased flight of the affluent from our inner-city public schools, and an erosion of the resources available to those schools. An enlightened society would, we believe, avoid such destructive social policies. More enlightened policies are easy to imagine: policies that promote integration rather than segregation by social class and race, ordinances calling for a mix of high- and low-cost housing in new developments, policies to equalize the resources available for inner-

[1]See Table 13.

city and suburban schools. It is more difficult to imagine our society having the courage and commitment to implement such policies.

Some Negative Results

Several often recommended ideas about school improvement receive little or no support in our results. Among these are (a) student participation in school decision making, and (b) small class size. We caution readers that we have examined only the *naturally occurring* range of student participation and class size. Conceivable but rare instances of very small classes or very great student participation may have some of the consequences their advocates (e.g., Office for Juvenile Justice and Delinquency Prevention, 1980) hope for. And, we have examined school orderliness and not the range of other outcomes these arrangements may be related to. At the very least, the results of the present research argue for circumspection in recommending student participation or small class size as an approach to increasing school orderliness.

Schools Can Make a Big Difference

In earlier chapters we have taken two alternative approaches to learning about school characteristics that influence the amount of disorder they experience. In Chapter 10 we attempted to isolate the effects of specific features of schools in a fine-grained way, with the result that any one specific feature of schools appears to have only modest influence. In contrast, in Chapter 11 we examined the contributions of broad underlying factors of school structure and organization to school disorder, with the result that school administration, considered broadly, appears to make major contributions to school orderliness. We interpret these results to mean that piecemeal attempts at school improvement will result at best in small improvements. Broad attempts at school improvement—hitting the system several places at once—should lead to bigger gains in school orderliness and the quality of life in schools.

LEARNING TO DO BETTER

The strategies for preventing school disruption we have described are based on the best evidence, the best analytical skill, and the best judgment we have been able to apply. Nevertheless, the evidence and the analytical tools used are far from perfect. The strategies suggested appear particularly worthy of attention and trial, but we cannot confidently state that they will definitely prevent school disruption. The following paragraphs describe how more trustworthy knowledge about the prevention of disruption in schools may be achieved.

The most straightforward way to test a prevention strategy is to conduct an experiment. This means implementing a specifiable strategy in a number of schools (chosen by lot), monitoring the implementation of the strategy to make sure that it is actually being followed, and determining whether the strategy has reduced school disruption. This requires dependably measuring the amount of disruption experienced by these schools and an equal number of comparable schools (which have not implemented the strategy merely because schools selected to test it and the comparison schools were chosen by lot). If the two groups of schools show reliable differences in their levels of disruption, then one can be reasonably confident that the difference is due to the strategy being tested. Unfortunately, such experiments are unlikely to be performed, if only because the faithful implementation of programs in schools distinguished primarily by their random selection is unlikely.

This procedure is not the only way to determine the effectiveness of prevention strategies. Evaluation researchers have at their disposal a number of powerful quasi-experimental designs that allow reasonably strong inferences about program effectiveness. One of the most potent of these involves the systematic, uniform collection of data about levels of disorder over time. If these levels change after a new school policy or systematic practice is implemented—and when evidence indicates that the change in practices was implemented with fidelity—then a reasonable inference is that the new policy or practice caused the change in levels of disruption. When similar evidence is accumulated for different schools, in different places, and at different times, then strong inferences about the effectiveness of the strategy may be made.

Seldom are experiments of the sort described here attempted, and uniform, high-quality information about levels of school disruption is rarely routinely collected over time. Evaluating school programs is not a popular activity. School administrators sometimes fear that data about school disorder will be misused, or used against them. Also, the evaluation of social programs is often frustrating—often all one learns is that the intended program was never really implemented as planned, or that the program cannot be demonstrated to be effective. Yet because preventing violence and disruption in public schools is an important goal, learning how this goal can be achieved is important. Courage, effort, and skill are required to learn to do better. Even learning that a particular prevention strategy was not implemented as intended is a positive contribution. It points the way for further efforts directed at achieving program implementation.

In his remarks at the oversight hearing on the Safe School Study, Congressman Ike Andrews (1978), Chair of the House Subcommittee on Economic Opportunity, illustrated a central issue to be faced in learning to do a better job of preventing school disorder.[2]

> I would suggest that the conclusions in your study and your recommendations are probably accurate and wise. I say that because my wife, a seventh-grade teacher, and my mother who taught for some 30-odd years, and my daughter who has now taught for 8 years, could have told you the same things before you started the study.... [It] is like the farmer who did not buy the book on agriculture. He said he did not need to learn any more. He was not doing half as well as he already knew how to do. (pp. 31–32)

The irony is that American agriculture is a high-technology, innovative business enterprise with a clear bottom line. Schools are not. A large part of the task of learning to reduce disorder is learning how to bring about the adoption and faithful implementation of effective programs. Many approaches to increasing school orderliness are already being recommended by educational leaders. We will learn to improve schools and decrease disruption only by trying to implement promising ideas and creating the conditions that lead to successful implementation. Elsewhere (G. D. Gottfredson, 1984c; G. D. Gottfredson, Rickert, D. C. Gottfredson, & Advani, 1984), a method for practitioner–researcher collaboration in creating these conditions is described in detail.

The path to surer knowledge and more orderly schools is not an easy path to tread. The active cooperation of policymakers, adminis-

---

[2]Congressman Andrews may be right about the failure of educators and policymakers to implement what is supposed to be effective, but at the same time he overestimates the accuracy of some common perceptions about effective strategies. For example, although many would argue for smaller class sizes as a way to reduce disorder, there is no support for such a strategy in our analyses. Similarly, arguments that increasing student influence in school decision making will reduce disruption receive no support. Other remedies specifically mentioned by the Congressman in the full text of his remarks, such as more psychotherapists to help youngsters who show signs of problems, are ideas that have received no research support or negative support in the literature (McCord, 1978).

trators, teachers, the public, and evaluation researchers will be required. Immediate, large-scale reductions in school disorder are not to be expected. Instead, the best that can be hoped for, at least in the short run, is a gradual increase in knowledge and a modest improvement in the orderliness of schools. The failure to follow this path, however, will probably result in little improvement, or even in the deterioration of the quality of American public education.

A POLICYMAKER'S GUIDE

Publicized congressional hearings do not solve social problems, whatever their contribution to winning elections. Dramatic announcements of new programs do not by themselves reduce the problems that schools face, whatever the degree of adulation they bring to their sponsors. Avoiding the systematic collection of data about school violence and disorder will not make the problem go away. Neither will ignoring social problems diminish their malignant influence.

Diligent and resourceful attention to social problems can be productive. In attempting to reduce school disorder the wise policymaker will:

1. Recognize that spectacular results are not to be expected immediately.
2. Be skeptical about any particular claim that *the* solution to school disorder is in hand.
3. Try to implement promising ideas to reduce school disorder. This might include:
   a. focusing resources and technical assistance on schools with the highest risks of problems, to assist them in reducing school size, increasing the instructional resources, and reorganizing instruction so each teacher deals more closely with a limited number of students;
   b. developing and implementing model disciplinary procedures with clearly specified rules, fair and consistent enforcement methods, and procedures that separate academic from disciplinary problems, and that provide a humane, responsive, and appropriate consequences for behavior;
   c. creating arrangements so that all students can obtain rewards for their performance, and so that the contributions and

behavior of each student are valuable to the school's inhabitants;

d. implementing any of a range of educational practices suggested by other bodies of theory and research, the rationale for which can be clearly explicated.[3]

4. Provide mechanisms to monitor the implementation of those programs, to see if they are really implemented as planned.

5. Make explicit plans to evaluate programs, using the most powerful designs possible.

6. Put one's favorite ideas for reducing school disorder on the line by subjecting them to rigorous tests.

7. Expect some failures. Honest evaluations of honest efforts do not always produce positive results. Try to learn from the experience, design a new program, and evaluate that.

8. Make the conditions under which implementation is achieved a major topic of study. We may know more about what should be done than we know about how we can do what we should do.

9. Persevere. There is reason to believe not only that broad social interventions, but also rather specific steps taken by schools can succeed in reducing school disorder. Accumulating knowledge about what works, and about ways to encourage the adoption of sound practices in schools, will require programmatic effort.

---

[3]For some suggestions see, for example, Atkeson and Forehand (1979), Barth (1979), G. D. Gottfredson (1983), Johnson, Bird, and Little (1978), and Office of Juvenile Justice and Delinquency Prevention (1980).

CHAPTER 13

Some Speculations
and Extensions

Education is perhaps the most important function of state
and local governments.

—*Brown v. Board of Education*, 347 U.S. 483, 493 (1954)

American schools don't need vast new sums of money as
much as they need a few fundamental reforms.

—Ronald Reagan, December 8, 1983

We do not believe that a public commitment to excellence
and educational reform must be made at the expense of a
strong public commitment to the equitable treatment of our
diverse population.

—National Commission on Excellence in
Education, April 1983

In this final chapter, we go beyond the specific results of the research
reported in earlier chapters. Public debate about the condition of our
schools proceeds at a pace that exceeds the pace at which careful

research can contribute knowledge, and it often makes little use of the knowledge that is available. Some of the research reported earlier in this book bears on this debate, as does other research that has accumulated in recent years. Accordingly, in this chapter we offer our speculations and best guesses about useful public policies that will affect education and the safety of America's schools. As far as is possible, we will base these speculations and extensions on other recent research and on the research reported in earlier chapters.

Our speculations offer hope that schools can be improved and be made safer places, but they diverge from some of the recent recommendations for reform. Changes in public policies that affect secondary education are required. Making these changes will require a greater degree of agreement about the goals of secondary education than now exists. In particular, they will require some consensus on the desirability of achieving greater equity as well as high-quality education for everyone. They will require as well not only the will but also the resources to bring about beneficial change.

WE HAVE CHRONIC PROBLEMS OF DISCIPLINE IN SOME SCHOOLS—NOT AN ACUTE NATIONAL CRISIS

Recent reports have implicated discipline in determining the quality of education in our nation. In *A Nation at Risk: The Imperative for Educational Reform*, the National Commission on Excellence in Education (1983) recommended that "the burden on teachers for maintaining discipline should be reduced through the development of firm and fair codes of student conduct that are enforced consistently" (p. 29). Less than a year after that report was issued, a Cabinet Council on Human Resources (CCHR, 1984) working group (composed of officials from the Department of Education, the Department of Justice, and the White House Office of Policy Development) released a report arguing that the public schools are (as the Educational Research Sevice School Research Forum, 1984, p. 9, put it) "racked by disorder as a result of court interference and timid leadership by school administrators." The CCHR report states that "many, probably most, urban schools" have ineffectively coped with discipline because of "the lack of 'will' of school officials to take action," and because of "perceived and at times actual legal obstacles which stand in their way" (p. 15). The report fostered notions that (a) school disorder is an acute crisis, (b) problems of school disorder can be solved without the expenditure of money, and (c) the simple expedient of freeing the hands of school personnel to deal with disciplinary problems will solve this crisis.

Each of these three notions is misleading. The evidence suggests not that we have an acute crisis in school discipline or an increasing rebellion against order; it suggests rather that we have some chronic disciplinary problems in many schools. Unfortunately, there are no truly dependable survey data about the extent of disorder in schools over time. But pieces of the picture can be assembled from the National Crime Surveys (Moles, 1983), and in Chapter 1 we reviewed the best available evidence about the extent of teacher and student victimization in the nation's public schools.

Although the percentage of students experiencing serious victimizations in a given month is small, millions of students attend the public schools, so this small percentage translates into the large numbers cited by the CCHR (1984) report and repeated by the national media: almost 17,000 secondary students are injured badly enough to seek medical attention as a result of robberies or attacks in school in a typical month. Different methods of estimating rates produce different results: questionnaire surveys produced the high rates often cited from the Safe School Study surveys. The rates estimated using interviews are much lower.[1]

In short, although most victimizations in schools involve relatively minor incidents, victimization in schools resembles the kinds and levels of victimization elsewhere. Most of the robberies students experience appear to be minor "shakedowns" for small amounts of money, and although clearly a problem, do not conform to the popular image of robbery. Similarly, most attacks in schools result either in no injury or in personal injury that does not require a physician's attention. Nevertheless, the frequency of minor victimizations and indignities, the absolute numbers of victimizations of a more serious nature, and public opinions about school disorder imply that in-school victimization is a serious national problem. These experiences of victimization are of importance because they disrupt the orderly conduct of education, undermine teacher job satisfaction, result in personal physical and

---

[1]More detailed information about the extent of victimization of teachers and students is provided in Exhibits A through H accompanying testimony by G. D. Gottfredson (1984b).

psychological harm to teachers and students, and help to create widespread impressions of some schools as places in which no one would really want to work or study.

Is Disorder Increasing?

Our nation does not systematically collect good data on disorder or victimization in schools over time. The best available information on trends over time has been compiled by Moles (1983). He secured the assistance of the Justice Department in isolating reports of victimization of persons aged 12–19 who had last attended grades 7–12 during the September through June period using the National Crime Surveys conducted each year from 1973 to 1980. The following kinds of incidents that occurred in schools were examined in a parallel way for each year: completed and attempted assault, robbery, and theft. The rates estimated using these data do not support a contention that the personal victimization of students in school increased between 1973 and 1980, the most recent year for which data are available. (See Figure 12.)

Some difficult to interpret information on teacher victimization over time is also available from National Education Association surveys

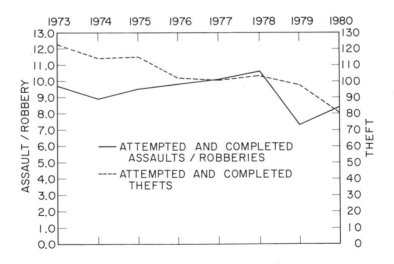

FIGURE 12: Completed or attempted victimization in school per thousand students, 1973–1980 (Source: National Crime Survey data; Moles, 1983).

of teachers. Unfortunately those surveys are illsuited to examining trends over time because the questions asked were changed from time to time and the sampling procedures are uncertain. Moles (1983) summarized his interpretations of the National Education Association data as follows: "These figures contradict the notion of a progressive worsening of the school crime problem. What increases there were came a long time ago" (p. 10). Our own interpretation is that the National Education Association data are of little use in discovering trends over time due to ambiguities resulting from problems with sampling and the wording of questions.

A general picture of a more or less stable level of disorder in schools conforms with other evidence (Laub, 1983) that serious juvenile crime has persisted at a relatively stable level in recent years.

Are Educators' Hands Tied?

There appears to be some misunderstanding among some teachers, administrators, and government officials about what courts have said about the treatment of students (Currence, 1984). The CCHR (1984) report is especially misleading. It suggested that legal procedures prevent effective prosecution of student misdeeds. For instance, the CCHR report quotes an article by Grant (1982) as follows:

> A teacher was still shaking as she told us about a group of students who had verbally assaulted her and made sexually degrading comments about her in the hall. When we asked why she didn't report the students, she responded, "Well, it couldn't have done any good." "Why not?" we pressed. "I didn't have any witnesses" she replied. (p.15)

Although the CCHR report grants that the failure to employ meaningful disciplinary responses to student misconduct "may result from overly timid readings of court decisions that . . . may have been extended beyond their original meanings by government and school officials" (pp. 15–16), it notes with favor Justice Department readiness to file *amicus* briefs in cases before the courts "on the side of increasing the authority of teachers, principals and school administrators to deal with school discipline problems" (p.21).

We believe that although some educators may *feel* restrained, there is no major problem with court-imposed limitations on the ability of educators to respond appropriately to student misconduct. The major Supreme Court case often believed to tie educators hands is *Goss v. Lopez* (419 U.S. 565, 95 S.Ct. 729, 42 L.Ed.2d 725, 1975). This case involved several Ohio public school students who had been suspended for misconduct for up to 10 days without a hearing. The Court held that the due process clause of the Fourteenth Amendment requires that public school students be informed of the charges against them and be given a simple opportunity to present their version of the incident before being suspended, or as shortly thereafter as is practicable.

The case involved a variety of students, members of a class of persons, who had allegedly engaged in various misdeeds. Some of the suspensions involved are instructive:

> Betty Crome was suspended for conduct which did not occur on school grounds, and for which mass arrests were made—hardly guaranteeing individualized factfinding by the police or by the school principal. She claims to have been involved in no misconduct. However, she was suspended for 10 days without ever being told what she was accused of doing or being given an opportunity to explain her presence among those arrested. (*Id.* at 580–581)

If administrators and others who regard *Goss* as tying their hands read the Court's opinion, they should find it reassuring. The Court stated that, "the interpretation and application of the Due Process Clause are intensely practical matters" (*Id.* at 578), and that "the fundamental requisite of due process of law is the opportunity to be heard" (*Id.* at 579, citing *Grannis v. Ordean*, 234 U.S. 385, 394, 1914). The Court was careful to guard against creating the impression that cumbersome due process procedures are required:

> The prospect of imposing elaborate hearing requirements in every suspension case is viewed with great concern, and many school authorities may well prefer the untrammeled power to act unilaterally, unhampered by rules about notice and hearing. But it would be a strange disciplinary system in an educational institution if no communication was sought by the disciplinarian with the student in an effort to inform him of his dereliction and to let him tell his side of the story in order to make sure that an injustice is not done. (*Id.* at 580)
>
> There need be no delay between the time "notice" is given and the time of the hearing. In the great majority of cases the disciplinarian may informally discuss the alleged misconduct with the student minutes after it has occurred. We hold only that, in being given an opportunity to explain his version of the facts at this discussion, the student first be told what he is accused of doing and what the basis of the accusation is. (*Id.* at 582)
>
> In holding as we do, we do not believe that we have imposed procedures on school disciplinarians which are inappropriate in a classroom setting. Instead we have imposed requirements which are, if anything, less than a fair-minded school principal would impose upon himself in order to avoid

> unfair suspensions . . . . We stop short of construing the Due Process Clause
> to require, countrywide, that hearings in connection with short suspensions
> must afford the student the opportunity to secure counsel, to confront and
> cross-examine witnesses supporting the charge, or to call his own witnesses
> to verify his version of the incident. (583)

Other court cases sometimes believed to tie the hands of educators in dealing with school discipline are not really relevant to maintaining order in schools. The case of *New Jersey v. T.L.O.*, currently under review by the Supreme Court (docket number 83–712), involves issues of search and seizure in an attempt to secure a *criminal* conviction in an instance of alleged drug distribution. It is difficult to argue that the courts do not have a proper role in interpreting Constitutional protections against unwarranted searches and seizures in cases of criminal prosecution. However the Court decides the *T.L.O.* case, the case simply does not deal with the usual and ordinary process of maintaining discipline in schools on a day-to-day basis.[2]

In short, educators' hands are not unduly fettered by the courts in disciplinary actions involving sanctions as severe as a suspension of up to 10 days. The real problem is the failure of schools to be clear about what their disciplinary procedures are and to actually follow those procedures. Beyond efforts to disseminate information about what is and is not legal, placing emphasis on court decisions relating to school disciplinary procedures or illegal searches and seizures will misdirect attention from the real problem of establishing and maintaining firm, fair, and consistently applied disciplinary procedures.

SHOULD WE ESTABLISH POLICIES TO REMOVE TROUBLEMAKERS FROM SCHOOLS?

In Ronald Reagan's radio address to the nation on 7 January 1984, he quoted Albert Shanker (of the American Federation of Teachers) as saying,

---

[2]In the unreported decision (New Jersey v. T.L.O., U.S. Supreme Court, 1985), the Court adopted a standard allowing a school official to search when there are "reasonable grounds" for suspecting that evidence of a violation of law or school rules will be found. This decision cannot be viewed as tying educators' hands.

> We're not going to get people interested in English or mathematics or
> social studies and languages, unless we solve discipline problems and take
> out of our schools those students who prevent teachers from teaching.

In the same address, Mr. Reagan announced that he had directed the Justice Department to file court briefs to help school administrators enforce school discipline. Apparently, many who make or recommend policy agree with sociologist Jackson Toby (1983b) who wrote that,

> social changes . . . that made it burdensome for school administrators to
> expel students guilty of violent behavior or suspend them for more than ten
> days partially explain the erosion of the authority of the teacher. (pp. 34–
> 35)

Toby suggests that compulsory school attendance laws be changed to require attendance only for younger students, allowing students who do not wish to remain in school to drop out.

Toby's (1980, 1983b) arguments in favor of policies that would result in fewer troublesome youths in the public schools are interesting. He argues that it may be useful "to establish minimum behavioral standards for students in public schools that are enforceable by credible threats, including possible termination of enrollment" (1983b, p. 42). In addition, Toby sees obstacles to creating more orderly schools in compulsory attendance laws that discourage students from voluntarily leaving school or school officials from expelling them. He notes that unless a juvenile court sends a violent young person to a correctional institution, the youngster will be expected to attend the school in which he or she may have been committing offenses. In short, public policies intended to do good for the individual juvenile may undermine the effectiveness of entire schools.

As attractive and reasonable as these suggested policy reforms may sound, they lead in the wrong direction. The primary reason they do so is that they do not address the fundamental problems suggested by the evidence in our earlier chapters. School disorder tends to be greatest in schools serving communities characterized by social disorganization and largely minority populations; therefore, many of the students removed from school by such policies would tend to be minority youth and youths from disorganized neighborhoods. The likely effect of such policies would be to maintain or exacerbate inequality in the educational attainment of minority groups and the perpetuation of social disorganization in communities.

A second reason that such a policy may be misguided is provided by evidence Toby (1983b) adduces. He argues, contrary to the conclusions drawn by the National Institute of Education (1978), that large proportions of the violent offenses committed in urban schools are committed by intruders. (To make this inference he uses data from the National Crime Surveys about the percentage of offenders who were reported to be "strangers" by the victims. Evidence adduced in earlier chapters implies that victimization is more common in larger schools, where attachment to school is low, and where the typical teacher teaches many different pupils, implying that many of Toby's strangers may in fact have been students who were simply unknown to the victim.) Toby's (1983b) data also show, however, that the "intruders" who commit these offenses are of about the same age as the students in the school (see his Table 6). Only 5% of the offenders against students aged 16–19 were perceived to be aged 21 or older, and only 4% of the offenders against students aged 12–15 were perceived to be 18 or older.[3] In other words, if Toby's inference that the offenders unknown to these student victims were intruders is correct, these intruders are mostly of school age. They would not be intruders if they were attending a school they were supposed to be attending. One must wonder how many of these "intruders" are students who were suspended from a school.

In addition to making dropout easier by inducing states to lower compulsory attendance ages and making suspension or expulsion easier by making these actions less cumbersome, Toby (1983a) recommends that the federal government provide incentives to urban schools to use security guards to exclude youthful intruders. He also urges Congress to change federal laws that he believes "give youngsters uninterested in education an incentive to remain enrolled in school, such as statutes governing welfare benefits under the program of Aid to Families with Dependent Children" and sections of the Social Security Act that exclude the earnings of dependent children in calculating family eligibility for benefits.

What are we to make of these policy recommendations? The most obvious objection to these recommendations is that they would all work

[3]Higher proportions of the offenders against teachers in Toby's (1983b) Table 6 were perceived to be aged 21 or older, but it is not clear what proportion of the teachers were teaching in elementary or secondary schools or some other kind of school and whether the offenders were intruders, strangers, other faculty members, or even administrators.

to make it easier for schools to exclude from their rolls the young people they now serve least well. Toby examines the issue of whether lowered compulsory school attendance requirements would result in lowered enrollment in school as well as lowered crime rates using state-level data on attendance laws, enrollment rates, and rates of crime reported to the police. His data (Table 3 in Toby, 1983a) show higher enrollment rates in four states requiring attendance through age 18 than in five states requiring attendance only through age 15 or less (the difference approaches but is never larger than 5% for any age of student between 14 and 18). His data (Table 4 in Toby, 1983a) also show that there is a tendency for rates of crime reported to the police to increase slightly as the compulsory attendance age increases across states. The number of police reports per thousand students increases from 8.0 for 15 states with compulsory attendance ages of 15 or less to 11.4 for 8 states with compulsory attendance ages of 17 or more. (This excludes the outlier state of Hawaii, a state with a compulsory attendance age of 18 and a very high rate of reported crimes.) Toby (1983a) interprets the lowered crime rates as important and the lowered attendance rates as "a minor factor in enrollment and very likely a less important factor in actual attendance" (p. 77).

In an earlier report, G. D. Gottfredson (1979) urged caution in interpreting state-level data in the ways Toby has interpreted them in making his policy recommendations. Gottfredson used some of the very same data Toby (1983a) tabulated. In Gottfredson's analyses, compulsory attendance laws were correlated with reported crime rates (just as they are in Toby's table); but when other state demographic characteristics were statistically controlled, the analyses provided no evidence of a significant effect of attendance laws on crime rates. Enrollment rates were not significantly correlated with crime rates, nor was average daily attendance correlated with crime rates. Other results reported by Gottfredson (1979) imply that attempts to interpret state-level correlations of this type can often produce absurd results, but among those other results was an estimate that the *total* effect of attendance laws on crime (i.e., the direct influence of attendance laws plus any effect operating through any of the intermediary variables examined) is smaller than the *direct* effect of attendance laws on school enrollment, and that attendance laws have near zero indirect effects on crime rates via either enrollment or attendance. In short, alternative analyses of essentially the same data adduced by Toby (1983a) do not support his interpretations.

Wilson's (1983) interpretation of Toby's suggestions is instructive:

> Unteachable youths, or at least youths who are unteachable *given the realities of most public school systems*, are kept in school by a combination of compulsory attendance laws, welfare regulations, and minimum wage laws. (p. 283, emphasis added)

We think Wilson's statement captures an important element of the policy question. Substantial evidence implies that it is youths who do not do well in school who most often drop out early and who engage in more delinquent behavior (G. D. Gottfredson, 1981). Excluding the more unruly students from school would be excluding those students who are not now helped to perform well in school.

Toby may be correct in suggesting that students who do not do well in school should not be compelled to attend (and if they misbehave that they be compelled not to attend). Despite evidence (Blau & Duncan, 1967; Jencks, 1977) that persistence in school pays off in terms of occupational attainment and income, there is really no evidence on which to base a policy regarding the effects of compelling young people to persist in schooling. We do not know if compelling young people to remain in school would increase their rebellion or decrease it. We do not know if compelling young people to remain in school would enhance their career prospects or decrease them. Experiments to determine the effects of compulsory attendance have not been done. That they should be done is clear, but the lack of evidence one way or the other about the likely effects provides little guidance to the policymaker.

The evidence presented in the earlier chapters may help somewhat. In those chapters, we presented results that imply schools can reduce disorder by taking steps to improve the ways they are run. In other words, changes in school environments that move the reality of contemporary public education in a direction that increases ordinary social controls can help make them safer. This possibility deserves at least as much policy attention as the possibility that excluding troublesome youths would make schools safer. Working to make schools safer by strengthening ordinary social controls has the potential advantage that it does not depend on denying participation in schooling to a class of youth.

Ordinary Controls

Behavioral scientists often talk about problems of delinquency as problems of control (Empey, 1978; Hirschi, 1969). A key task for society in general, and schools in particular, is to maintain social control. Social control can in principle take several forms, but we distinguish between *ordinary* social control and *extraordinary* social control. Ordinary social control is exercised daily by each of us in our interactions with others. Mothers and fathers exercise ordinary social control when they create expectations for the behavior of their children and award desired conduct with approval and undesired conduct with disapproval or household punishments. Teachers and school administrators exercise ordinary control when they specify rules for conduct, when they smile at students who are well behaved and avoid interaction with others, or when they send a student who has violated a rule out of class for a brief period of time.

Hirshci (1969) has provided a useful perspective on ordinary social control that implies that most of us have stakes in conformity that provide sources of ordinary social control. We engage in certain behavior, and avoid other behavior, because we see that it is in our short-term or long-range benefit to do so. Not all students in our public schools have developed stakes in conformity in a powerful enough form to restrain them from aggressive or predatory behavior. Developing these restraints in the form of attachments to school or to teachers, belief in the validity of school rules, expectations that desired educational goals (in school and later in life) will be achieved through conformity in school rather than misbehavior, and accurate perceptions of the consequences of our behavior in everyday life is what ordinary control involves.

In contrast, extraordinary social controls—suspension, expulsion, arrest, prosecution, confinement, and other extreme sanctions—are often suggested as ways of reducing misconduct in schools. For example, the recent concern about the outcome of the U.S. Supreme Court review of *New Jersey v. T.L.O.*, reflects a concern that the authority of school officials to engage in effective prosecution of juveniles will be hampered by procedural rules for search and seizure. We believe that these extraordinary controls are unlikely to work as well as strengthened ordinary controls. Ordinary controls are easier to apply in a timely fashion, are manipulable, and are less costly than extraordinary controls (G. D. Gottfredson, 1984a). Strengthened ordinary controls can be powerful restraints against misconduct. Ordinary controls may offer greater promise of reducing school disorder than do cumbersome, difficult-to-apply, or counterproductive extraordinary controls.

Evidence implies that efforts to change the aspects of school governance and climate shown in the earlier chapters to be associated with school victimization can indeed make schools safer (G. D. Gottfredson, D. C. Gottfredson, & Cook, 1983; D. C. Gottfredson, 1984). Demonstration programs aimed at reducing the risk of delinquent behavior through school-based interventions, that aimed to increase the clarity, firmness, or responsiveness of school rule enforcement, or that aimed at increasing student stakes in conformity by providing appropriate educational environments, produced safer schools. Therefore, the possibility that the ways schools are currently run can be improved to increase school orderliness deserves equal attention in policy debates. Policymakers may view it as desirable to remove "bad" students to make the environment better for those who conform and perform well in existing environments, or they can take seriously the task of designing environments in which more students are able to conform and learn. Our preference is the latter.

HOLDING SCHOOLS ACCOUNTABLE FOR SAFE ENVIRONMENTS

In 1980, California's Attorney General (now that state's Governor, Duke Dukmejein) sued the Los Angeles city school district for not providing a safe environment for students. The suit sought declaratory relief rather than any specific remedy, apparently because the Attorney General's intent was to demonstrate that schools do have an obligation to provide safe environments. Although that suit was well publicized in the media, it was on shaky ground from the beginning, based as it was on the theory that requiring students to attend unsafe schools constituted cruel and unusual punishment. (The case was dismissed by the trial court.) More recently, the State of California amended its constitution (Article I, section 28(c), 1982) to read:

> *Right to Safe Schools.* All students and staff of public primary, elementary, junior high and senior high schools have the inalienable right to attend campuses which are safe, secure and peaceful.

We know little of the response of school systems in California to the state's constitutional amendment, and we know of no important litigation alleging that his right has been violated. But the wording of the amendment opens a number of questions about how one would know if the schools are safe, secure, and peaceful. Even in states where students and teachers do not have a constitutionally provided "inalienable right" to safe schools, most members of the public and most school administrators would agree that safe schools are a desirable goal. Yet reasonable monitoring mechanisms that would enable a determination about whether schools are safe places are rare.

State legislatures have from time to time proposed monitoring schemes based on reports of violence or other crimes by school officials. One such proposal (AB 2483) is currently before the California legislature. That bill would require the compilation of school crime statistics based on a standard school crime reporting form. These reports would be forwarded to the State Superintendent via the District Superintendents. This is probably not a good way to monitor school safety. Evidence from the Safe School Study data implies that school principals complete incident reporting forms in highly idiosyncratic ways, and testimony by school officials at a hearing held in 1980 in New Jersey to consider such reports suggested that many administrators are likely to resist the accurate completion of such reports. Furthermore, there is little reason to believe that school officials will be aware of most crimes (let alone the entire range of incivilities) that occur in schools.

School System Self-Monitoring

An alternative way to monitor school safety would be through the use of periodic surveys of the kind conducted in 1976 by the National Institute of Education. A field-tested set of instruments for conducting this kind of survey is available (G. D. Gottfredson, 1985), and could be used as one way to conduct such monitoring. Surveys of students are currently used nearly everywhere to assess the academic outcomes of schooling, and despite psychometric difficulties in their unambiguous interpretation as measures of school effectiveness, surveys based on academic achievement tests have been used as a logical approach to the public's demand for accountability in education.

Our best school districts can be expected to monitor their safety on their own and to take corrective action when it is needed because this kind of use of information is a characteristic of effective organizations

(G. D. Gottfredson, 1984c). But schools that lack safe environments also tend to be the schools that engage in little systematic planning for school improvement and where people in the school do not believe they can count on others to contribute to school improvement (G. D. Gottfredson, 1985).

Accordingly, it would be very useful for school systems to put systematic monitoring systems into place that will inform local policy-makers about the degree of safety that characterize each school in their systems. The manner in which such monitoring information is used is of the utmost importance. The use of standardized educational tests in accountability programs is often objected to by school personnel because they perceive it as unfair. Output in terms of student performance on such standardized achievement tests is largely predictable from student input (Coleman et al., 1966). Consequently, school officials often feel that they are in a no-win situation: schools that receive large populations of students who perform poorly on standardized tests when they arrive are likely to have populations that perform poorly on the accountability tests. Test score results then contribute to the deterioration of the image of these schools. This difficulty is exacerbated when the schools receive little in the way of assistance in improving their students' academic performance.

In contrast, routine systematic monitoring of school safety and school climate more generally could form a platform on which school improvement programs are based. Although the research reported in earlier chapters implies that to a large extent the disorder a school displays is predictable from the community the school serves and the demographic composition of the school, it also implies that the extent of disorder is also predictable from school policies and practices. Schools with climate profiles that suggest improvement is needed might be targeted for special assistance in school improvement by local education agencies. Data about school safety and other aspects of school climate would help school staff and administrators pinpoint problems that can form the basis of program planning for school improvement, and would provide school system administrators with information useful in allocating monetary and organizational development resources.

Of course, the effective use of school climate surveys requires cooperation from school administrators, and herein lies a potential problem-however unlikely it is to occur. Timid school administrators may wish to avoid collecting survey data for fear that the results could be used as evidence of the school's lack of safety in a suit against the school system (such as the suit against the Los Angeles Unified School District noted previously). This kind of evidentiary use of the survey would therefore discourage its primary use and purpose: namely, to enable school administrators to examine disciplinary problems in the school systems and deal with them. Any public official who attempted to make this kind of unintended use of school diagnostic information would be defeating the purpose of school climate and safety monitoring.

Perhaps the best protection against this kind of double bind would be for state legislatures to mandate periodic climate surveys to monitor school safety. Because fear of the improper use of assessment results could work against the collection of needed information, legislatures should make clear that the mandated monitoring of school climates implies no private right of action. Legislative action may also be necessary to ensure that sufficient resources are allocated for climate assessment and for the implementation of interventions to improve school safety when improvement is needed.

At the same time, the potential misuse of survey data by zealous complainants does not seem likely to occur. Although a number of states have provisions of law calling for "thorough and efficient education," and although nearly all states routinely use standardized educational tests as part of accountability or assessment programs, we know of no successful litigation against school systems based on these survey data.

We speculate that the greatest impediment to the collection and use of information about school safety and other aspects of school climate arises not from any fear of litigation but rather from fear of responses by school system administrators. Our experience implies that far too often central or regional school system administrators respond negatively to the open discussion and confrontation of problems. This creates a situation in which school personnel try to hide problems rather than to discover and cope with them. This situation poses a special challenge for American public education. We will most likely succeed in creating better and safer schools only if we openly examine and address problems. School officials must learn that it is a sign of professional competence to identify problems rather than to hide them.

Monitoring Imposed by the Courts

The recent amendment to the California constitution creating a "right to safe schools" did not specify how this right would be secured, or how a determination would be made about whether a school were safe. A clear possibility exists, however, that some day a suit may be brought against a school system alleging that it is denying this right to students or teachers. The courts will have to decide somehow whether the complaint has merit. How should the vague assertion in the constitutional amendments be interpreted?

It is possible, of course, that a specific person or persons injured in a school may bring suit arguing that the fact of their injury implies that the right was violated. More likely than suits involving individual action, however, are civil suits alleging that schools are not safe in terms of the general environments they provide. Some assessment will have to be made by the courts of the degree of safety in schools as a whole and of the reasonableness of the steps taken by school officials to secure a safe school environment. It is likely, therefore, that many of the issues raised in court cases involving educational equity and school segregation will arise in school safety cases.

When courts issue a desegregation order, they have seldom grappled directly with efforts to determine whether the order was effective. Occasionally the courts have taken steps to determine whether a school district is complying with the order, and in *Brown II* (349 U.S. 294, 301, 1955) the Supreme Court specifically stated that the lower court was to retain jurisdiction so the judge could monitor school board compliance with the desegregation order. Recently, Crain and Mahard (1982) have argued that courts can monitor school system performance after a desegregation order using statistical data. Monitoring school safety by using victimization surveys, or more comprehensive instruments to assess school climate such as the *Effective School Battery* (G. D. Gottfredson, 1985), would provide one tool for the courts to determine whether their orders are carried out.

BROADENING THE SCOPE OF EDUCATIONAL ASSESSMENT

Organizations probably get what they measure. Measuring school disruption is one way to give a clear signal that the school system cares about safety and school orderliness. A number of reports in the past few years have exhorted our schools to attend to the problem of disorderliness and to do something about it. Political leaders have made similar exhortations. These vague and general calls to do better are likely to be ineffective unless they are tied to specific instruments to measure school orderliness in ways that pinpoint problem areas. Currently school effectiveness is monitored largely by use of standardized achievement test scores, and attendance and graduation rates. Much is to be gained by broadening the scope of measurement to include school safety and other aspects of school management and school climate. The previous chapters illustrate that these elements of school effectiveness can be measured. School systems should now move in the direction of broader assessments of organizational effectiveness.

WILL CREATING MORE ORDERLY SCHOOLS COST MONEY?

Making our less effective schools safer will require the expenditure of money. One of the lessons we have learned over the past several decades is that simply throwing money at a problem does not solve it. There can be no debate about that. But the development of techniques that are easy to implement, well designed, and are likely to be implemented in faithful form will require the targeted expenditure of money on that development. The following are some areas where federal leadership is required to solve some general school problems related to discipline:

- Development, evaluation, and demonstration of discipline guidelines for schools to follow. In particular, we need to know more about how to design disciplinary procedures that are adhered to and applied in fair, consistent, and immediate ways.

- Development, evaluation, and demonstration of school improvement or organizational development techniques that can be used to alter the ways schools are run. In particular, we need to know more about the obstacles that prevent schools from taking actions to improve discipline, school climate, and learning. How do we create the will to do what is necessary?

- Development, evaluation, and demonstration of quality assurance indicators that can be used by school districts, local school boards, the government, and researchers to monitor the orderliness of all schools. We need systematic measures of school orderliness to determine whether the situation is getting better or worse, to pinpoint troubled schools, and to structure the priorities of school administrators and faculties. A general principal of organizational psychology is that you get what you measure. We should measure school orderliness to focus attention where attention is needed.

- Development, evaluation, and demonstration of effective procedures for coping with disruptive, failing, and drop-out prone youths in schools. Suspending these youths will not solve the problem of our inability to serve them well. Finding ways to alter school environments so that students' stakes in conformity are increased should help. We must create techniques that are effective and find ways to increase the use of effective techniques in schools.

None of these things will happen unless we work on the problem, and working on the problem will cost some money. Federal leadership is very much needed in this area.

Student and Teacher Questionnaires

SAFE SCHOOL STUDY

National Institute of Education

STUDENT QUESTIONNAIRE

This questionnaire is part of a study that is being done for the U.S. Congress. The study was planned to find out how safe people are in school, to learn about any trouble they may have had, and to figure out how schools that have a problem can be made safer.

You were selected <u>randomly</u> from among the students at your school to be part of this study. This is exactly like having your name drawn out of a hat.

THIS IS NOT A TEST. There are no right or wrong answers. What we need is your honest answer to these questions about your school.

Your participation in this study is <u>voluntary</u> and you have the right not to respond to certain or all of the questions in this questionnaire. However, RTI would like to stress that your participation is important to the validity and success of the study and we encourage your full cooperation.

DO NOT WRITE YOUR NAME ON THIS BOOKLET. Then there will be no way to tell whose answers these are. All we need are the answers, not your names. One more important thing — do not talk or compare answers. It must be quiet, so each of you can give your own answers.

If you have a question at any point, raise your hand.

O.K., please open the booklet to the first page.

```
FOR OFFICE USE ONLY
Response Code _____
```

INSTRUCTIONS

There are several kinds of questions in this booklet.

THE FIRST KIND is a multiple choice question. After the question it will say (CIRCLE ONE NUMBER). This means to circle the number beside the answer that fits you best, like this:

EXAMPLE 1

How tall are you?

(Circle one number.)

Less than 5 feet 1
Between 5 and 6 feet . . . . ②
More than 6 feet 3

THE SECOND KIND will ask you to circle all the numbers beside answers that fit you, like this:

EXAMPLE 2

What courses do you take at school?

(Circle all that apply.)

English . . . . ①
Math . . . . ②
Social Studies 3
Science 4
Industrial Arts . . . . ⑤
Other 6

THE THIRD KIND asks a set of questions with the answers to the right of each one. Each answer is labeled as below.

EXAMPLE 3

How do you feel about each of these ideas?

(Circle one number on each line.)

	Agree	Undecided	Disagree
a. Students should decide what is taught in school	1	②	3
b. Parents and teachers should work together	①	2	3
c. Teachers know all the answers	1	2	③

THE FOURTH KIND asks you to circle the number beside "Yes" or "No." If the answer is "Yes," follow the arrow to the next question and answer it by writing a number on the line.

EXAMPLE 4

In the last month did anyone damage something of yours at school?

1   No
2   Yes   →   a.   How many times in a
                      classroom?   **2**
                                                      number
                 b.   How many times in other   l
                      places at school?   number

THE FIFTH KIND just asks you to write in an answer. Please write as clearly as possible.

EXAMPLE 5

How many minutes long is your lunch period?   **30**
                                                    minutes

1.   Are you:

(Circle one number.)

Male 1
Female 2

2. How old are you?

(Circle one number.)

```
11 years old or younger . . . . . . . . . . . . .  1
12 years . . . . . . . . . . . . . . . . . . . . .  2
13 years . . . . . . . . . . . . . . . . . . . . .  3
14 years . . . . . . . . . . . . . . . . . . . . .  4
15 years . . . . . . . . . . . . . . . . . . . . .  5
16 years . . . . . . . . . . . . . . . . . . . . .  6
17 years . . . . . . . . . . . . . . . . . . . . .  7
18 years . . . . . . . . . . . . . . . . . . . . .  8
19 years or over . . . . . . . . . . . . . . . .  9
```

3. How do you describe yourself?

(Circle one number.)

```
American Indian or Alaskan Native . . . . . . . . . . . . . . . . . . . . . . .  1
Asian-American or Pacific Islander (Chinese, Japanese,
    Hawaiian, etc.) . . . . . . . . . . . . . . . . . . . . . . . . . . . . . . . . . . . .  2
Spanish-American (Mexican, Puerto Rican, Cuban or
    other Latin American) . . . . . . . . . . . . . . . . . . . . . . . . . . . . .  3
Black or Afro-American or Negro (other than Spanish-
    American) . . . . . . . . . . . . . . . . . . . . . . . . . . . . . . . . . . . . . .  4
White (Other than Spanish-American) . . . . . . . . . . . . . . . . . . . . .  5
Other (Write in) _____  6
```

4. How long have you gone to this school?

(Circle one number.)

```
1 month or less . . . . . . . . . . . . . . . .  1
Less than 1 year but more than 1 month. . . . .  2
1 or 2 years . . . . . . . . . . . . . . . . . .  3
3 or 4 years . . . . . . . . . . . . . . . . . .  4
5 or more years. . . . . . . . . . . . . . . . .  5
```

5. What grade are you in?

(Circle one number.)

```
1st Grade  . . . . . . . . . . . . . . . . . . .  1
2nd Grade . . . . . . . . . . . . . . . . . . . .  2
3rd Grade . . . . . . . . . . . . . . . . . . . .  3
4th Grade . . . . . . . . . . . . . . . . . . . .  4
5th Grade . . . . . . . . . . . . . . . . . . . .  5
6th Grade . . . . . . . . . . . . . . . . . . . .  6
7th Grade . . . . . . . . . . . . . . . . . . . .  7
8th Grade . . . . . . . . . . . . . . . . . . . .  8
9th Grade (Freshman) . . . . . . . . . . . . . .  9
10th Grade (Sophomore) . . . . . . . . . . . . . 10
11th Grade (Junior). . . . . . . . . . . . . . . 11
12th Grade (Senior). . . . . . . . . . . . . . . 12
Ungraded . . . . . . . . . . . . . . . . . . . . 13
```

6. Do you take part in any of the following school activities?

(Circle one number on each line.)

	Yes	No
a. Athletics outside of gym class	1	2
b. Band, orchestra, or chorus	1	2
c. School clubs	1	2
d. Student government	1	2
e. Other activities not part of class work	1	2

7. How good are your school's athletic teams compared to other school's athletic teams in this area?

(Circle one number.)

```
Much better  . . . . . . . . . . . . . . . . .  1
A little better . . . . . . . . . . . . . . . . .  2
```

About the same 3
Not quite as good 4
Not nearly as good 5
No teams at my school that play regularly 6

8.   In other ways, how good is your school compared to other schools in this area?

(Circle one number.)

Much better 1
A little better 2
About the same 3
Not quite as good 4
Not nearly as good 5

9.   Why do you go to this school and not some other school?

(Circle all that apply.)

I chose this school for its special courses or programs 1
I was expelled from another school 2
I was assigned to this school as it serves my neighborhood 3
I was assigned here so that more black and white students
   can be at school together 4
Some other reason (What?)_____ 5

10.   How well do you like the following:

(Circle one number on each line.)

	Don't Like	Like Fairly Well	Like Very Well
a. This school	1	2	3
b. The students	1	2	3
c. The principal	1	2	3
d. The classes you are taking	1	2	3

11.   How many close friends do you have at this school?

(Circle one number.)

None 1
1 - 2 2
3 - 4 3
5 - 9 4
10 - 19 5
20 or more 6

12.   How often are the following things true of your school?

(Circle one number on each line.)

	Almost Never	Sometimes	Almost Always
a. Everyone knows what the school rules are . .	1	2	3
b. The school rules are fair	1	2	3
c. The punishment for breaking school rules is the same no matter who you are . . .	1	2	3
d. The school rules are strictly enforced	1	2	3
e. If a school rule is broken, students know what kind of punishment will follow	1	2	3
f. Students can get an unfair school rule changed	1	2	3

13.   How often is your school like this?

(Circle one number on each line.)

	Almost Never	Sometimes	Almost Always
a. Students need permission to do anything around here	1	2	3

b. Students are paddled for serious rule-
   breaking 1   2   3
c. Students are treated like children here 1   2   3

14. How much do you agree or disagree with each of the following statements?

(Circle one number on each line.)

	Agree	Undecided	Disagree
a. Schools should have rules about the way students can dress	1	2	3
b. It is all right for schools to suspend students without a hearing	1	2	3
c. If students are in a fist fight, let them settle it by themselves	1	2	3
d. If students use drugs around schools, it is their own business	1	2	3
e. Students do have a lot to say about how this school is run	1	2	3
f. Students should have a lot to say about how this school is run	1	2	3

15. How easy or hard is it for students to get the following things at your school?

(Circle one number on each line.)

	Very Easy	Fairly Easy	Fairly Hard	Very Hard	Impossible	Don't Know
a. Beer or wine	1	2	3	4	5	9
b. Marijuana	1	2	3	4	5	9
c. Heroin	1	2	3	4	5	9
d. Stolen things for sale	1	2	3	4	5	9

16. Do you stay away from any of the following places because someone might hurt or bother you there?

(Circle one number on each line.)

	Yes	No
a. The shortest route to school	1	2
b. Any entrances into the school	1	2
c. Any hallways or stairs in the school	1	2
d. Parts of the school cafeteria	1	2
e. Any school restrooms	1	2
f. Other places inside school building	1	2
g. School parking lot	1	2
h. Other places on school grounds	1	2

17. How often are you afraid that someone will hurt or bother you at school?

(Circle one number.)

Most of the time 1
Sometimes 2
Almost never 3
Never 4

18. How often do you bring something to school to protect yourself?

(Circle one number.)

Most of the time 1
Sometimes 2
Almost never 3
Never 4

19. At school in November did anyone force you to hand over money or things worth less than $1?

(Circle one number. If "Yes," follow the arrow.)

1   No

2   Yes   →   How many times? _____
                                                  Number

20. Besides things under a dollar, did anyone take money or things directly from you by force, weapons or threats at school in November?

(Circle one number. If "Yes," follow the arrow.)

1   No
2   Yes   →   a. How many times did this involve losses
                     of $1 to $10?
                  b. How many times did this involve losses   Number
                     of more than $10?   _____

21. In November did anyone steal something <u>worth less than $1</u> from your desk, locker, or other place at school?

(Circle one number. If "Yes," follow the arrow.)

1   No
2   Yes   →   How many times? _____
                                                  Number

22. Besides things under a dollar, in November, did anyone steal things of yours from your desk, locker, or other place at school?

(Circle one number. If "Yes," follow the arrow.)

1   No
2   Yes   →   a. How many times did this involve thefts
                     of $1 to $10?
                  b. How many times did this involve thefts   Number
                     of more than $10?   _____
                                                                     Number

23. At school in November did anyone physically attack and hurt you?

(Circle one number. If "Yes," follow the arrow.)

1   No
2   Yes   →   a. How many times were you attacked
                     and hurt badly enough to have to
                     see a doctor?
                  b. How many times were you attacked   Number
                     and hurt but <u>not</u> badly enough to
                     have to see a doctor?   _____
                                                                     Number

24. Did you stay at home any time in November because someone might hurt you or bother you at school?

(Circle one number.)

Yes 1
No   2

25. Are there fighting gangs in your neighborhood?

(Circle one number.)

Yes 1
No 2

26. In the last year has either of your parents been robbed on the streets of your neighborhood?

(Circle one number.)

Yes 1
No 2

27. In the last year has anyone broken into your home?

(Circle one number.)

Yes 1
No   2

28. Does your mother or a stepmother live at home with you?

(Circle one number.)

Yes 1
No 2

29. If your mother or stepmother lives at home with you, does she have a full-time job?

(Circle one number.)

Yes 1
No 2
She does not live with me 3

30. If your mother or stepmother lives at home with you, how far in school did she go?

(Circle one number.)

8th grade or less 1
Some high school 2
Finished high school 3
Some college or other schooling after
   high school 4
Finished college 5
Don't know 6
She does not live with me 7

31. Does your father or a stepfather live at home with you?

(Circle one number.)

Yes 1
No 2

32. If your father or stepfather lives at home with you, does he have a full-time job?

(Circle one number.)

Yes 1
No 2
Ile does not live with me 3

33. If your father or stepfather lives at home with you, how far in school did he go?

(Circle one number.)

8th grade or less 1
Some high school 2
Finished high school 3
Some college or other schooling after
   high school 4
Finished college 5
Don't know 6
He does not live with me 7

34. Is English spoken most of the time in your home?

(Circle one number.)

Yes 1
No 2

35. How often do you and your parents talk about school or school work?

(Circle one number.)

Almost never 1
Once or twice a month 2
Once or twice a week 3
Almost every day 4

36. How do you get to and from school most of the time?

(Circle one number.)

Walk 1
School bus 2
Public bus, subway, train. 3
Car 4
Bicycle, motorbike, or motorcycle 5
Some other way (How?) _____ 6

37. How many minutes does it usually take you to get home from school?

(Circle one number.)

10 minutes or less 1
11 to 20 minutes 2
21 to 30 minutes 3
31 to 40 minutes 4
41 to 50 minutes 5
51 to 60 minutes 6
More than 60 minutes 7

38. How often do you feel afraid that someone will hurt or bother you on the way to school?

(Circle one number.)

Almost never 1
Once or twice a month 2
Once or twice a week 3
Almost every day 4

39. How do you usually get your lunch on school days?

(Circle one number.)

Pay full price at school cafeteria 1
Pay reduced price at school cafeteria. 2
Get free lunch at school cafeteria 3
Bring lunch to school 4
Go home for lunch 5
Have lunch at nearby restaurant or
  lunch counter. 6
Do not eat lunch 7

40. Do you have a part-time or a full-time job?

(Circle one number.)

Yes 1
No 2

41. In the last four weeks how many days of school did you miss?

(Circle one number.)

None 1
1 - 2 days 2
3 - 5 days 3
6 - 10 days 4
More than 10 days 5

42. Have you ever been suspended from this school?

(Circle one number.)

Yes 1
No 2

43. How well do the following people get along at your school?

(Circle one number for each item.)

	Not Well	Fairly Well	Very Well
a. Students of different races	1	2	3
b. Students of different nationalities	1	2	3
c. Students without much money and students with money	1	2	3

44. How much do you agree or disagree with each of the following statements?

(Circle one number on each line.)

	Agree	Undecided	Disagree	No Minorities Here
a. Racial minority groups (Blacks, Spanish-Americans, etc.) are treated fairly in this school	1	2	3	9
b. Racial minority groups (Blacks, Spanish-Americans, etc.) are treated fairly in this country	1	2	3	

45. In general, how often are teachers at your school like this?

(Circle one number on each line.)

	Almost Never	Sometimes	Almost Always
a. Teachers expect a lot of work from students	1	2	3
b. They are teaching me what I want to learn	1	2	3
c. They keep order in the class	1	2	3
d. The teachers are fair	1	2	3
e. They are interested in the students	1	2	3
f. They let everyone know who gets high and low grades	1	2	3
g. Teachers let students learn from each other in class	1	2	3

46. How easy would it be to do the following things if you wanted to?

(Circle one number on each line.)

	Not Easy	Fairly Easy	Very Easy
a. Get an unfair grade changed	1	2	3
b. Work faster or slower than the rest of the class	1	2	3
c. Have your ideas listened to in class	1	2	3
d. Talk over school work problems with a teacher	1	2	3
e. Talk over personal problems with a school counselor	1	2	3

47. Most of the classes here are:

(Circle all that apply.)

Easy 1
Interesting 2
Hard 3
Boring 4
Worth taking. 5

48. Which one of these things should your teachers work hardest to do?

(Circle only one number.)

Teach basic subjects and skills 1
Help students develop good character 2
Prepare students for later jobs 3
Prepare students for college 4
Keep control in class 5
Make students interested in learning 6
Teach respect for other races and
    nationalities 7

49. Is there a lot of competition for grades in this school?

(Circle one number.)

Yes 1
No 2

50. Do most of your friends think getting good grades is important?

(Circle one number.)

Yes 1
No 2

51. At the end of the last semester, were your course grades mostly:

(Circle one number.)

High (mostly A's) 1
Above average (mostly B's) 2
Average (mostly C's) 3
Below average (mostly D's). 4
Low (mostly E's or F's) 5

52. Could you have chosen to be in a harder English class in your present grade if you had wanted to?

(Circle one number.)

Yes 1
No 2
Don't know 3
In hardest class already 4
All English classes the same 5

53. How would you rate yourself in reading ability?

(Circle one number.)

Well below average 1
Slightly below average 2
Average 3
Slightly above average 4
Well above average 5

54. Have you ever had to repeat a year in school because you failed?

(Circle one number.)

Yes 1
No 2

55. How important is each of the following to you?

(Circle one number on each line.)

	Not Important	Fairly Important	Very Important
a. What teachers think about you	1	2	3

b. The grade you get at school 1	2	3	
c. Being a leader in school activities 1	2	3	
d. What the other students at school			
think about you 1	2	3	

56. How much do you agree or disagree with each of the following statements?

(Circle one number on each line.)

	Agree	Undecided	Disagree
a. The principal is doing a good job 1	2	3	
b. The teachers are friendly 1	2	3	
c. The principal runs the school with			
a firm hand 1	2	3	
d. The teachers are doing a good job. 1	2	3	
e. The principal gets out of his office			
and talks with the students 1	2	3	
f. The principal is tough and strict 1	2	3	
g. The principal is fair 1	2	3	
h. The principal is friendly. 1	2	3	

57. How often is each of the following statements true of your school?

(Circle one number on each line.)

	Almost Never	Sometimes	Almost Always
a. Students help decide how courses			
are taught 1	2	3	
b. Students can rate the teachers 1	2	3	
c. If the school does something wrong			
and a group of students complain,			
they can get a fair deal 1	2	3	
d. Students have a say in making			
school rules 1	2	3	

58. What kind of television program do you like best?

(Circle one number.)

Comedies 1
Sports 2
Police or detective shows 3
Love stories 4
Other kinds of shows (What kinds?)
_____ 5

59. If some other students here tore up things in a classroom at night and you knew who did it, what would you do?

(Circle all that apply.)

a. Tell your friends 1
b. Tell your parents 2
c. Tell a teacher or the principal. 3
d. Agree with the students who did it 4
e. Do nothing 5
f. Do something else (What?)
_____ 6

60. How do you feel about each of the following ideas?

(Circle one number on each line.)

	Agree	Undecided	Disagree
a. People who leave things around			
deserve it if their things get taken 1	2	3	

b. Taking things from stores doesn't
   hurt anyone 1   2   3
c. People who get beat up usually
   asked for it 1   2   3
d. If you want to get ahead, you
   can't always be honest 1   2   3

61. Would you do any of the following things if you knew you could get away with it?

(Circle one number on each line.)

	No	It Depends	Yes
a. Cheat on a test	1	2	3
b. Spray paint on school walls	1	2	3
c. Take money from other students	1	2	3
d. Skip school	1	2	3

62. If you got into serious trouble at school with the teachers, how often would your parents do the following?

(Circle one number on each line.)

	Almost Never	Sometimes	Almost Always
a. Listen to your side	1	2	3
b. Agree with you	1	2	3
c. Come to school to take your side	1	2	3
d. Punish you	1	2	3

63. Who would you go to <u>first</u> if you needed help with a personal problem?

(Circle one number.)

A school counselor 1
A teacher 2
Parents 3
Brother or sister 4
Someone else (Who?)
_____ 5

64. How do you feel about each of the following ideas?

(Circle one number on each line.)

	Agree	Undecided	Disagree
a. Every time I try to get ahead, something or someone stops me	1	2	3
b. If I study hard, I will get good grades	1	2	3
c. If I plan things right, they will come out O.K.	1	2	3

65. What do you <u>want to do most</u> in the year after you leave high school?

(Circle one number.)

Go to college 1
Go to business or trade school 2
Join the armed forces 3
Get a job 4
Get married 5
Something else (What?)
_____ 6
I don't know 7

66. How much is school helping you get ready for what you want to do after high school?

(Circle one number.)

Very much 1
Some 2
A little 3
Not at all 4
I don't know what I want to do
    after high school 5

67. What do you <u>expect</u> you will actually do in the year after high school?

(Circle as many as apply.)

Go to college 1
Go to business or trade school 2
Join the armed forces 3
Get a job 4
Get married 5
Something else (What?)
_____ 6

68. If a school had a problem with personal attacks, theft, and property destruction, what could be done to make it safer?

_____

_____

_____

69. Do you have any comments on the questions in this booklet?

_____

_____

Please check back to make sure you have answered every question.

Thank you for your help with this study.

APPENDIX A
(Continued)

SAFE SCHOOL STUDY

National Institute of Education

TEACHER QUESTIONNAIRE

This study has been mandated by the U.S. Congress and is being conducted by the Research Triangle Institute for the National Institute of Education.

We are asking principals, teachers, and students in schools across the country to tell us their experiences with vandalism, personal attacks, and theft in schools. Each group has its own perspective on the problem and its own particular concerns. The information provided by teachers like you is crucial to understanding the nature and extent of this problem in schools.

Your participation in this study is **voluntary** and you have the right not to respond to certain or all of the questions in this questionnaire. However, RTI would like to stress that your participation is important to the validity and success of the study and we encourage your full cooperation.

THE INFORMATION YOU FURNISH IN THIS QUESTIONNAIRE WILL BE TREATED CONFIDENTIALLY AND NEVER LINKED TO YOU PERSONALLY. NO NAMES OF INDIVIDUALS, SCHOOLS, DISTRICTS OR STATES WILL BE USED IN ANY REPORTS. THE ID NUMBER IN THE UPPER CORNER OF THE QUESTIONNAIRE IS USED ONLY SO THAT INFORMATION FROM VARIOUS SOURCES CAN BE COMBINED FOR PURPOSES OF ANALYSIS.

PLEASE TRY TO COMPLETE THE QUESTIONNAIRE AS SOON AS POSSIBLE AND RETURN IT TO THE LOCATION INDICATED BY THE SCHOOL PRINCIPAL. WITHIN THE NEXT 24 HOURS, PLACE THE COMPLETED QUESTIONNAIRE IN THE ENVELOPE AND DROP IT IN THE BALLOT BOX. THEN MARK OFF YOUR NAME ON THE ROSTER NEXT TO THE BALLOT BOX.

FOR OFFICE USE ONLY

Response Code _____

215

Read carefully each question you answer. It is important that you follow the directions for responding, which are:

- (Circle one number.)
- (Circle as many as apply.)
- (Circle one number on each line.)
- (Circle one number for each item.)
- (Circle one number for each month.)

Sometimes you are asked to fill in a blank—in these cases, simply write your response on the line provided.

PART I
Background Information

1. How many years have you taught full-time?   _____
                                                                                     years

2. How many years have you been teaching in this school?

                                                        (Circle one number.)

                        Less than 1 year 1
                        1 to 4 years 2
                        5 to 9 years 3
                        10 to 14 years 4
                        15 or more years 5

3. Are you:

        (Circle one number.)

            Male 1
            Female 2

4. When were you born?

                                                        (Circle one number.)

                        Before 1920 1
                        1920 - 1929 2
                        1930 - 1939 3
                        1940 - 1949 4
                        1950 or later 5

5. Circle the number that best describes you.

                                                             (Circle one number.)

        American Indian or Alaskan Native 1
        Asian-American or Pacific Islander (Chinese, Japanese, Hawaiian, etc.) 2
        Spanish-American (Mexican, Puerto Rican, Cuban, or other Latin American) . . 3
        Black or Afro-American or Negro (other than Spanish-American) 4
        White (other than Spanish-American) 5
        Other (specify) _____ 6

6. What is the highest level of education you have attained?

                                                        (Circle one number.)

                        Some college or less 1
                        Bachelor's degree 2
                        Some graduate courses 3
                        Master's degree 4
                        Courses beyond the master's degree 5
                        Doctor's degree 6
                        Other (specify)_____ 7

7. How much in-service training have you had in each of these areas in the last 24 months?

(Circle one number on each line.)

		None	About A Half Day	1-2 Days	3-4 Days	5 Days or More
a.	Teaching methods or curriculum content	1	2	3	4	5
b.	Interpersonal or intergroup relations	1	2	3	4	5

8. In what school program do you do most of your teaching?

(Circle one number.)

College preparatory or academic 1
General 2
Commercial or business 3
Music or art 4
Trade or industrial arts 5
Agricultural 6
Special education 7
Physical education 8
Other (specify) _____ 9

9. Within an average week, how many different students do you teach ?   _____
number

10. At what grade level(s) do you currently teach?

(Circle as many as apply.)

Kindergarten 0	Grade 7 7
Grade 1 1	Grade 8 8
Grade 2 2	Grade 9 9
Grade 3 3	Grade 10 10
Grade 4 4	Grade 11 11
Grade 5 5	Grade 12 12
Grade 6 6	

PART II

Personal Safety

11. In your opinion, how much of a problem are vandalism, personal attacks and theft in the neighborhood surrounding your school?

(Circle one number.)

None or Almost None	A Little	Some	Fairly Much	Very Much
1	2	3	4	5

12. At your school during school hours how safe from vandalism, personal attacks and theft is each of the following places?

(Circle one number on each line.)

		Very Unsafe	Fairly Unsafe	Average	Fairly Safe	Very Safe	Does Not Apply
a.	Your classroom while teaching . . .	1	2	3	4	5	9
b.	Empty classrooms	1	2	3	4	5	9
c.	Hallways and stairs	1	2	3	4	5	9
d.	The cafeteria	1	2	3	4	5	9
e.	Restrooms used by students	1	2	3	4	5	9
f.	Lounges or restrooms used by teachers	1	2	3	4	5	9
g.	Locker room or gym	1	2	3	4	5	9
h.	Parking lot	1	2	3	4	5	9
i.	Elsewhere outside on school grounds	1	2	3	4	5	9

13. Did anyone take things directly from you by force, weapons, or threats at school in:

(Circle one number for each month. If "yes" answer
follow-up questions a and b.)

NOVEMBER   1   No

2   Yes →   a. How many times did this involve
losses of $10 or less?   _____

b. How many times did this involve   number
losses of more than $10?   _____
                                              number

OCTOBER   1   No

2   Yes →   a. How many times did this involve
losses of $10 or less?   _____

b. How many times did this involve   number
losses of more than $10?   _____
                                              number

14. Did anyone steal things of yours from your desk, coat closet, or other place at school in:

(Circle one number for each month. If "yes" answer
follow-up questions a, b, and c.)

NOVEMBER   1   No

2   Yes →   a. How many times did this involve
thefts of less than $1?   _____

b. How many times did this involve   number
thefts of $1 to $10?   _____

c. How many times did this involve   number
thefts of more than $10?   _____
                                              number

OCTOBER   1   No

2   Yes →   a. How many times did this involve
thefts of less than $1?   _____

b. How many times did this involve   number
thefts of $1 to $10?   _____

c. How many times did this involve   number
thefts of more than $10?   _____
                                              number

15. Were you a victim of rape or attempted rape at school in:

(Circle one number for each month. If "yes" answer
follow-up questions a and b.)

NOVEMBER   1   No

2   Yes →   a. How many times were you a victim
of rape?   _____

b. How many times were you a victim   number
of attempted rape?   _____
                                              number

OCTOBER   1   No

2   Yes →   a. How many times were you a victim
of rape?   _____

b. How many times were you a victim   number
of attempted rape?   _____
                                              number

**16. Did anyone physically attack and hurt you (not including rape
or rape attempts reported in Question 15) at school in:**

(Circle one number for each month. If "yes" answer
follow-up questions a and b.)

NOVEMBER   1   No

2   Yes →   a. How many times were you attacked
and hurt so badly that you saw a
doctor?   _____

b. How many times were you attacked   number
and hurt but not so badly that you
saw a doctor?   _____
                                              number

OCTOBER   1   No

                 2   Yes   →   a.   How many times were you attacked and hurt so badly that you saw a doctor?

                                 b.   How many times were you attacked and hurt but <u>not</u> badly enough that you saw a doctor?

                                                 number

                                                 number

IF YOU ANSWERED "NO" TO ALL OF THE ABOVE INCIDENTS (QUESTIONS 13-16) CIRCLE "10" IN THE LIST BELOW AND GO TO QUESTION 19.

17. If you answered "yes" to one or more of the above questions, 13-16, think back to the <u>most recent or only thing</u> that happened to you and circle the number or numbers below which describe that incident.

                                                      (Circle as many as apply.)

Took something directly from you worth $10 or less 1

Took something directly from you worth more than $10 2

Stole something of yours worth less than $1 3

Stole something of yours worth $1 - $10 4

Stole something of yours worth more than $10 5

Raped you 6

Attempted to rape you 7

Hurt you so badly that you saw a doctor 8

Hurt you, but <u>not</u> so badly that you saw a doctor 9

Nothing happened (GO TO QUESTION 19) 10

18. Please answer the following questions about the <u>most recent or only thing</u> that has happened to you in OCTOBER or NOVEMBER.

                                                      (Circle one number.)

a. How many people did it?

One 1
Two 2
Three or more 3
Don't know 4

b. How many were current students at this school?

None 0
One 1
Two 2
Three or more 3
Don't know 4

c. How many were other school-age youths?

None 0
One 1
Two 2
Three or more 3
Don't know 4

d. How many were males?

None 0
One 1
Two 2
Three or more 3
Don't know 4

e. How many were of the same race as you?

None 0
One 1
Two 2
Three or more 3
Don't know 4

f. Where did this incident take place?

Hallway or stairs 1
Your classroom during classes 2
Empty classroom 3
An office 4

A storeroom 5
Student restroom 6
Gym, locker room, or athletic field 7
Parking lot 8
Elsewhere on school ground 9
Other place (specify)_____ 10

(Circle as many as apply.)

g.   To whom did you report this incident?   Principal's Office or head of department . 1
School security division 2
Police 3
Other teachers 4
Other (specify) _____ 5

Did not report this incident 6

(Circle one number.)

h.   If you did not report it to the principal,   Too small or common to matter 1
head of school security division, or   No evidence or proof 2
police department, why was this?   They would not have done anything
about it 3
Took care of it myself 4
My own fault that this incident occurred . 5
Other reasons (specify) _____ 6

Incident was reported 7

i.   If something was taken directly from
you or stolen in this incident: a.   What was it? _____

b.   What would it cost to replace it?

19. In October did any students swear at you or make obscene remarks or gestures to you?

(Circle one number.)

Never 1
Once or twice 2
A few times 3
Many times 4

20. In October how many times did any students threaten to hurt you?

(Circle one number.)

Never 1
Once or twice 2
A few times 3
Many times 4

21. In October how many times did you hesitate to confront misbehaving students for fear of your own safety?

(Circle one number.)

Never 1

```
Once or twice  . . . . . . . . . . . . . 2
A few times   . . . . . . . . . . . . . 3
Many times    . . . . . . . . . . . . . 4
```

PART III
Student Conduct

22. In your dealing with misbehaving students how often do you do the following things?

(Circle one number on each line.)

		Never	Seldom	Sometimes	Often	Very Often
a.	Send them out of class	1	2	3	4	5
b.	Give additional school work	1	2	3	4	5
c.	Use or threaten to use physical punishment	1	2	3	4	5
d.	Lower their grades if it is repeated .	1	2	3	4	5
e.	Give privileges to increase positive involvement	1	2	3	4	5
f.	Ignore it when students talk back . .	1	2	3	4	5

23. During an average week, how many hours <u>at school</u> do you spend on the following?

a. Administrative and clerical tasks (grading papers, filling out forms, etc.) . . . . _____
   hours

b. Preparation and planning . . . . _____
   hours

c. Supervisory duties outside class . . . . _____
   hours

d. Teaching students . . . . _____
   hours

24. At your school, how is each of the following measures determined—by a specific administrative rule, a general policy to be interpreted by the teacher, by individual teachers setting their own policies, or is it not possible to say?

(Circle one number on each line.)

		Specific Administrative Rule	General Policy Interpreted By Teacher	Individual Teacher Sets Own Policy	Not Possible To Say
a.	Deciding on standards for passing and failing	1	2	3	9
b.	Controlling classroom disorder . . .	1	2	3	9
c.	Dealing with serious behavior problems (e.g., fighting, disobedience, etc.)	1	2	3	9
d.	Discussing matters about students with parents	1	2	3	9

25. How much does each of the following statements describe your school?

(Circle one number on each line.)

		Not At All	A Little	Fairly Much	Very Much
a.	All students are treated equally . . .	1	2	3	4
b.	Students have a say about how this school is run	1	2	3	4

		Not Well	Fairly Well	Very Well	Does Not Apply
c.	Parents have a say about how this school is run	1	2	3	4
d.	Counselors give me advice about handling misbehaving students . . .	1	2	3	4

26. In your opinion, how well do the following groups get along at your school?

(Circle one number on each line.)

		Not Well	Fairly Well	Very Well	Does Not Apply
a.	Students of different races	1	2	3	9
b.	Students of different nationality backgrounds	1	2	3	9
c.	Students of different socioeconomic groups	1	2	3	9
d.	Teachers and students	1	2	3	
e.	Teachers and administrators	1	2	3	
f.	Parents and teachers	1	2	3	

27. How much do you disagree or agree with each of the following statements?

(Circle one number on each line.)

		Strongly Disagree	Disagree	Undecided	Agree	Strongly Agree
a.	Schools should have rules about the way students can dress	1	2	3	4	5
b.	It is all right for schools to suspend students without a hearing	1	2	3	4	5
c.	If students are in a fist fight, let them settle it themselves	1	2	3	4	5
d.	If students use drugs around school, it is their own business	1	2	3	4	5
e.	Students should have a lot to say about how this school is run	1	2	3	4	5
f.	Parents should have a lot to say about how this school is run	1	2	3	4	5
g.	I want to keep on teaching the kind of students I have now	1	2	3	4	5
h.	I want to continue teaching at this school rather than move	1	2	3	4	5

28. How well does your school supply you with the materials and equipment you need for teaching?

(Circle one number.)

Not well at all 1
A little 2
Fairly well 3
Very well 4

29. How well do each of the following characteristics describe the principal of your building?

(Circle one number on each line.)

		Not At All	A Little	Fairly Well	Very Well
a.	Friendly	1	2	3	4
b.	Fair	1	2	3	4
c.	Permissive	1	2	3	4
d.	Informal	1	2	3	4
e.	Shares decision-making	1	2	3	4

PART IV
Student Characteristics and Teaching Practices

30. **What is the average number of students in the classes you teach?** _____
number

31. **Of the students you teach, about what percent are:**

(Write in percentages; answers should total 100%)

American Indian or Alaskan Native . . . .   _____%

Asian-American or Pacific Islander (Chinese, Japanese, Hawaiian, etc.) . . . .   _____%

Spanish-American (Mexican, Puerto Rican, Cuban, or other Latin American) . . . . . .   _____%

Black or Negro (other than Spanish American) . . . .   _____%

White (other than Spanish-American) . . . .   _____%

Other (specify) . . . .   _____%
100%

32. a.   **Of the students you teach, what percentage would you say are:**

(Write in percentages; answers should total 100%)

    a.   High ability. . . . .   _____%

    b.   Average ability . . . .   _____%

    c.   Low ability . . . .   _____%
100%

   b.   **Of the students you teach how many are:**

(Write in number.)

    a.   Underachievers . . . .   _____
students

    b.   Behavior problems . . . .   _____
students

    c.   Genuinely interested in school . . .   _____
students

33. **Answer each of the following questions by filling in the blank with the appropriate number.**

(Write in number. If none write in "0".)

   a.   Each month, on the average, how many students discuss their personal problems
with you? . . . .   _____
students

   b.   Each month, on the average, how many students do you send to the principal or
assistant principal's office for discipline? . . . .   _____
students

   c.   How many hours each month, on the average, do you spend with students on
school athletic and extra-curricular activities? . . . .   _____
hours

   d.   How many hours each month on the average do you spend outside of class helping
students with school work? . . . .   _____
hours

34. **How often do you give different students in the same class continuing assignments at different levels?**

(Circle one number.)

Often 1
Sometimes 2
Never 3

35. **Which one of the following do you emphasize most?**

(Circle one number.)

Teaching basic subjects and skills 1
Helping students develop good character 2
Preparing students for later jobs 3
Preparing students for college 4
Keeping control in class 5

Developing student interest in learning 6
Developing respect for other races and nationalities 7

36. Which one of the following does your principal emphasize most?

(Circle one number.)

Teaching basic subjects and skills 1
Helping students develop good character 2
Preparing students for later jobs 3
Preparing students for college 4
Keeping control in class 5
Developing student interest in learning 6
Developing respect for other races and nationalities 7

37. In your opinion, how important are the following in deciding whether students take your courses?

(Circle one number on each line.)

		Of Little Importance	Moderately Important	Very Important
a.	Student's desires	1	2	3
b.	Student's grades	1	2	3
c.	Student's test scores	1	2	3
d.	Parent's desires	1	2	3
e.	Teacher's evaluation	1	2	3

38. How often does each of the following occur at your school?

(Circle one number on each line.)

		Never	Occasion-ally	About Half The Time	Most of The Time	Always
a.	Teachers are provided with up-to-date information on problem students by the school's administration	1	2	3	4	5
b.	Teachers hear about problem students from other teachers	1	2	3	4	5
c.	Teachers maintain control in class .	1	2	3	4	5
d.	Outsiders can go anywhere in this school without being stopped	1	2	3	4	5
e.	Adults monitor the halls between classes including teachers, other staff, or parents	1	2	3	4	5
f.	Parent volunteers are at school during the school day	1	2	3	4	5

39. Following are 10 statements about schools, teachers, and pupils. Please indicate your personal opinion about each statement by circling the appropriate number at the right of each statement.

		Strongly Disagree	Disagree	Undecided	Agree	Strongly Agree
a.	Pupils are usually not capable of solving their problems through logical reasoning	1	2	3	4	5
b.	Beginning teachers are not likely to maintain strict enough control over their pupils	1	2	3	4	5
c.	The best principal gives unquestioning support to teachers in disciplining pupils	1	2	3	4	5
d.	It is justifiable to have pupils learn many facts about subjects even if they have no immediate application .	1	2	3	4	5

e.	Being friendly with pupils often leads them to become too familiar	1	2	3	4	5
f.	Student governments are a good "safety valve" but should not have much influence on school policy ..	1	2	3	4	5
g.	If a pupil uses obscene or profane language in school, it must be considered a moral offense	1	2	3	4	5
h.	A few pupils are just young hoodlums and should be treated accordingly..............	1	2	3	4	5
i.	A pupil who destroys school material or property should be severely punished	1	2	3	4	5
j.	Pupils often misbehave in order to make the teacher look bad	1	2	3	4	5

40. What measures would you recommend to schools having problems with vandalism, personal attacks, and theft?

_____

_____

_____

_____

_____

_____

_____

_____

_____

THANK YOU FOR YOUR HELP ON THIS STUDY!

Item Content of the Scales

A list of questionnaire items used to form composites described in the body of the report is provided here. Scales are listed in alphabetical order. All items are from the phase II student, teacher, or principal questionnaires, and are designated S, T, or P, accordingly. The numbers and lower case letters refer to the specific items in the corresponding questionnaires. These questionnaires are reproduced in Appendix A. Items are scored with appropriate sign (refer to the factor analysis results in the body of the report).

Ambiguous Sanctions
    T22d, T22f
Belief in Conventional Social Rules
    S60a, S60b, S60c, S60d, S61b, S61c
Clear Sanctions
    P31b, T22b, T22c, T22e
College Preparation
    T35 (percent choosing alternative 4), T36 (alternative 4), T33d (senior high only), T34 (senior high only), P58 (senior high only)
College vs. Job Orientation
    S45a, S47 (alternative 4), S49, S50, S65 (alternatives 1 and 4), S67 (alternatives 1, 4, and 5), S48 (alternatives 3 and 4)
Community Crime
    P68, S25, S26, S27, T11 (Note: In the analyses reported in Chapter 10, the teacher item was dropped when the criterion was teacher victimization, and the student items were dropped when the criterion was student victimization.)
Delinquent Youth Culture
    S14d, S15a, S15b, S15c, S15d, S59c, S59e, S61a, S61d
Democratic Orientation
    T27e, T27f
Desegregation
    P64a, P64b, P62/P48, Absolute value (50% − percentage of students white)

Firm and Clear Enforcement
    S12d, S12e, S13a, S13b, S56c, S56f
Good Principal
    S56a, S56e, S56g, S56h
Good Teachers
    S56b, S56d
Isolation and Referral
    P31a, P31f, P31g, P31h, P32 (all relative to school enrollment)
Overall Disruption
    P26e, T13, T14, T15, T16, T19, T20, T21, S18, S19, S20, S21, S18, S19,
    S20, S21, S22, S23
Parental Education and Self-Reported Ability
    S30, S33, S35, S53
Parent–Student Influence
    T25b, T25c
Peer and Nonacademic Ties
    S6a, S6b, S6c (senior high only), S6e, S10b, S40, S45f, S55b, S55d (senior
    high only)
Perceived Fairness and Clarity of Rules
    S12a, S12b, S12c, S13c, S45d, S56g
Policy Confusion
    T24a, T24b, T24c, T24d (percent replying not possible to say)
Principal Intervention
    T22a, T33b, P31 (relative to enrollment)
Punishment Orientation
    T27b, T39b, T39h, T39i
Race Relations
    S43a, S43b, S44a
School Attachment
    S8, S10a, S10c, S10d (senior high only), S45b, S45e, S45g, S46c, S46d, S47
    (alternatives 2, 4, and 5), S50 (junior high only), S55a, S55b (junior high
    only), S66
Security Measures
    P17a, P17c, P18a, P18b, P18c, P18d, P18e, P20b, P20c, P20d, P20f (Note:
    Items based on P20 refer to school days only)
    Social and Educational Disadvantage
    P51, P52e, P56, average of percentage of students white according to
    aggregated student (S3) and teacher (T31) reports, average of percentage of
    students Spanish-American according to aggregated student (S3) and
    teacher (T31) reports, S29, S31
Strict Principal
    S56c, S56f
Student Influence
    S12f, S14e, S46a, S57a, S57b, S57c, S57d
Student Victimization
    S19, S20, S21, S22, S23

Teacher–Administration Cooperation
    T25a, T25d, T26e, T38a
Teacher Culture
    T33a, T38b
Teacher Victimization
    T13, T14, T15, T16, T19, T20, T21
Vocational vs. Basic Skills Climate
    T34 (senior high only), T35 (alternatives 1 and 3), T36 (alternatives 1 and 3), T39d (senior high only), P59 (senior high only)

References

Adorno, T. W., Frenkel-Brunswick, E., Levinson, D. J., & Sanford, R. N. *The authoritarian personality*. New York: Harper, 1950.

Alinsky, S. *Rules for radicals*. New York: Random House, 1971.

Alwin, D. F. *Structural equation models of contextual effects*. Paper prepared for a conference on Methodology for Aggregating Data in Educational Research, L. Burstein & M. T. Hannon, organizers, Stanford University, October 1976.

Alwin, D. F., & Hauser, R. M. The decomposition of effects in path analysis. *American Sociological Review*, 1975, 40, 37–47.

Andrews, I. (Chair). *Oversight hearing on Safe School Study*. Hearing before the Subcommittee on Economic Opportunity of the Committee on Education and Labor, House of Representatives, 24 January 1978. Washington, D.C.: U.S. Government Printing Office, 1978.

Antunes, G. E., Cook, F. L., Cook, T. D., & Skogan, W. G. *Patterns of personal crime against the elderly: Findings from a national survey*. Unpublished manuscript, University of Houston, no date (1977 or later).

Atkeson, B. M., & Forehand, R. Home-based reinforcement programs designed to modify classroom behavior. *Psychological Bulletin*, 1979, 86, 1298–1308.

Bahner, J. M. Testimony at the oversight hearing on American secondary education. In *Hearings before the Subcommittee on Elementary, Secondary, and Vocational Education, U.S. House of Representatives*. Washington, DC: U.S. Government Printing Office, 1980.

Baldwin, J. Ecological and areal studies in Great Britain and the United States. In N. Morris & M. Tonry (Eds.), *Crime and justice: An annual review of research* (Vol. 1). Chicago: University of Chicago Press, 1979.

Barker, R. *Ecological psychology*. Stanford, Calif.: Stanford University Press, 1968.

Barth, R. Home-based reinforcement of school behavior: A review and analysis. *Review of Educational Research*, 1979, 49, 436–458.

Beasley, R. W., & Antunes, G. The etiology of urban crime: An ecological analysis. *Criminology*, 1974, 11, 439–461.

Bechtel, R. B. Undermanning theory. In D. H. Carson (Ed.), *Proceedings of the Environmental Design and Research Association--5*. Stroubsburg, Pa.: Dowden, Hutchinson & Ross, 1974.

Berg, I. *Education and jobs: The great training robbery*. Boston: Beacon Press, 1971.

Bidwell, C. E., & Kasarda, J. D. School district organization and student achievement. *American Sociological Review*, 1975, *40*, 55–70.

Biderman, A., Johnson, L., McIntyre, J., & Weir, A. *Report on a pilot study in the District of Columbia on victimization and attitudes toward law enforcement. Field surveys*. Washington, D.C.: U.S. Government Printing Office, 1967.

Blau, P. M., & Duncan, O. D. *The American occupational structure*. New York: Wiley, 1967.

Blalock, H. M. *Causal inferences in non-experimental research*. Chapel Hill: University of North Carolina Press, 1964.

Block, R. Community, environment, and violent crime. *Criminology*, 1979, *17*(1), 46–57.

Boesel, D. P. *Political factors in the initiation of the NIE safe school study*. Paper presented at the American Psychological Association Convention, Toronto, August 1978.

Boggs, S. L. Urban crime patterns. *American Sociological Review*, 1965, *30*, 899–908.

Bollen, K. A., & Ward, S. Ratio variables in aggregate data analyses: Their uses, problems, and alternatives. *Sociological Methods and Research*, 1979, 7(4), 431–450.

Bordua, D. J. Juvenile delinquency and "anomie": An attempt at replication. *Social Problems*, 1958–59 (sic), *6*, 230–238.

Brophy, J. Successful teaching strategies for the inner-city child. *Phi Delta Kappan*, 1982, *63*, 527–530.

Burack, R., & Downing, D. *Schools initiative evaluation technical report* (Prepared under National Institute for Juvenile Justice and Delinquency Prevention grants nos. 77-NI-99-0012 and 78-JN-AX-0016). San Rafael, CA: Social Action Research Center, 1980.

Cabinet Council on Human Resources Working Group on School Violence/ Discipline. *Disorder in our public schools* (Memorandum to the Cabinet Council on Human Resources). Washington, DC: The White House, 1984.

Carnegie Council on Policy Studies in Higher Education. *Giving youth a better chance*. San Francisco: Jossey-Bass, 1979.

Chase-Dunn, C. K., Meyer, J. W., & Inverarity, J. *State formation and the expansion of the autonomy of youth: The problems of order in secondary schools*. Unpublished paper, Johns Hopkins University, Center for Metroplitan Planning and Research, September 1977.

Chilton, R. J. Continuity in delinquency area research: A comparison of studies for Baltimore, Detroit, and Indianapolis. *American Sociological Review*, 1964, *29*, 71–83.

Chilton, R. J., & Dussich, J. P. J. Methodological issues in delinquency reseach: Some alternative analyses of geographically distributed data. *Social Forces*, 1974, *53*, 73–82.

City schools in crisis. *Newsweek*, September 12, 1977, pp. 62–64; 67–68; 70.

Cohen, A. J. *Delinquent boys*. New York: Free Press, 1955.

Cohen, L. E., & Felson, M. Social change and crime rate trends: A routine activity approach. *American Sociological Review*, 1979, *44*, 588–608.

Coleman, J. S., Campbell, E. Q., Hobson, C. J., McPartland, J. M., Mood, A., Weinfeld, F. D., & York, R. L. *Equality of educational opportunity*. Washington, D.C.: U.S. Government Printing Office, 1966.

Coleman, J. S., Hoffer, T., & Kilgore, S. *High school achievement: Public, Catholic, and private schools compared*. New York: Basic, 1982.

Cook, T. D., & Campbell, D. T. The design and conduct of quasi-experiments and true experiments in field settings. In M. D. Dunnette (Ed.), *Handbook of industrial and organizational psychology*. Chicago: Rand McNally, 1976.

Cook, F. L., & Cook, T. D. Evaluating the rhetoric of crisis: A case study of criminal victimization of the elderly. *Social Service Review*, 1976, *50*(4), 632–646.

Crain, R. L., & Mahard, R. E. How desegregation orders may improve minority academic achievement. *Harvard Civil Rights Civil Liberties Law Review*, 1982, *16*, 693–733.

Crain, R. L., & Wu, S. C. *The role of the school in determining school crime rates*. Paper presented at the American Psychological Association Convention, Toronto, August 1978.

Currence, C. Discipline codes must foster balance of order, autonomy (Interview with Henry S. Lufler, Jr.). *Education Week*, 18 January 1984, pp. 8, 18.

Daily, C. A. *The assessment of lives*. San Francisco: Jossey Bass, 1971.

David, R. L. & Lincoln, A. J. School crime power, and the student subculture. In E. Wenk & N. Harlow (Eds.), *School crime and disruption: Prevention models*. Washington, D.C.: National Institute of Education, 1978.

Davis, N. J. *Sociological construction of deviance*. Dubuque, Iowa: Brown, 1975.

Decker, S. H. Official crime rates and victim surveys: An empirical comparison. *Journal of Criminal Justice*, 1977, *5*, 47–54.

DiPrete, T. A. *Discipline and order in American high schools* (NCES 82–202). Washington, DC: National Center for Education Statistics, 1981.

Dixon, W. J., & Brown, M. B. *Biomedical computer programs, P-series*. Berkeley: University of California Press, 1977.

Draper, N. R., & Smith, H. *Applied regression analysis*. New York: Wiley, 1966.

Duncan, B. L. Differential social perception and attribution of intergroup violence: Testing the lower limits of stereotyping of blacks. *Journal of Personality and Social Psychology*, 1976, *34*, 590–598.

Educational Research Service School Research Forum. *Discipline in the public schools: Educator responses to the Reagan administration policies.* Arlington, VA: Educational Research Service, 1984.

Empey, L. T. *American delinquency.* Homewood, Ill.: Dorsey, 1978.

Emrich, R. L. The safe school study report to Congress: Evaluation and recommendations. *Crime and Delinquency*, 1978, *24*, 258–276.

England, R. W. A theory of middle-class juvenile delinquency. *Journal of Criminal Law, Criminology, and Police Science*, 1960, *50*, 535–540.

Ennis, P. *Criminal victimization in the United States. A report of a national survey. Field surveys II.* Washington, D.C.: U.S. Government Printing Office, 1967.

Featherman, D. L., & Hauser, R. M *Opportunity and change.* New York: Academic Press, 1978.

Feldman, K. A., & Newcomb, T. M. *The impact of college on students.* San Francisco: Jossey-Bass, 1969.

Ferguson, T. *The young delinquent in his social setting.* London: Oxford, 1952.

Firebaugh, G. *A rule for inferring individual-level relationships from aggregate data.* Unpublished manuscript, Department of Sociology and Anthropology, Vanderbilt University, 1979.

Gallup, G. H. Sixth annual Gallup poll of public attitudes toward education. *Phi Delta Kappan*, 1974, *56*, 20–32.

Gallup, G. H. The 16th annual Gallup poll of the public's attitudes toward the public schools. *Phi Delta Kappan*, 1984, *66*, 23–38.

Garbarino, J. The human ecology of school crime: A case for small schools. In E. Wenk & N Harlow (Eds.), *School crime and disruption: Prevention models.* Washington, D.C.: National Institute of Education, 1978.

Gold, M. Scholastic experiences, self-esteem, and delinquent behavior: A theory for alternative schools. *Crime and Delinquency*, 1978, *24*, 290–308.

Gold, M., & Moles, O. C. *Delinquency in schools and the community.* Paper presented at the meeting of the American Society of Criminology, Atlanta, November 1977.

Gold, M., & Reimer, D. J. Changing patterns of delinquent behavior among Americans 13 through 16 years old: 1967–72. *Crime and Delinquency Literature*, 1975, *1*, 483–517.

Gordon, R. A. Issues in the ecological study of delinquency. *American Sociological Review*, 1967, *32*, 927–944.

Gordon, R. A. Issues in multiple regression. *American Journal of Sociology*, 1968, *73*, 592–616.

Gottfredson, D. C. *Environmental change strategies to prevent school disruption.* Paper presented at the annual meeting of the American Psychological Association, Toronto, August, 1984.

Gottfredson, D. M., Neithercutt, M. G, Venezia, P. S., & Wenk, E. A. *A national uniform parole reporting system*. Davis, Calif.: National Council on Crime and Delinquency Research Center, 1970.

Gottfredson, G. D. Organizing crime: A classificatory scheme based on offense transitions. *Journal of Criminal Justice*, 1975, *3*, 321–332.

Gottfredson, G. D. Models and muddles: An ecological examination of high school crime rates. *Journal of Research in Crime and Delinquency*, 1979, *16*, 307–331.

Gottfredson, G. D. Schooling and delinquency. In S. E. Martin, L. B. Sechrest, & R. Redner (Eds.), *New directions in the rehabilitation of criminal offenders* (Report of the Panel on Research on Rehabilitative Techniques, National Reseach Council). Washington, D.C.: National Academy Press, 1981.

Gottfredson, G. D. (Ed.). *School Action Effectiveness Study: First interim report*. Baltimore: Johns Hopkins University, Center for Social Organization of Schools, 1982.

Gottfredson, G. D. Schooling and delinquency prevention: Some practical ideas for educators, parents, program developers, and researchers. *Journal of Child Care*, 1983, *1* (3), 51–64.

Gottfredson, G. D. Preventing repeat delinquency. In R. P. Gowen (Ed.), *Proceedings of the Conference on Juvenile Repeat Offenders* (pp. 121–136). College Park, MD: Institue for Criminal Justice and Criminology, University of Maryland, 1984. (a)

Gottfredson, G. D. Testimony before the Subcommittee on Elementary, Secondary, and Vocational Education, U.S. House of Representatives, 23 January 1984, on the topic of School Disorder. Pp. 3–45 in *Oversight on school discipline*. Washington, DC: U.S. Government Printing Office, 1984. (b)

Gottfredson, G. D. A theory-ridden approach to program evaluation: A method for researcher–implementer collaboration. *American Psychologist*, 1984, *39*, 1101–1112. (c)

Gottfredson, G. D. *Effective School Battery: User's manual*. Odessa, FL: Psychological Assessment Resources, 1985.

Gottfredson, G. D., Gottfredson, D. C., & Cook, M. S. (Eds.). *The School Action Effectiveness Study: Second interim report (Report No. 342)*. Baltimore: The Johns Hopkins University, Center for Social Organization of Schools, 1983.

Gottfredson, G. D., Rickert, D. E., Gottfredson, D. C., & Advani, N. *Standards for Program Development Evaluation plans. Psychological Documents*, 1984, *14*, 32 (Ms. No. 2668).

Gottfredson, M. R. *The classification of crimes and victims*. Unpublished doctoral dissertation, State University of New York at Albany, School of Criminal Justice, 1976.

Gottfredson, M. R., & Hindelang, M. J. Victims of personal crimes: A methodological disquistion. *Proceedings of the Social Statistics Section of the American Statistical Association*, 1975, pp. 178–184.

Gottfredson, M. R., & Hindelang, M. J. A consideration of telescoping and memory decay biases in victimization surveys. *Journal of Criminal Justice,* 1977, *5,* 205–216.

Gough, H. G. *Manual for the California Psychological Inventory.* Palo Alto, Calif.: Consulting Psychologists Press, 1964.

Gove, W. R., & Hughes, M. Reexamining the ecological fallacy: A study in which aggregate data are critical in investigating the pathological effects of living alone. *Social Forces,* 1980, *58,* 1157–1177.

Grant, G. Children's rights and adult confusions. *Public Interest,* 1982 (Fall).

Grant, J., Daniels, D., Neto, V., & Yamasaki, C. *School team approach phase I evaluation* (Prepared under National Institute for Juvenile Justice and Delinquency Prevention grants nos. 77-NI-99-0012 and 78-JN-AX-0016). San Rafael, CA: Social Action Research Center, 1979.

Greenberg, D. F. Delinquency and the age structure of society. *Contemporary Crisis,* 1977, *1,* 189–223.

Hadden, J. K., & Borgatta, E. F. *American cities: Their social characteristics.* Chicago: Rand McNally, 1965.

Hannan, N., & Burstein, L. Estimation for grouped observations. *American Sociological Review,* 1974, *39,* 374–392.

Hanushek, E. A., & Jackson, J. E. *Statistical methods for social scientists.* New York: Academic, 1977.

Harman, H. H. *Modern factor analysis.* Chicago: University of Chicago Press, 1967.

Harries, K. D. *The geography of crime and justice.* New York: McGraw-Hill, 1974.

Harries, K. D. Cities and crime: A geographic model. *Criminology,* 1976, *14,* 369–386.

Harvey, D. *Explanation in geography.* London: Arnold, 1969.

Hawley, A. H. *Human ecology: A theory of community structure.* New York: Ronald, 1950.

Help! Teacher can't teach? *Time,* June 16, 1980, pp. 54–63.

Hiatovsky, Y. Multicollinearity in regression analysis: A comment. *Review of Economics and Statistics,* 1969, *51*(4), 586–589.

High schools under fire. *Time,* November 14, 1977, pp. 62–75.

Hindelang, M. J., & Gottfredon, M. R. *A multivariate analysis of rates of personal victimization.* Unpublished manuscript, Criminal Justice Research Center, Albany, New York, 1976.

Hirschi, T. *Causes of delinquency.* Berkeley: University of California Press, 1969.

Hoerl, A. E., & Kennard, R. W. Ridge regression: Biased estimation for nonorthogonal problems. *Technometrics,* 1970, *12(1),* 55–82.

Hollifield, J. H. Safe school study describes problems, points to potential solutions. *Educational R. &. D. Report,* 1978, *1,* 1–3. (Published by Council for Educational Development and Research, Washington, D. C.)

Howard, E. R. *School discipline desk book.* West Nyack, N.Y.: Parker, 1978.

How safe are the nation's schools? *Hypotenuse*, February 1978, pp.10–16.

Ianni, F. A. J. The social organization of the high school: School specific aspects of school crime. In E. Wenk & N. Harlow (Eds.), *School crime and disruption: Prevention models.* Washington, D.C.: National Institute of Education, 1978.

Janowitz, M. Where is the cutting edge of sociology? *Sociological Quarterly,* 1979, *20,* 591–593.

Jencks, C. *Who gets ahead? The determinants of economic success in America.* New York: Basic, 1977.

Johnson, G., Bird, T., & Little, J. W. *Delinquency prevention: Theories and strategies.* Washington, D.C.: U.S. Dept. of Justice, Office of Juvenile Justice and Delinquency Prevention, 1979.

Johnston, L. *The American high school: Its social system and effects.* Ann Arbor, Mich.: Institute for Social Research, 1973.

Jonassen, C. T., & Peres, S. H. *Interrelationships of dimensions of community systems: A factor analysis of eighty-two variables.* Columbus: Ohio State University Press, 1960.

Jöreskog, K. G. A general method for estimating a linear structural equation system. In A. S. Goldberger & O. D. Duncan (Eds.), *Structural equation models in the social sciences.* New York: Seminar Press, 1973.

Jöreskog, K. G., & Sörbom, D. *LISREL IV: Analysis of linear structural relationships by the method of maximum likelihood.* Chicago: National Educational Resources, 1978.

Karweit, N. L., Fennessey, J., & Daiger, D. C. *Examining the credibility of offsetting contextual effects* (Report No. 150). Baltimore: Johns Hopkins University, Center for Social Organization of Schools, 1978.

Kelley, C. M. *Uniform crime reports for the United States.* Washington, D.C.: U.S. Government Printing Office, 1976.

Kelly, G. A. *The psychology of personal constructs.* New York: Norton, 1955.

Kerlinger, F. N., & Pedhazer, E. *Multiple regression in behavioral research.* New York: Holt, Rinehart, & Winston, 1973.

Kim, J. O. Factor analysis. In N. H. Nie, C. H. Hull, J. G. Jenkins, K. Steinbrenner, & D. H. Bent, *Statistical package for the social sciences.* New York: McGraw-Hill, 1975.

Kim, J. O., & Kohout, F. J. Multiple regression analysis: Subprogram regression. In N. H. Nie, C. H. Hull, J. G. Jenkins, K. Steinbrenner, & D. H. Bent, *Statistical package for the social sciences.* New York: McGraw-Hill, 1975. (a)

Kim, J. O., & Kohout, F. J. Special topics in general linear models. In N. H. Nie, C. H. Hull, J. G. Jenkins, K. Steinbrenner, & D. H. Bent, *Statistical package for the social sciences.* New York: McGraw-Hill, 1975. (b)

Kim, J. O., & Mueller, C. A. Standardized and unstandardized coefficients in causal analysis. *Sociological Methods and Research,* 1976, *4,* 423–438.

Kobrin, S. The Chicago area project—A 25-year assessment. *Annals of the American Academy of Political and Social Science,* 1959, *322,* 19–29.

Kvaraceus, W. C., & Miller, W. B. *Delinquent behavior: Culture and the individual*. Washington, D.C.: National Education Association, 1959.

Lander, B. *Toward an understanding of juvenile disruption*. New York: Columbia University Press, 1954.

Laub, J. H. Trends in serious juvenile crime. *Criminal Justice and Behavior*, 1983, *10*, 485–506.

Law Enforcement Assistance Administration. *San Jose methods test of known crime victims* (Statistics Technical Report No. 1). Washington, D.C.: Author, 1972.

Little, C. B. *Delinquent behavior and trouble with the police: An assessment of some competing explanations*. Unpublished manuscript, State University of New York at Cortland, 1979.

Liazos, A. School, alienation, and delinquency. *Crime and Delinquency*, 1978, *24*, 355–370.

Lord, F. M., & Novick, M. R. *Statistical theories of mental test scores*. Reading, MA: Addison-Wesley, 1968.

Mays, J. B. *Growing up in the city: A study of juvenile disruption in an urban neighborhood*. Liverpool: University Press of Liverpool, 1954.

McCord, J. A thirty-year follow-up of treatment effects. *American Psychologist*, 1978, *33*, 284–289.

McDermott, M. J., & Hindelang, M. J. *Criminal victimization in urban schools* (Analytic Report SD-VAD-15). Unpublished manuscript, Criminal Justice Research Center, Albany, New York, 1977.

McDill, E. L., & Rigsby, L. C. *Structure and process in secondary schools: The academic impact of educational climates*. Baltimore: Johns Hopkins University Press, 1973.

McPartland, J. M., & McDill, E. L. *The unique role of schools in the causes of youthful crime* (Report No. 216). Baltimore: Johns Hopkins University, Center for Social Organization of Schools, 1976.

McPartland, J. M., & McDill, E. L. *Violence in schools: Perspectives, programs, and positions*. Lexington, Mass.: Lexington, 1977.

Miller, W. B. Lower class culture as a generating milieu of gang delinquency. *Journal of Social Issues*, 1958, *14*, 5–19.

Mills, C. W. The professional ideology of social pathologists. *American Journal of Sociology*, 1943, *49*, 165–180.

Moles, O. C. *Trends in interpersonal crime in schools*. Paper presented at the annual meeting of the American Educational Research Association, Montreal, April 1983.

Moos, R. H., & Trickett, E. J. *Manual for the Classroom Climate Scale*. Palo Alto, Calif.: Consulting Psychologists Press, 1974.

National Commission on Excellence in Education. *A nation at risk: The imperative for educational reform*. Washington, D.C.: U.S. Department of Education, 1983.

National Conference on Prevention and Control of Juvenile Delinquency. *Report on housing and juvenile disruption*. Washington, D.C.: U.S. Government Printing Office, 1947.

National Council on Crime and Delinquency (Eds.). *Theoretical perspectives on school crime.* Hackensack, N.J.: National Council on Crime and Delinquency, 1978. (NTIS No. PB–279–529)

National Institute of Education. *Violent schools—Safe schools: The safe school study report to Congress.* Washington, D.C.: Author, 1978.

Nunnally, J. C. *Psychometric theory.* New York: McGraw-Hill, 1967.

Office of Juvenile Justice and Delinquency Prevention. *Program announcement: Prevention of delinquency through alternative education.* Washington, D.C.: Author, 1980.

Pearson, K. On a form of spurious correlation which may arise when indices are used in the measurement of organs. *Proceedings of the Royal Society of London,* 1897, *60,* 489–498.

Pence, E. C., & Taylor, R. B. Extending manning theory and exploring its limitations. Paper presented at the meeting of the American Psychological Association, Toronto, September 1978.

Peterson, P. L., & Walberg, H. J. *Research on teaching.* Berkeley, Calif.: McCutchan, 1979.

Polikoff, A. *Housing the poor: The case for heroism.* Cambridge, Mass.: Ballinger, 1978.

Polk, K., & Schafer, W. E. *Schools and delinquency.* Englewood Cliffs, N.J.: Prentice-Hall, 1972.

Pope, C. E. *Victimization rates and neighborhood characteristics: Some preliminary findings.* Paper presented at the meeting of the American Society of Criminology, Dallas, 1978.

Price, B. Ridge regression: Application to nonexperimental data. *Psychological Bulletin,* 1977, *84,* 759–766.

Quetelet, L. A. J. *A treatise on man and the development of his faculties* (R. Knox, trans.). Gainesville, Florida: Scholars' Facsimiles & Reprints, 1969. (Originally published, 1842.)

Richards, J. M., Jr. *Human ecological techniques in the study of population-environment interactions.* Paper presented at the American Psychological Association Convention, Toronto, August 1978.

Richards, J. M., Jr. *Standardized vs. unstandardized regression coefficients: Once more into the breach.* Unpublished manuscript, Johns Hopkins University, Center for Social Organization of Schools, 1979.

Robinson, W. S. Ecological correlations and the behavior of individuals. *American Sociological Review,* 1950, *15,* 351–357.

Rockwell, R. C. Assessment of multicollinearity: The Haitovsky test of the determinant. *Sociological Methods and Research,* 1975, *3*(3), 308–319.

Ross, P. J., Bluestone, H., & Hines, F. K. *Indicators of social well-being for U.S. counties* (Rural Development Research Report No. 10). Washington, D.C.: U.S. Department of Agriculture, 1979.

Rotter, J. B. Generalized expectations for internal vs. external control. *Psychological Monographs,* 1966, *80.*

Rozeboom, W. W. Ridge regression: Bonanza or beguilement? *Psychological Bulletin,* 1979, *86*(2), 242–249.

Rubel, R. J. Analysis and critique of HEW's safe school study report to Congress. *Crime and Delinquency*, 1978, 24, 257–265.

Rutter, M., Maughan, B., Mortimore, P., & Ouston, J. *Fifteen thousand hours: Secondary schools and their effects on children*. Cambridge, Mass.: Harvard University Press, 1979.

Shaw, C. R. *Delinquency areas*. Chicago: University of Chicago Press, 1929.

Shaw, C. R., & McKay, H. D. *Juvenile delinquency in urban areas*. Chicago: University of Chicago Press, 1969.

Skolnick, J. H. *Justice without trial: Law enforcement in a democratic society* (2nd ed.). New York: Wiley, 1975.

Slavin, R. E. *Cooperative learning and the alterable elements of classroom instruction*. Paper presented at the meeting of the American Educational Research Association, New York, 1982.

Smith, D. M. *The geography of social well-being in the United States*. New York: McGraw-Hill, 1973.

Sokal, R. R. Classification: Purposes, principles, progress, prospects. *Science*, 1974, *185*, 1115–1123.

Spady, W. G. The authority system of the school and student unrest: A theoretical exploration. In C. W. Gordon (Ed.). *Uses of the sociology of education: The seventy-third yearbook of the National Society for the Study of Education* (Part II). Chicago: National Society for the Study of Education, 1974.

Sparks, R. F. *Research on victims of crime: Accomplishments, issues, and new directions* (ADM 82–1091). Washington, D.C.: U.S. Government Printing Office, 1982.

Stanley, J. C. Reliability. In R. L. Thorndike (Ed.), *Educational measurement*. Washington, D.C: American Council on Education, 1971.

Stinchcombe, A. L. *Rebellion in a high school*, Chicago: Quadrangle, 1964.

Toby, J. Crime in American public schools. *Public Interest*, 1980, *58* (Winter), 18–42.

Toby, J. Crime in the schools. In J. Q. Willson (Ed.), *Crime and public policy*. San Francisco: ICS Press, 1983. (a)

Toby, J. Violence in school. In M. Tonry & N. Morris (Eds.), *Crime and justice: An annual review of research, Volume 4*. Chicago: University of Chicago Press, 1983. (b)

Tocqueville, A. de. *Democracy in America*. New York: Vintage Books, 1898/1945.

U.S. Bureau of the Census. *1970 Census users' guide*. Washington, D.C.: U.S. Government Printing Office, 1970.

U.S. Bureau of the Census. *National crime survey: Central cities sample—Five largest cities—Survey documentation*. Washington, D.C.: Author, 1974.

U.S. Bureau of the Census. *Census geography* (DAD No. 33). Washington, D.C.: U.S. Government Printing Office, 1978.

U.S. Department of Commerce. *Social indicators 1976*. Washington, D.C.: U.S. Government Printing Office, 1977.

U.S. House of Representatives. Committee on Education and Labor, Subcommittee on Economic Opportunity. *Oversight hearing on safe school study*. Washington, D.C.: U.S. Government Printing Office, 1978.

U.S. House of Representatives. *Oversight hearings on American secondary education* (Hearings before the Subcommittee on Elementary, Secondary, and Vocational Education). Washington, D.C.: U.S. Government Printing Office, 1980.

U.S. Senate, Committee on the Judiciary. *Our nation's schools—A report card: "A" in school violence and vandalism.* Preliminary report of the Subcommittee to Investigate Juvenile Delinquency. Washington, D.C.: U.S. Government Printing Office, 1975.

U.S. Senate, Committee on the Judiciary. *School violence and vandalism: Models and Strategies for change.* Hearing before the Subcommittee to Investigate Juvenile Delinquency. Washington, D.C.: U.S. Government Printing Office, 1976. (a)

U.S. Senate, Committee on the Judiciary. *School violence and vandalism: The nature, extent and cost of violence and vandalism in our nation's schools.* Hearings before the Subcommittee to Investigate Juvenile Delinquency. Washington, D.C.: U.S. Government Printing Office, 1976. (b)

U.S. Senate, Committee on the Judiciary. *Maryland: Juvenile justice.* Hearings before the Subcommittee to Investigate Juvenile Delinquency. Washington, D.C.: U.S. Government Printing Office, 1976. (c)

U.S. Senate, Committee on the Judiciary. *Challenge for the third century: Education in a safe environment—Final report on the nature and prevention of school violence and vandalism.* Washington, D.C.: U.S. Government Printing Office, 1977.

Van Patten, J. J. Violence and vandalism in our schools. *Journal of Thought,* 1976, *11*(3), 180–189.

Weis, J. G., & Hawkins, J. D. Background paper for the delinquency prevention research and development program. Unpublished manuscript, Center for Law and Justice, University of Washington, Seattle, 1980.

Welsh, R. S. Delinquency, corporal punishment, and the schools. *Crime and Delinquency,* 1978, *24*, 336–354.

White, R. C. The relation of felonies to environmental factors in Indianapolis. *Social Forces,* 1932, *10*, 498–509.

Wiatrowski, M. D., Roberts M. K., & Gottfredson, G. D. Classifying school environments to understand school behavior disruption. *Environment and Behavior,* 1983, *15*, 53–76.

Wilks, J. A. Ecological correlates of crime and disruption. In President's Commission on Law Enforcement and the Administration of Justice, *Task force report: Crime and its impact—An assessment.* Washington, D.C.: U.S. Government Printing Office, 1967.

Williams, T., Moles, O., & Boesel, D. *The NIE safe school study: Concepts and design.* Unpublished manuscript, National Institute of Education, 1975. (Portions of this document are reproduced in Volume 2 of the Safe School Study report, NIE, 1977.)

Wilson, J. Q. Crime and public policy. In J. Q. Wilson (Ed.), *Crime and public policy.* San Francisco: ICS Press, 1983.

Wittes, S. *People and power: A study of crisis in secondary schools.* Ann Arbor, Mich.: Center for Research on Utilization of Scientific Knowledge, 1970.

Woodall, M. V. *Manual for improving student discipline.* Milford, DE: Longfield Institute, 1979.

Wyne, M. D. *The national safe school study: Overview and implications.* Paper presented at the American Educational Research Association Convention, San Francisco, April 1979.

Yule, G. U. On the interpretation of correlations between indices or ratios. *Journal of the Royal Statistical Society,* 1910, 73, 644–647.

Author Index

Subject Index